A Note about the Author

I was fifteen years old when the war began. I jc
eighteen. I became a navigator and eventually was posted along with my
pilot, Reg Everson, whom I had crewed up with at an OTU (Operational
Training Unit) at Swanton Morley in East Anglia. There we trained on the
Mosquito 6 Fighter Bomber.

When we joined 305 (Polish) Squadron flying our Mosquito, it meant
flying from France at an airfield at Epinoy, half way between Douai and
Cambrai. On this squadron we were part of 138 Wing of 2 Group in
Second TAF (Tactical Air Force), flying in tactical support of our ground
forces. We operated at night flying at an average height of 1500 ft.

My pilot, Reg was a wonderful pilot to whom I owe my life. We had the
misfortune, very near the end of the war, on the night of 9 April 1945,
when we were flying home from a patrol near Berlin, to be shot down by
an American night fighter who was obviously trying to increase, or even
start his score, thinking he was shooting down a Ju88. It was a case of
friendly fire as this kind of incident is still known. Due to Reg's very cool
and very skilful handling of our stricken plane, the starboard engine of
which had become a blazing inferno, and from the nacelle of which the
starboard wheel had dropped down and was revolving like a six foot wide
Catherine wheel, he achieved some twenty seconds of continuing flight
which enabled us to bale out and parachute safely to the ground.
Unfortunately, we were in what was still German territory. Indeed, we
had fallen into the southern rim of the Ruhr pocket. Reg got back to
Epinoy ahead of me and we had a completely different set of experiences.
I ended up getting back to Epinoy with two American aircrew who had
been shot down in their Mitchell. We 'liberated' a Mercedes car, painted
in police markings, in good working order, but it only had three wheels
which wasn't enough for a four wheel car. Mercifully we found a spare
and drove home.

Subsequently, having got my commission like the rest of us from that famous airman, Air Vice Marshal Sir Basil Embry, AOC of 2 Group up in Brussels, I finally ended up in RAF Gütersloh in Germany. I was released early in 1947 and went directly back to Oxford.

I have had a varied career since, covering the Bank of England, a year and a bit in Washington DC at the Fund, a financial journalist on the Manchester Guardian ending up as a broker in the City with some freelance journalism thrown in.

Tony Rudd – December 2010

Winged Victory
1940
Battle of Britain Day by Day

Tony Rudd

Published 2010 by arima publishing

www.arimapublishing.com

ISBN 978 1 84549 459 9

© Tony Rudd 2010

Printed and bound in the United Kingdom

Typeset in Garamond 11pt

arima publishing
ASK House, Northgate Avenue
Bury St Edmunds, Suffolk IP32 6BB

t: (+44) 01284 700321
www.arimapublishing.com

Table of Contents

Acknowledgements

Creating this blog and turning it into this book has been a team affair. Originally a couple of years ago, I had, with my son-in law, the idea for the blog. But without the help of a team that I formed, it would never have happened.

The first and most important member of our small group is Dr. Zoë Varnals Bagley. She has been particularly well qualified to make the venture possible. After getting her MA in history at Reading University, she got a job as an Assistant Curator at the RAF Museum at Hendon. She spent two years at Hendon and became hugely knowledgeable about the RAF, and, particularly, about the Battle of Britain. Meanwhile, she finished her thesis on wartime entertainment of the Forces (ENSA), a revised version of which is shortly to be published. Having earned her doctorate from King's College London, she has followed this by putting in a serious stint of research for our blog and its book version.

The second member of the team is my son-in-law James Dunford Wood, himself the son of an RAF pilot. In addition to creative input, he has contributed vital expertise in the technical and design aspects of the blog. He built it using Wordpress technology.

The third member of our team has been Harriet O'Grady who has typed the manuscript of the blog. Our thanks are due to her tireless energy.

Lastly, what I need to do is to thank all three for their forbearance and patience in dealing with me in the light of the fact that I am virtually blind. How they have faced and dealt with such a challenge, I just don't know. Anyhow I am immensely grateful to them.

I would also like to thank the many readers of the blog who sent in comments and who have given their permission for their reproduction in this book.

Special thanks are also due to the following for their assistance in preparing the blog and this book: Air Commodore Ian Morrison, Squadron Leader Liz Jones, Squadron Leader Stuart Balfour, Group Captain Patrick Tootal, OBE, Wing Commander Martin Tinworth, Cyril Shoesmith, Edith Kup, the RAF Museum at Hendon and the Air Historical Branch of the RAF. We should also acknowledge the invaluable resources provided by the online RAF Campaign Diary and the National Archives in Kew in enabling us to provide daily and weekly battle statistics.

Glossary

AA – Anti-aircraft fire; also commonly referred to as Ack Ack
A/C – aircraft
AOC – Air Officer Commanding
ARP – Air Raid Precautions
AM – Air Marshal
ACM – Air Chief Marshal
AVM – Air Vice Marshal
BEF – British Expeditionary Force
Cpl – Corporal
CO – Commanding Officer
DFC – Distinguished Flying Cross
DSO – Distinguished Service Order
Do17 – Dornier 17
e/a – enemy aircraft
ERKs – Ground Crew
FAA – Fleet Air Arm
Flt Lt – Flight Lieutenant
FO – Flying Officer
GPO – General Post Office
He111 – Heinkel 111
Ju87 – Junkers 87 – Stuka
Ju88 – Junkers 88
LDV – Local Defence Volunteer
MAP – Ministry of Aircraft Production
MC – Military Cross
Me109 – Messerschmitt Bf 109
Me110 – Messerschmitt Bf 110
MM – Military Medal
NCO – Non Commissioned Officer
OTU – Operational Training Unit
PO – Pilot Officer

POW – Prisoner of War

RADAR – Radio Detection and Ranging

RAAF – Royal Australian Air Force

RAF – Royal Air Force

RAFVR – Royal Air Force Volunteer Reserve

RCAF – Royal Canadian Air Force

RDF – Radio Direction Finding

RFC – Royal Flying Corps

RNAS – Royal Naval Air Service

RN – Royal Navy

R/T – Radio Telephony

Sgt – Sergeant

Sqdn Ldr – Squadron Leader

WAAF – Women's Auxiliary Air Force

WO – Warrant Officer

Introduction

There have been hundreds of books on the Battle of Britain published since the war, but there is, so far as we know, only one blog of the Battle and that is ours, Winged Victory. This story started on the day that Churchill became Prime Minister and also the day that Hitler launched his invasion of France and the Low Countries. It was May 10 1940. Hitler's French campaign of 1940 was won in 60 days. Bearing in mind that in the First World War it had taken over four years of continuous trench warfare to achieve an outcome, which, anyhow had ended in German defeat, no wonder Hitler's fantasy of world domination suddenly became not a fantasy but a real aspiration. If he could achieve what he had just done that summer, he could achieve anything.

However, after winning the battle in France, Britain became the only European country that still opposed Hitler. What Hitler had expected was that Britain would see sense and would be willing to sue for peace. Instead, Britain opted for war. This was what made Britain and the RAF the inevitable target of a wholesale attack by Germany's air force, the Luftwaffe.

But we were not the easy push over which the Luftwaffe had expected. We had spent the previous five years modernising the RAF and building an extremely effective system of air defence. So instead of a quick victory, the battle was to go on day by day for three and a half months.

This country had had to fight in the past to maintain its independence. But those battles, both on land and sea, had been fought and concluded in a single day. This was until the First World War when industrial warfare, with its millions of casualties became the new model. What is interesting about the Battle of Britain is that it neither resembled a one-day event like Waterloo and Trafalgar, nor did it have much to do with the trench warfare of 1914-18. Instead, it was fought out in the air by fighter pilots in aircraft designed for fighting. It lasted three and a half months because that was the time it took to prove to the Germans that they just weren't going to overwhelm the RAF. Yet, because the Battle lasted virtually the whole of the summer, it took a terrible toll on those who did the fighting or were affected by it. It was, in effect, a battle of attrition. There can be few forms of combat more demanding on the human frame, both physical and mental, than air fighting. Yet this went on engaging hundreds of aircraft on both sides, day after day, for over a hundred days. This was the reality of the Battle of Britain.

In order to get the real 'feel' of such an encounter we created our blog which allowed us to give an account of the Battle on a day-to-day basis in a unique form which had not been done before in this way. The historical blog has arrived. Ours may be the first, but many will follow.

But how, it may be asked, is it going to be possible to translate the immediacy provided by a day-to-day blog, into the format of a book? The answer is that, though this work may be in book form, it is still fundamentally the same shape as the original blog. This means that the day to day accounts of the Battle are interspersed with short comments on pilots, squadrons, aircraft, airfields, the commanders, the support teams together with a weekly commentary on the progress of the Battle. The blog we are happy to say appears to have been a success with over 120,000 hits. We have had many comments, some of which we have reproduced in this book.

The Lead up to the Battle
May 10 – July 9 1940

The Lead up to the Battle
May 10 – July 9 1940

May 10 1940 – The End of the Phoney War

May 10 1940 was the day the real war started and the Phoney War ended. It was today that Hitler's armoured divisions launched their Blitzkrieg attack in the west that in a matter of days would break through at Sedan and successfully cross the River Meuse. The same day, in the United Kingdom, Neville Chamberlain resigned as Prime Minister and was succeeded by Winston Churchill and a new Coalition Government. For Britain, these events brought about a complete change of attitude to the war.

Events were to move fast. Within a week, Hitler's Panzer divisions were streaking for the Channel coast. However, there were many, in England, who still thought France would survive this attack, as she had survived in the First World War. Churchill, a strong admirer of the French Army, very much held this view. Air Chief Marshal Sir Hugh Dowding, the head of Fighter Command, was for his part aware that the new Prime Minister had every faith in the French. Dowding's worry was that they would soon be asking for support, in particular in the air. He could foresee that sending such reinforcements to France would be a worrying temptation. There were, after all, dozens of squadrons of fighters sitting idly on airfields in England.

The trouble was that Britain had another strategy up its sleeve. Since he had been appointed leader of the new Fighter Command back in 1936, Dowding had seen his job as safeguarding the British homeland. He had built up his fighter force for this purpose, not to send it to France. As he saw it, he was in charge of the country's ultimate insurance policy. He had no intention of losing it in a failed campaign in France. Moreover, the whole idea of sending the British Expeditionary Force to France had only been decided in the previous spring, as a gesture of solidarity with our Allies. When war had seemed inevitable, Dowding's view was that we wished them luck, but he still had to keep his powder dry for the ultimate test when it came. The way the campaign in France was shaping, it looked increasingly likely that come it would.

The French Prime Minister, Paul Reynaud, and General Gamelin, Commander-in-Chief of the French Army, unsurprisingly, requested that extra RAF fighter squadrons be sent to France. On May 15, Churchill asked for Dowding's views. Dowding urged the War Cabinet not to send any more aircraft; it was imperative that they were available for the defence of Britain. He set out his views, in no uncertain terms, in the now famous 10 Point Memorandum. The next day, Churchill flew to Paris, where he was again pressed for an extra ten squadrons. Churchill was conscious that history might judge Britain poorly if France fell due to a lack of RAF fighter support, and he asked the War Cabinet to send six squadrons to France. The request was met with some horrified reactions and it was eventually decided to use six squadrons, based in Britain, working in rotation to provide cover in France. Thus, three squadrons worked a 'morning' shift, and three different squadrons an 'afternoon' shift.

Whilst Churchill was in France, he was to see for himself the completely defeated attitude of the French. In their view, they had already lost the war. Indeed, Reynaud had said as much, in a telephone conversation with Churchill, on 15 May. Churchill had reluctantly, but finally, seen the writing on the wall. Britain was soon to be on her own.

Comments:

Bill Glennon: My father Albert (Bert) Glennon had joined the London Fire Brigade from the Navy in 1920. During that time he had spent most of his time at Manchester Square fire station and by 1939 had almost 20 years experience in fire fighting. As war seemed inevitable the London Fire Brigade began to make preparations and looked for long service personnel to head small squads of fire fighters spread out over London.

So it was that, in 1939, my father became the Acting station officer of station 3Z in Princes Row, a few streets away from Buckingham Palace with some 40 men (mostly AFS volunteers) in three watches under his command.

Between 28 September 1940 and 20 April 1941 he kept a list of all the fire calls he attended.

May 17 1940 – The Disaster Unfolds

The next few days of May, the second week of Churchill's premiership, were to put the new leader under severe strain. Would the circumstances arise under which the British Government would have to seek terms from Hitler? There were, undoubtedly, waverers who thought that if the situation deteriorated further, we would be forced to seek terms. But Churchill was absolutely firm and determined. In his view, there should be no parley, no negotiations. But if Britain was attacked following the fall of France, Churchill would have to rely on the preparations to repel such an attack which had already been made, and made, furthermore, under his predecessor, Chamberlain. The problem here was that for the previous five years, Churchill had personally led a campaign in the House of Commons against, first, Stanley Baldwin's Government, then the Chamberlain Government, for what he considered to be their alleged failure to take Hitler seriously.

In particular, he was critical of the failure of the Government to modernise the Royal Air Force, bearing in mind the huge advances which appeared to be taking place in the development of the Luftwaffe. In response to the widely held fear of bombing, which was so starkly voiced by Baldwin when he declared in 1932 that 'the bomber will always get through', development of the RAF had initially focussed on Bomber Command.

Another major contribution to Britain's defences that began under the Chamberlain Government, was the development of radar. Churchill had had his own adviser on these matters, a certain Professor Lindemann, who had suddenly become the scientific adviser to the new Government, at least in all but name. Could he, Churchill, or his adviser Lindemann, have any confidence in what had been done, particularly, by the Chamberlain Government? Interestingly enough, the question never arose. It was in any case too late to ask. There was every chance that within a week or so the German onslaught on Britain would begin. Churchill just had to hope that what had been built over the past five years was going to withstand such a test. It either would, in which case, the country would be safe. Or it wouldn't, in which case, Churchill would soon be gone and we'd have a government led by such a figure as Lord Halifax, who would have to do the negotiations with Hitler. It was as stark as that.

Meanwhile, Dowding would have to try and avoid suffering too serious a diminution in the strength of Fighter Command. Following a meeting, on 19 May, between Dowding, Churchill and the Head of Bomber Command, to discuss air support in the increasingly likely case of the evacuation of the BEF from France, it was decided no more squadrons would be sent to France. Extra air support would be provided from bases in Britain.

Comments:

Vivienne: Dear Tony, I read with great interest about your blog recently as my 10 year old son is a real history fan and is very interested in all things World War Two. The fact that I don't have to prize him away from the computer to read all about it is a real bonus, this is a great idea.

I knew someone who served in the RAF during the war. He is sadly no longer with us, but he gave me a first hand account of his experiences and I will never forget what he told me. This is a great way to keep this in the minds of the younger generation which I think is so important.

May 24 1940 – Hectic Days

France was in its death agonies. The Commander-in-Chief of the French Army, General Gamelin, had been dismissed. General Maxime Weygand, fresh from Syria, had been appointed in his place. Meanwhile, nothing could stop the pell-mell advance of the Wehrmacht. The RAF Advanced Air Striking Force, consisting mainly of Fairey Battles, along with a number of Blenheims, had been decimated as they were committed to the bombing of bridges which the retreating armies had failed to blow up. Several squadrons of Hurricanes were operating as cover for the BEF, and had been holding their own in the air, but so continuously that their losses too were now very serious.

Still, the BEF was managing to retreat along with substantial French forces to Dunkirk. On 24 May, the evacuation from France began with 1,000 men being picked up at Boulogne. That same day, the British Government began planning the evacuation from Dunkirk. The early estimates were that we would be unlikely to get more than 30 to 40 thousand troops safely away. This out of a total of over 300,000 troops in all. By the evening of 26 May, the order for Operation Dynamo to commence had been given, and on 27 May, the first evacuation from Dunkirk took place. The following day, the Belgian army surrendered.

Comments:

Mark: Today, 26 May is the 70th annniversary of 46 Squadron flying off HMS Glorious to take part in the operations around Narvik. Of the names listed all except Sqdn Ldr Cross (who survived the sinking of Glorious) PO Lydall KIA PO Bunker, FS Shackley, PO Cowles, PO Mee, PO Frost PO Knight, Sgt Taylor (lost from Glorious on June 8) took part in the Battle of Britain

26 May 1940

Ten aircraft flew from H.M.S. GLORIOUS to SKAANLAND
P2632 Sqdn Ldr CROSS Pilot 20:30 22:30
L1980 FO FROST Pilot
L1814 PO LEFEVRE Pilot
L1815 FO COWLES Pilot
L1988 PO BUNKER Pilot
L1961 Sgt EARP Pilot
L1892 Flt Lt STEWART Pilot
L1794 FS SHACKLEY Pilot
L1793 SGT ANDREW Pilot
L1816 SGT EDWORTHY Pilot
N2543 Flt Lt JAMESON Pilot
L1892 Flt Lt STEWART Pilot
N3652 FO MEE Pilot
L1806 FO LYDALL Pilot
L1812 FO KNIGHT Pilot
L1980 FO FROST Pilot
L1804 PO DRUMMOND Pilot
L1988 PO JOHNSON Pilot
N2633 PO McGREGOR Pilot
L1853 Sgt TAYLOR Pilot

Spitfire Site: The apex of Operation Dynamo had been developing this week, with a rather dramatic start on 27 May and 'little ships' joining the action on the 30. I find the air battle over Dunkirk most interesting, and relatively poorly covered in literature.

May 31 1940 – The Great Evacuation

All British eyes by now were focussed on Dunkirk. The great evacuation was reaching its peak. Completely contrary to expectations 30 to 40 thousand troops a day were being taken off. However, the waiting men, standing in long queues on the beaches, were having a very trying time. There can be few worse experiences than standing in disciplined lines for hours on end while being bombed.

Unhappily, whilst the RAF was flying hundreds of missions – in total 2,739 fighter sorties were flown over Dunkirk – their impact was little felt by the troops on the beaches. Dowding's determination not to send more fighters to France, coupled with the fact that Dunkirk was at the maximum range for single-engine fighters, meant that, despite the hard work and bravery of the pilots, the patrols were relatively ineffective. However, the evacuation was able to transport just under 340,000 troops back to Britain. Just over 68,000 were killed, wounded, or taken prisoner by ground forces during the evacuation from France.

Still, the RAF pilots who were shot down over the beaches didn't have much of an experience either. Alan Deere whose Spitfire had taken a burst of enemy fire in its engine, put his aircraft down in shallow water. He managed to get out and, eventually, to get to the beach. When he finally got on a craft, he was greeted by the Major in charge, with the remark 'for all the good you've done you really needn't have come'. There it was. In the end, most of them got away and that's what counted.

The events of May and early June impacted heavily on Fighter Command's strength with the loss of around 500 of their aircraft. The losses were such that Dowding told the War Cabinet on 2 June that he could not guarantee air superiority for more that 48 hours.

Comments:

Andrew: The evacuation of Dunkirk may not have been as succesful without RAF Fighter Command's efforts. Several hundred sorties were flown, many Luftwaffe raids were succesfully intercepted and broken up. The troops on the ground couldn't see the impact of the RAF as the aerial battle was high and behind the beaches.

June 7 1940 – The Lull Before the Storm

After the momentous events of the last few weeks, June was to constitute a relative lull for the British. The political crisis endured by Churchill in the first few weeks of his premiership was now over. He had achieved a remarkably smooth working relationship with Chamberlain, one of the five members of his War Cabinet. Bearing in mind that Chamberlain was Churchill's former boss and previous antagonist, when it had come to the question of whether talks with Hitler should be entertained, he had made it absolutely clear that in his, Chamberlain's view, the man could not be trusted, and there was simply no point in thinking of it. Chamberlain carried the day and Halifax was given the job of telling Hitler there was to be no parley. In Parliament, Churchill was establishing his ascendancy. This was, of course, hugely helped by his wonderful oratory. He had started by telling the truth: 'I have nothing to offer but blood, toil, tears and sweat'.

This was the month when both the RAF and the Luftwaffe spent valuable weeks getting ready, filling gaps, doing repairs and generally catching up, following the extremely demanding weeks they'd just been through. For Fighter Command, it was a crucially important period to start rebuilding its strength. Following the French campaign, it only had 520 operational fighters. Production of aircraft was a priority. In May, Churchill had appointed Lord Beaverbrook as Minister of Aircraft Production. A combination of Beaverbrook's bullying, the effects of the 'shadow factory' scheme starting to bear fruit, and sheer hard work by factory workers, saw production dramatically increase during June.

For the RAF, a good example of what was involved occurred in 242 Squadron up in Coltishall in 12 Group, above London. The squadron had returned from France in tatters. They'd had an extremely difficult time during the fighting there – flying at all times of the day in combat, for much of the time seeing their comrades shot down, and losing their CO.

All the while, they had been scrambling from one inhospitable airfield to another. Finally, they had suddenly to pack up and get out before the Germans arrived. Now back in Britain, they had few possessions, other than their Hurricanes parked outside. They looked a motley bunch down at the dispersals where they lounged about in a disconsolate manner.

But this day their lives were, so to speak, to be switched on again. A strange figure had walked into the dispersal. He lurched a bit when he walked. Not surprising really, he had artificial legs. Quite a feat to walk at all. But more than that, he purported to be a pilot on active service. And to cap it all, he was about to be their CO. One of the Canadians, who was half asleep on a sofa, cocked an eye at the apparition and then shut it again. To send them this figure as their CO was the last straw.

Douglas Bader took in the scene. He obviously had a problem. Talk wouldn't get him out of the difficulty. These chaps needed more than that, if he was to lift them out of their lethargy and depression. So he walked out of the dispersal, over to his Hurricane. With the ground crew's assistance he got into the cockpit, strapped himself in and taxied out. He took off and then proceeded to cut the sky into ribbons. He had, at least, to show them he could fly. As he landed and taxied in, the Canadians had got up and were all watching as he returned. Bader strode in. He got chatting to them straight away. He heard their stories. He ticked them off for being scruffy in the Mess. One of them, however, spoke up, 'We've nothing but what we are standing up in. We lost all our kit in France'.

'Ok' said Bader, 'there's an outfitter in town, go down and order yourselves uniforms and put it down to me. Tomorrow we fly at 8' o clock. See you in the Mess'. He stumped out.

Fighter Command was having to repair the ravages it had suffered in the battle of France and the retreat to the coast, together with providing cover for the evacuation. All had cost it dear. Now it would have to work hard to get itself ready for a new battle – this time, the big one.

Comments:

Battle of Britain TV: The lull before heading into the storm of war…. Churchill's 'Fight them on the beaches' speech on 4 June 1940, shone light on the underplayed role of the RAF in the Dunkirk evacuation and prepared the country for to the storm they were heading into. With new 'dunkirk' spirit we would get through it together, and 'never surrender'.

The stage was set for the young fighter boys…

May it not be that the cause of civilization itself will he defended by the skill and devotion of a few thousand airmen?

Spitfire Site: Not sure I'd agree with the term 'lull' during the first two weeks after Dunkirk. The experience for any individual unit may well have been so. But many of the RAF units in France were struggling for another two weeks, and HMS Glorious was sunk in the Norwegian Sea together with the entire No. 46 Hurricane Squadron. Not much 'lull' for Dowding or the government, I suppose.

10 June, Italy declared war on France and Britain. It would eventually bring their air force over Britain, in October 1940.

June 14 1940 – The Luftwaffe Prepares

Over in France, the scene was of methodical but urgent activity. On 14 June, the Germans had marched into Paris. The Luftwaffe was doing the job it did best. As a tactical air force it was settling in to new quarters. The French campaign had been hugely successful but at the same time it had been costly. A large number of aircraft had been lost. Air operations as part of a successful campaign involving hugely ambitious thrusts on the ground inevitably meant taking big risks. Most of them came off but even when they did, there was a high cost to pay. Many replacements were needed. At the same time, new headquarters had to be set up. Luftflotte 2, under the command of Generalfeldmarschall Albert Kesselring, chose Brussels for theirs. It was a city with excellent communications. Down in France, the airfield at Epinoy, halfway between Cambrai and Douai, was extensive but still needed to be put shipshape, German fashion. Communications had to be established with headquarters in Brussels. Spares and ammunition had to brought in, workshops set up, catering staff had to be recruited, food ordered, but in a couple of weeks this was all done. The Luftwaffe was used to it. It was their purpose in life. Now they were at least operating without opposition. For them it was a relatively easy task.

Luftflotte 3, had its headquarters in Paris, with its fighter HQ in Cherbourg. From there, it controlled a number of bases in Brittany and Normandy. They were under the command of Generalfeldmarschall Hugo Sperrle, a very large bear-like man, who was, nonetheless, a very professional man. He liked everything done properly. Under his command it was. Preparations were in hand from Brittany in France right along the coast up to the northern most tip of Norway. It was here that Luftflotte 5 was based, to cover the North Sea, with headquarters at Stavenger and under the command of Generaloberst Hans-Jürgen Stumpff.

Britain was faced, therefore, with the enemy getting ready across the sea on the western coast of Europe. It was still too early to be clear about what would happen next. But the Luftwaffe was preparing for every eventuality, even an air battle over Britain itself.

Comments:

Spitfire Site: Good post. There were so many events during that week that it would be hard to follow them all. Some of the others:

- RAF's final withdrawal from France
- The Lancastria disaster
- Churchill's 'Finest Hour' speech

June 28 1940 – Radar to the Rescue

The whole defence system of Fighter Command in 1940 was based on radar. The experiments had been successful. The new device worked. There were some 32 Chain Home radar stations, each involving 350 foot steel lattice masts, side by side, with 250 foot wooden masts. These were complemented by the Chain Home Low stations which had been developed by army scientists to detect aircraft flying at low altitude. On the steel masts were the radar devices sending out the pulse signals which got reflected from incoming aircraft. These reflections were picked up on the apparatus on the wooden masts. In their hut below, Airmen and WAAFs, known as Clerks-Special Duties, watched their cathode ray screens for the tell tale blips generated by incoming aircraft. Each such station was connected by landline, laid specially by the GPO to Bentley Priory. There, the signals came into a filter room designed to weed out false messages. Having got through that, the signal went on to the control room where a set of WAAFs, circulated around a very large scale map of Britain. There, they used the signals to place small blocks of wood representing the aircraft, red for the Germans which they called Bandits and black for ours. Above all this was a platform on which Dowding and his staff could watch the proceedings, as the WAAFs pushed the markers around.

Another important ancillary part of the organisation was played by the Observer Corps. With its 30,000 strong membership, spread amongst the one thousand observer posts dotted around the country, they fed their sightings of aircraft, enemy and friendly, through to their headquarters and from that to Bentley Priory. Each Observer Corps post was equipped with tin hats, apparatus for measuring the height of aircraft, telephones which connected them with the system, and, most important of all, tea making apparatus. The Observer Corps role was to keep track of aircraft over land. Radar only observed over the sea, pointing outward from the coast.

All this information which came into Bentley Priory was disseminated onwards to the four Groups. Each Group had a similar setup with WAAFs pushing markers around a map of their area. Executive responsibility for instituting action was held at Group level. The Group Commander decided which squadrons to send up, in what number, and which should be held in reserve. He actually fought the battle. It was on his skill and judgement that the outcome and confrontation with the enemy would depend. Each Group had its sector stations. These had the controllers who were in direct contact with the squadrons. They remained in touch with them after take off, giving them interception courses to fly which were marked on the Sector plotting tables. This is how Fighter Command was to operate throughout the battle. Its operations were invariably in response to what the radar was showing, which was plotted at HQ Control and then at Group Control. The whole thing worked like a coordinated machine. At the time, the system was absolutely unique, there was nothing else like it. It was to play a vital part in the battle.

Comments:

Paul Handley: How were the radar sites defended? What knowledge did the Nazis have of them, and how and to what extent were they attacked, and with what results?

Tony Rudd: Reference to your query concerning the radar sites. You will get more information on the subject as the blog develops along with the battle. But briefly, the sites were defended by Fighter Command intercepting German aircraft that attacked them. Of course, occasionally, they managed to get in and out before being attacked by the RAF. The Germans seemed to have very little knowledge of the system. However, we were very good at putting them back into service when they were damaged by attacks. So much so that Goering, half way through the battle, ordered that attacks on them be discontinued as, apparently, they were not being effective.

Battleofbritaintv: In the words of so many, RDF, or the 'Dowding System' was so vital to our success in the Battle of Britain…

I would love to share with you some exerpts from my interview with one of the WAAF's who worked at the control room of Uxbridge.

RDF

RDF was absolutely vital. Aircraft in those days didn't have a long time to stay up because they ran out of petrol. The RDF ran from the coast outwards and we could monitor the stations in France and Belgium, and we could see when they were taking off. We could see that the fighter aircraft were in the sky at the right time, but not too soon. They weren't just hanging about there. They would go up and be there, ready to intercept as soon as the raid got within range. So RDF was absolutely vital. It was the thing that made all the difference.

Command and Control

We got our information from the filter room at Stanmore who got it from the RDF, as it was called then, and from the Royal Observer Corps. The Corps haven't really been talked about very much, but they did a lot because the RDF was round the coast. So what happened as soon as enemy raids crossed the coast? It wasn't recorded by the RDF, it was recorded by the Royal Observer Corps – people standing on steeples, church towers and things like that – and phoning in!

It all went into Stanmore – the filter room, to people who were going to operate on it. We received it by headphones, and also by teleprinter tape. There was a teleprinter – a small, square machine, by each plotting station. The tape came out with all the information on:

First you would see map coordinates
Next the direction that the aircraft were flying
Next the number of aircraft
Then the height

You put that up on the block, but unless it was up to date it was no good. It was useless to know where they were ten minutes ago. You had to know then. That's why they had this colour system of plots.

The colour altered so that the controller would know how old the lot was. At the end of each run you took the oldest colour off. You swept them all off, put them in a box. So you had to be pretty quick and pretty dextrous.

The thing I've often been a bit surprised about was that all the girls on the watch had had a very good education. Everybody had what was the equivalent of 'O' Levels at least. In fact we were locally called 'The Boarding School Girls' (which most of us weren't actually). But I can see now that you couldn't have done it unless you were pretty bright. You had to be able to work quickly and accurately. "

Flt Lt Hazel Gregory, Clerk Special-duties, Uxbridge Control Room, 11 Group, May- Dec 1940

Excerpt from interview 11 November 2009

Spitfire Site: There were also other technology improvements prior to the Battle, for example constant-speed propellers to all RAF aircraft.

John Morris Bush: I helped to maintain the Radar transmitters after the Battle. You may be interested to know that there were three transmitters on our site, one up and running, one on standby in case of failure, and the other one under maintenance. Each transmitter consisted of two very large modules. In fact the two output valves were the size of a man's torso, and dissasembled for cleaning, the body of the valve was made of china, and there was a pump to extract the air in the valve to give the vacuum needed. It took about an hour to get a transmitter up and running, that is why one was on standby ready for use when the up and running one failed. We had three minutes to get back on air otherwise a report had to be submitted.

M B Bingham: I am a former plastics technologist and '52-'55 RAF wireless mechanic. Understand that using newly discovered polyethylene (ICI Polythene) as radar cable insulant gave superior preservation of detection signal than the earlier compounded rubber cable insulant. This increase in insulation properties known as K factor, provided an even earlier enemy aircraft approach warning, which allegedly puzzled the Germans.

I understand that (rather like penicillin's serendipitious discovery) polythene was discovered by ICI after ethylene had escaped from a high pressure gas cylinder and had become this wax-like polymer around the cylinder's leaky valve. ICI quickly went on to build a plant making a high pressure, low density version called Polythene.

I was told this story recently by a lady, who'd been in the wartime ICI Polythene lab at Runcorn and is now living in the same sheltered housing block in Cheshire where a D Day veteran pal lives.

Tim Pottle: Great stuff! My Grandfather was involved in the initial testing of the Radar system.

A Bristol Blenheim Mk. IV circles a British tanker on fire and sinking in the English Channel after a German attack

Scramble!

*Heinkel III over
the Isle of Dogs*

Hurricanes of 85 Squadron

Dornier 17 bomber aircraft

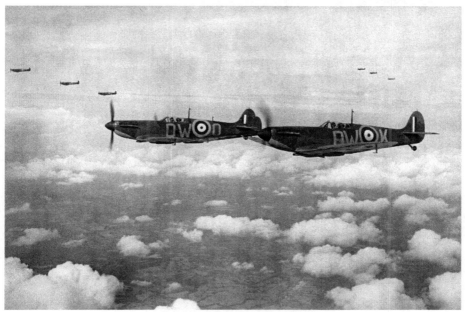

Spitfires flying in vic formation

Spitfires flying

Kanalkampf
July 10 – August 12 1940

Kanalkampf
July 10 – August 12 1940

Day 1 – July 10 1940

Weather: showery.

The German attack against coastal shipping had started at the beginning of July. However, the official date of the beginning of the Battle was fixed on July 10. The first German aircraft picked up by radar were reconnaissance planes looking for convoys which could be attacked. There were also the long range aircraft whose job was to fly deep into the Atlantic ascertaining what kind of weather could be expected over Britain in a day or so. The action began in the morning with an attack on a convoy and a sharp attack on Swansea which resulted in some thirty civilian deaths. This was followed by serious action in the afternoon. Around 1:30pm the tell-tale blips indicating a large concentration of Luftwaffe aircraft had begun to appear on the cathode ray tubes of the receiving sets in the radar scanning huts in which WAAFs were on the lookout for exactly this kind of warning. What they indicated was a flight of some twenty-six Dornier 17 bombers accompanied by twenty-six Me109 fighters plus forty Me110s.

The convoy was being patrolled by half a dozen Hurricanes. The latter were soon to be joined by elements of four squadrons from 11 Group. In the fight which followed the Luftwaffe lost four planes shot down. The RAF lost three Hurricanes, one of which collided with a German bomber losing half its wing and crashing into the sea. The damage was one coastal ship sunk.

The tally for the day was thirteen Luftwaffe aircraft shot down at the cost of seven RAF fighters lost. The RAF had flown 609 sorties in the day and had managed to achieve a two to one victory over the enemy. Not bad in its first encounter with its much more experienced adversary. A particular feature of the day was the relatively indifferent performance of the twin-engine fighter, the Me110. These aircraft had been forced to fly in a tight circle to defend themselves, relying on their rear gunners. But it also became clear that the RAF was going to be outnumbered in the Battle to follow. They were only going to be able to intercept many of the raids of the Luftwaffe by flying a large number of sorties each day.

54 Squadron Operational Record Book, 10 July

As a result of the first phase of the Battle for Britain, the squadron could only muster eight aircraft and thirteen pilots.

242 Squadron Operational Record Book, 10 July

Convoy patrol over sea. First enemy bomber shot down by Squadron in this section. Shot down by Sub-Lt Gardner. Two others damaged.

Top Gun Gallery
Robert Stanford Tuck

Tuck was a regular who joined the air force in 1935. He came from a Jewish family and had a not particularly brilliant record at school, however, in 1935 having achieved his pilot wings, he joined 65 Squadron and remained on it until 1940 when he joined 92 Squadron.

He experienced his first combat in the Battle of France and his first success over Dunkirk, opening his score with three German Me109s shot down all on the same day. He went on to score a number of further kills for which he was awarded his first DFC. He participated in the Battle of Britain, with a string of victories. These were not without incident.

In mid-August, damaged by return fire from a Ju88, Tuck had to bale out. He then suffered another incident when attacking a Dornier 17. He ended up with a dead engine, ten miles out over the Channel, but succeeded in gliding back to dry land, where he crash landed his aircraft but emerged unscathed. On 11 September he was promoted to Squadron Leader and was made Commanding Officer of 257 Squadron which was flying Hurricanes. During the Battle he was awarded two Bars to his original DFC and finally in January 1941 he was awarded the DSO.

After the Battle, indeed the next year, in 1941 Tuck was shot down in an engagement with a German fighter over the Channel, but was rescued by a coal barge which, having seen him descend by parachute, went out and brought him to dry land. Later that year, he had an unfortunate incident when he chased a German bomber flying towards Wales. Under attack the bomber jettisoned its bombs. One of them fell on an army camp, and by an appalling coincidence killed a soldier who turned out to have been married to his sister. In other words, his brother-in-law. However, in July 1941, he was promoted to Wing Commander at Duxford. It was on a mission leading his wing across the Continent that he was shot down in January 1942 by ground fire. He remained a prisoner of war until February 1945 when he escaped and subsequently fought briefly with the Russians.

Stanford Tuck left the RAF in 1949, with a final number of kills to his name of twenty-seven enemy aircraft. He was one of the pilots who advised on the making of the film The Battle of Britain. He had a reputation as an extremely courageous and successful leader. He subsequently became a friend of the German ace fighter pilot, Adolf Galland. Indeed, Galland had asked Tuck for dinner when he was shot down. He died in 1987.

Day 2 – July 11 1940

Weather: cloudy, visibility fair.

The day started with radar picking up evidence of three groups of Luftwaffe aircraft flying northwards over Cherbourg. These Luftflotte 3 aircraft were soon flying on a course that would take them to the Dorset coast where a large convoy was heading westwards. To protect the convoy, half a dozen Spitfires plus another half a dozen Hurricanes had been scrambled from Warmwell, the forward airstrip close to the Dorset coast. The Hurricanes encountered a group of Ju87 Stuka dive bombers but the latter were covered by a number of Me109 fighters. These German fighters were successful in shooting down two of the Spitfires and a Hurricane. However, none of the convoy ships were sunk.

Skirmishes in the air were fought in many places along the South coast. In particular, 54 Squadron, flying from Manston in Kent was operating continuous sorties in an effort to cover convoys threading their way through the Straits of Dover. It was in these sorties that Alan Deere, the young New Zealand fighter pilot who was to survive an amazing number of hair raising incidents in the Battle, experienced one of them. In a dogfight, he was in a mid-air collision with a Me109. As a result, the propeller of the Spitfire was bent completely backwards while the engine of the aircraft was put out of action. Deere tried to leave the aircraft pulling at the cockpit canopy. But it would not budge. Deere did the only thing he could do which was to try and glide the doomed aircraft towards the coast several miles away. He just succeeded in reaching the English coast. He then managed to put his powerless aircraft down on the first field he came across. After a number of heavy bumps the aircraft eventually came to a standstill. Now his frantic efforts to pull the canopy back met with success. He wrenched it free running for his life in case the aircraft blew up. The Germans would have counted his crash as being a British aircraft downed. But as with many cases later on in the fighting, the RAF pilot survived to fight another day.

The action that day then switched back to the west of England. Radar had picked up the approach of a force of fifteen Ju87 Stukas with a covering force of some thirty Me110 aircraft which appeared to be heading towards Portland. Six Hurricanes, which had taken off from Tangmere, had been vectored to intercept. Furthermore, reinforcements from nearby airfields were immediately scrambled. The result was that two of the Stukas were shot down before the Me110s could interfere. A major dogfight then ensued.

The next contribution from Luftflotte 3 picked up by radar was noted as heading for Portsmouth. 601 Squadron was sent forward. They intercepted twelve He111s escorted by a similar number of Me110s. That day the RAF flew 432 sorties shooting down sixteen Luftwaffe aircraft for a cost of six British fighters.

54 Squadron Operational Record Book, 11 July 13:18 hours

Memories of the distant past were awakened this afternoon when eight a/c were ordered on a convoy patrol. There is one big difference however, between the present and past, the excitement was the exception, now it is common place. Unfortunately our aircraft were unable to discover any enemy aircraft.

242 Squadron Operational Record Book, 11 July

Dornier shot down by Sqdn Ldr Bader over sea on dawn patrol. PO Grassick crashed Hurricane – uninjured.

Aircraft of the Battle
The Spitfire

The two aircraft which won the Battle of Britain were the Hurricane and the Spitfire. The two came from very different stables. The Spitfire was the brilliant product of a genius, Reginald Mitchell. Mitchell had designed the winning entry in the Schneider Trophy of 1931 which, being the third consecutive win by Britain, won the Trophy outright. The Spitfire was the first all metal single seater fighter to see service with the RAF. The prototype emerged in March 1936. It was clearly a winner. But producing it was another matter. It was two and a half years before it at last emerged in sufficient numbers to go into squadron service. In August 1938 19 Squadron at Duxford was the first to receive Spitfires.

It was powered by the Rolls Royce Merlin engine which had virtually been built for it. Pilots loved the Spitfire. It was apparently a joy to fly. In combat it was the equal of the Me109. It had one significant advantage, it could turn in a tighter circle than its rival. This was due mainly to its thin wings.

In the Battle, the Spitfire behaved like a thoroughbred. Its maximum speed of 362 mph matched that of the Me109. In the Battle, it was the Mk1 which saw the most service. As a fighter machine it was the Me109's all round equal. In one respect, it might be said, to have had an advantage in that it gave the pilots who flew it the reassuring feeling that can only be compared with the jockey who finds himself in the saddle on the winning horse.

Comments

George Nicholas Himaras: We shall never forget!

Day 3 – July 12 1940

Weather: mainly cloudy.

The day began with two attacks by the Luftwaffe against convoys heading south past the coast of East Anglia. The heaviest attack was against one of the convoys heading towards the North Foreland area of the Kent coast. Four squadrons from 12 Group were scrambled to intercept the more northerly of the attacks. At the same time German aircraft were intercepted off the Scottish coast near to Aberdeen. However, the city suffered 26 casualties as a result of the bombing. Then, later that morning an interception of a He111 was made off the coast of the Isle of Wight with the German aircraft being shot down.

It was a day when interception was made difficult by the persistence of fog over much of the North Sea and Channel. However, the day yielded eight victories for the RAF whilst six RAF fighters were lost. The RAF flew 670 sorties.

74 Squadron Operational Record Book, 12 July, Hornchurch

At 16:30 hours Red Section left to investigate a raid fifteen miles NE of Margate. AA fire was sighted from a ship which was being bombed by a He 111. Flt Lt Malan DFC leading Red Section gave order to attack line eastern and opened attack closing to 300yds range. Heavy fire from the enemy aircraft's rear gunner and silenced by Red Leader. Sgt Mould and PO Stevenson also attacked in turn and enemy aircraft seen to crash into the sea.

The Squadrons

54 Squadron

Audax ominia perpeti – Boldness to Endure Anything

Originally formed in 1916 at Castle Bromwich, the squadron saw service in France during the First World War. It was disbanded in 1919. After only eleven years the squadron was reformed in 1930 at RAF Hornchurch. In March 1939 it was equipped with Spitfires. Based at RAF Hornchurch during July and August 1940, 54 Squadron was involved in some fierce engagements with the Luftwaffe, and in September 1940 it was moved to Catterick to rest.

Day 4 – July 13 1940

Weather: cold.

The fog of the previous day still persisted and didn't clear until midday. Despite this several convoys were attacked off the east coast. Attacks were also made on a convoy finding its way through the Straits of Dover. Finally, an attack was launched on a convoy off Lyme Regis by a formation of over 50 German aircraft. One RAF fighter was lost, but seven German aircraft were destroyed.

54 Operational Record Book - 13 July 17:14 hours

New Zealand to the fore again! This time in the person of PO Gray. Three sections were patrolling Manston when seasoned Blue section (Flt Lt Way, PO Gray and Sgt Norwell – all survivors of Dunkirk) were sighted by two Me109s. Better prepared than the earlier and less fortunate Green section of the squadron, the tables were turned on the 109s, chasing them back at sea level almost to the French coast. PO Gray shot down one which crashed into the sea (confirmed by 56 Squadron). Flt Lt Way was unfortunate for the 109 he was chasing escaped.

The Squadron now stands at:
a) enemy aircraft certain casualties – 39
b) enemy aircraft probable casualties – 21
c) our own pilots missing or killed – 6
d) our own aircraft lost whilst engaging the enemy – 13

PO DH Wissler - Diary, 13 July 1940

We were at readiness all morning but nothing happened, then as soon as we sat down to lunch we were told to take off for Martlesham. We did one patrol over the sea round up the E. Coast but we saw nothing although we were guided to where three bombers were meant to be. We returned about eight and on arriving back at Debden were instructed to do some formation flying so that photographers from Life could get some shots. Unfortunately I never felt less like formation and it wasn't really good.

(Reproduced with kind permission of the Imperial War Museum and Copyright holder)

The Airfields
Biggin Hill

This airfield built on the North Downs, just south of London to avoid the occasional fog which filled nearby valleys, became almost synonymous with the Battle of Britain itself. Being some only twenty miles from the centre of London it was inevitably both the site of an important fighter command station, and ultimately a major target for the Luftwaffe in the Battle. It was the first to claim, along with its sector airfields, 1000 enemy destroyed.

It had begun life in the First World War as an airfield forming part of the defensive ring of airfields around London. In 1930, its refurbishment was started. It was then occupied by several squadrons flying the biplanes of the time. The squadrons were amongst the first to be re-equipped with Hurricanes in 1938 and 1939.

Its first heavy use came during the dark days of Dunkirk in 1940 when 242 and 79 Squadrons flew their Hurricanes over the beaches in constantly rotating shifts.

In July and August, aircraft from this airfield played an increasingly significant role in the Battle. By now Spitfires of 92, 72, 74 and 610 Squadrons had largely replaced the Hurricanes. However, near the end of August the station became a prime target for attack by the Luftwaffe. On August 30, a squadron of Luftwaffe Ju88 Bombers attacked at low level with 1,000lb bombs, destroying a hangar, stores, accommodation blocks and repair shops, resulting in the death of thirty-nine people and several aircraft destroyed. Serious raids continued for the next two days. As a result of their bravery three WAAFs operating the teleprinters were awarded the Military Medal for continuing with their duties until the last moment before their ops room was destroyed by a 500lb bomb.

It was in early September when the Luftwaffe switched to targets in London that the day was saved for Biggin Hill. It was able to recover during the rest of that month.

Because of the central part it played in the Battle, it has become the site of the Chapel of Remembrance commemorating the Battle. It is dedicated to those who lost their lives flying from Biggin Hill. It is situated in what is now a largely civilian airfield.

Day 5 – July 14 1940

Weather: foggy but clearing later.

In the morning the Luftwaffe made attacks on a convoy rounding the Kent coast. At the same time the airfield near Ramsgate was attacked. A second convoy heading for the Straits of Dover was also attacked. Fighter Command was endeavouring to intercept all attacks made on convoys. But this day proved a difficult one. The RAF flew 597 sorties. However, it lost four aircraft whilst the German losses were only two aircraft.

A feature of the developing Battle was the use by the Luftwaffe of He59 seaplanes, ostensibly to pick up their pilots who had been forced to ditch in the sea. These aircraft carried Red Cross markings. However, in London there were serious misgivings. It was suspected that these seaplanes were not only being used to rescue downed pilots but also to spot the position of convoys that could then be attacked. The Government announced that it could no longer give immunity to these seaplanes. Fighter Command gave pilots orders to ignore the red crosses – the Air Ministry was, at this stage, still considering the issue.

That night German aircraft launched an attack against Avonmouth and did some damage to the docks and the railway line.

615 Squadron Operational Record Book - 14 July – Kenley

Squadron went down to Hawkinge again at 13:00hrs (thirteen aircraft). At 15:00hrs Red Section were patrolling convoy near Dover, when convoy was attacked by forty Ju87s which were escorted by Me109s. Pilot Officer M.R. Mudie (red 3) was shot down, and jumped by parachute. He was picked up by the Navy and sent to Dover Hospital severely wounded. Red 1 and 2 put several bursts into Ju87s but were unable to observe results as they were being attacked. Later our remaining nine aircraft took off from Hawkinge to assist Red Section.

FO Gayner shot down one Ju87 (confirmed by Yellow 2)

FO Collard also shot down one Ju87 (confirmed by Yellow 3)

PO Hugo shot down another Ju87 which he saw catch fire and fall into the sea.

Blue Section chased the Me109s and escaped, although they were damaged by their machine gun fire. Green Section missed the fun.

Results:

2 Ju87s destroyed confirmed

1 Ju87 destroyed unconfirmed

Our casualties: one pilot severely wounded.

This air battle was the subject of BBC news commentary which was broadcast the same evening by Charles Gardner. The Squadron also received congratulations from the Prime Minister. Squadron returned here at19:00hrs and returned to Hawkinge again the following morning.

Comments

Spitfire Site: That memorable BBC broadcast really brought the drama of the Battle of Britain to homes all around Britain.

David Asprey: Britain had to win four battles with her allies to survive and ensure that democracy and the rule of law was once again established on the continent of Europe, the Battle of Britain, the Battle of Alamein, the Battle of the Atlantic and the Battle of Normandy, none of the last three would have been possible without the skill and sacrifices of those who fought the Battle of Britain.

Captains and Commanders
Sir Hugh Dowding

When the RAF was reorganised into specialist commands back in mid-1936, and Fighter Command came into existence, the then Air Marshal Sir Hugh Dowding was chosen as its first commander, Air Officer Commanding in Chief. Thus, Dowding presided over the command during the vital four years when it was modernised for war. This was when ground breaking innovation of a radar based control system had been installed. It was also when many hundreds of new young pilots were brought onto the Squadrons and were provided with the new monoplane fighters, the Hurricanes and Spitfires. The Battle of Britain was, therefore, the battle which Dowding had been preparing for. Moreover, his influence had been crucial, well before his command had been set up. In the early Thirties, he had been the Air Member for Research. He had always been at the forefront of technical developments and showed interest in scientific innovation.

Born in 1882, Dowding had an early career in the Army in the Far East and the Mediterranean where he proved to be an effective commander. While at the Staff College at Camberley in 1913, he took flying lessons at Brooklands and gained his pilot's licence and consequently joined the RFC on the outbreak of the First World War. During this period he had fallen out with Trenchard over Dowding's desire to rest operational pilots at reasonable intervals in between battles. After service in France, he came back to Britain and worked in training and logistic roles.

What kind of a man was he? He was the perfect staff officer. He was totally devoted to his command and particularly to the young pilots in it. He wasn't an affable man. His nickname 'Stuffy' fitted him pretty well. During the Battle, he was at his post at Bentley Priory where command and control were located. Here, he would follow the Battle every day and every hour.

Comments

Gscurtis: Without Dowding we wouldn't be here. His brains saved the day.

Andrew: Agreed, without Dowding the RAF would have had only obsolete bombers to strike back with. His foresight and prewar effort rank him as one of the greatest military commanders of all time.

Day 6 – July 15 1940

Weather: overcast in the Channel.

The Luftwaffe sent out a force of fifteen Do17s which spotted a convoy passing along the south coast. However, the attack was turned back by a force of Hurricanes, but which did not manage to score.

Further to the west a small force of Luftflotte 3 aircraft attacked the RNAS airfield at Yeovil dropping some bombs on the runway and went on to attack the Westland works nearby. They also targeted further sites in the west of England including the local railways. The RAF flew that day 449 sorties. One Hurricane was lost but three enemy aircraft were shot down, including a He111.

266 Squadron Operational Record Book, 15 July – Wittering

Warm, visibility very good. Flying 17 hours 40 minutes. Ac Flight at readiness. B Flight at available. Practices included Beam attacks, and air fighting, night fighting circuits and landing. Spitfire aircraft N.3245 damaged after landing heavily during night flying practice. Pilot Flt Lt S.H. Bazley uninjured. Aircraft of Ac Flight carried out air raid investigation.

615 Squadron Operational Record Book, 15 July

Pilot Officer Mudie died from his wounds in Dover hospital.

The People in Support
The Ground Staff

Colloquially, they were called the ERKS. But without them, the aircraft, the Spitfires and the Hurricanes, could not have taken off and certainly could not have survived the Battle. They were not to be mistaken for parking attendants. They were highly trained, intelligent, resourceful and devoted members of a team, without which the RAF could not have operated. Every plane that took off in the Battle did so with the help of the ground staff. When a pilot took off early in the morning, the ground staff would have been working on his plane for several hours before, and perhaps right through the night.

The ground staff were part of the Battle. After each day's fighting, every aircraft which landed back from its operations had to be serviced. In particular, it had to be examined for battle damage. The most obvious would have been damage to the fuselage or the wings from hits delivered by Me109s firing and hitting the aircraft with their canons. All damage had to be assessed. The ground staff had to diagnose the problems that had arisen during the day. The question was, could the damage done be fixed on the squadron or did the damage require deeper surgery before the aircraft could be made safe to fly again. Different problems would require different skills. A problem with the aircraft's instruments would have to be looked at by the expert who did nothing else but tend to instrument problems. Electrical faults would require the electrical fitter to sort the problem out. Trouble with the coolant system would require attention by the expert in that area. Then there were the armourers who were responsible for rearming the aircraft in between operations. The Browning machine guns, all eight of them, had to function perfectly if their pilot was to survive. Then there was the team responsible for refuelling the aircraft. They had to work together as a team as if they were in the pits of a Formula One racing car. Moreover, unlike the Formula One team, they had to do their job often under fire. Literally, when Me109s strafed their airfields.

When you sum all this up, the picture that emerges is of a very demanding business, servicing fighter aircraft in 1940. Each aircraft had a couple or so of ERKS responsible for that aircraft, but each team could call on the expertise of all these different trades. If the pilots had come from Cranwell, the best of the experts on the ground had been trained by an equally demanding institution, namely Halton. The system required a senior NCO to sign off each aircraft as it took to the air. Each pilot had accepted the aircraft and had put his signature on the form, as well. Not only was expertise required, but so was speed. As an aircraft landed, it was in the hands of the ground crew. Once it had taken off, it was the responsibility of the pilot. The two worked hand in glove and relied on each other. On every fighter station, for each fighter pilot, there were at least three or four ground crew. After each day's operations, the question arose, how many fighters would be available at first light the next day. This vital question could only be answered by the senior NCOs who were running the show on the ground.

The strain on some squadrons during the Battle grew almost intolerable. As the demands on the pilots intensified, so did the strain on the ground crews. The ground crew had to snatch a bite to eat when they could, usually while on the job. Some worked and slept in the same uniform day in day out. The fighting record of each squadron depended as much on the efficiency and dedication of the ground crew, as it did on the pilots.

Comments

Andrew Rennie: I am working on a book about an Australian pilot who fought and died in the Battle of Britain. I have been lucky enough to be able to contact not only a pilot that was trained by the Australians, but also his ground crew in the lead up to the time he was killed. From these men I was able to glean the pride in the work that their pilots carried out. All of them said that for them it was the most exciting time of their life. The pilots are the ones glorified but the task of defending England fell to the whole of the RAF, and no more important task out there was keeping the aircraft armed and in the air.

Vivienne Allchin: My son Eddie was asking, in slightly different words to mine, were the various ground staff trained on the job or were they specifically recruited into the RAF because they already possessed some of the skills required? He marvelled at how they could learn so quickly in the circumstances. Does anyone know please?

Tony Rudd: The key professional ground staff got their training at Halton, the RAF Training Institute devoted to turning out skilled tradesmen in one or other of the ground crew specialisations. The Halton recruits formed the backbone of RAF ground staff in the same way as Cranwell did for the pilots. These were topped up by recruits that had, at least, some relevant engineering knowledge.

Day 7 – July 16 1940

Weather: mainly poor with fog extending from northern France across the Channel.

In a number of isolated encounters the Luftwaffe lost five aircraft while the RAF lost two fighters. The RAF flew 313 sorties.

It was on this day that Hitler issued his directive for the preparations for Sealion, the invasion of Britain. Thus ended the first week of the Battle. The RAF had performed reasonably well in combat against their adversary. Their pre-war tactics of flying in close formation and attacking according to a formula had soon to be abandoned. They had seen the loose German formations, in pairs with the leader flying slightly ahead of his wing man who flew slightly behind and above. This gave German pilots a serious advantage. The pair was called a rotte with two pairs being called the schwarm. The RAF was to adapt this formation into what they would call a 'finger four', in which the index finger would represent the leader. The German pilot, Werner Mölders, who had worked this formation out during his service in the Spanish Civil War, was to become the originator of the standard for air fighting, which lasted almost until the present day.

54 Squadron Operational Record Book, 16 July, 23:00 hours

For the first time during our stay at Rochford the majority of the squadron relaxed after release at a dance organised for the squadron by the doctors and nurses of the Southend General Hospital. This gesture was greatly appreciated and full advantage taken of it.

Adolf Hitler Directive No. 16 (16 July 1940)

As England, despite her hopeless military situation, still shows no sign of willingness to come to terms, I have decided to prepare and if necessary carry out a landing operation against her. The aim of this operation is to eliminate the English motherland as a base from which war against Germany can be continued and, if necessary, to occupy completely.

Week 1 Summary: Start of the Battle: Kanalkampf

This first confrontation between the Luftwaffe and the RAF arose from the persistence of the Admiralty in continuing with a traditional coastal trade, forming merchant ships into convoys. They arranged for protection both by convoy escorts, usually destroyers, and by air cover in the form of standing patrols by Fighter Command.

This turned out to be too much for the Germans, who could not resist attacking such a juicy target. From July 10 onwards, these convoys were under continuous attack by the Luftwaffe, who targeted the whole coastal trade with a view, presumably, to eliminating it. Certainly the Luftwaffe had its successes here. Several destroyers were sunk and the Navy was forced to withdraw them entirely from Dover to Harwich and Sheerness. From the RAF's point of view the campaign was not what Fighter Command had prepared for. Inevitably pilots involved in the dogfights risked drowning when they took to their parachutes, and a number were lost in this way. The RAF had no air sea rescue service to put into operation, whereas the Germans had their float planes for this very purpose. Indeed, during the Battle over land in August and September, Park issued orders hoping to prevent pilots being lost over the sea.

Some of the pilots during this first phase did question what they were doing fighting the Luftwaffe for this purpose. It is possible to ask even at this distance why the goods transported by sea at such cost to life continued. However, there are some who maintain that without this coal supply such vital industries such as aircraft construction would have been unable to continue to operate in the south of England.

Day 8 – July 17 1940

Weather: another dull day.

Fighter Command Serviceable Aircraft as at 09:00 hours:

- Blenheim – 67
- Spitfire – 237
- Hurricane – 331
- Defiant – 20
- **Total – 659**

The day was relatively quiet with just a few desultory attacks both in the Channel and the North Sea. There were 253 sorties during which the RAF lost one fighter and managed to shoot down two Luftwaffe aircraft.

PO DH Wissler – Diary, 17 July

The weather was filthy again this morning so we stayed in bed as long as possible. We did nothing all day although 'A' flight were called to readiness about lunch time. We are going to lose Sqdn Ldr Mcdougal as our CO today, in place Sqdn Ldr Williams, and first impressions of the latter aren't good. We all went to the Mead Hall and a terrific party ensued. Everyone got plastered and I did not get to bed until 2, having helped bring the ex-CO home.

(Reproduced with kind permission of the Imperial War Museum and Copyright holder)

Top Gun Gallery
Alan Deere

Deere was a New Zealander born in 1917. He was brought up in a rural environment. As a youngster he witnessed a civilian biplane land on the beach near to where he lived. He was shown over the aircraft by the pilot and thenceforward determined to learn to fly when he was old enough.

In his teens, he was recruited by an RAF team who was scouting for potential talent to fly the new monoplane aircraft coming into service with the RAF. He duly joined the RAF in 1937 in England.

He was granted a short service commission in 1938. He completed his flying training in that year and in September 1938, he joined 54 Squadron flying Gloster Gladiators. The Squadron was converted to Spitfires in January 1940. He fell in love with the new aircraft and thought it the most wonderful plane. He began his operational career over France when flying 'cover' for the BEF during the evacuation of Dunkirk. He flew on an extraordinary mission with a fellow pilot, escorting a Miles Magister light aircraft to rescue the CO of 74 Squadron who had been shot down over Calais. The mission was successful in finding and rescuing the stranded officer but during the operation the RAF fighters were attacked by Me109s. Deere promptly shot two of them down. Not content with that, later that afternoon, he shot down a third Me109.

He had several more victories over France, shooting down three Me110s, and was duly awarded the DFC, before being shot down himself on May 28. This time, he had to ditch his Spitfire and managed to do so in shallow water just off the Belgian coast. He then made his way to embark on a destroyer, meeting a somewhat cold reception in the ward room as the air force were thought not to be doing their bit to protect the troops waiting to embark from the beaches. He then arrived back at Hornchurch nineteen hours after taking off on this particular operation.

During the Battle of Britain, Deere played an extremely active part in operations. He scored a number of victories in the fighting and was shot down himself on several further occasions. He also experienced some remarkably narrow escapes. The most hair raising was when, together with two other aircraft, he was taking off during a German raid. The blast from an exploding bomb hit all three aircraft. Deere's plane was turned on its back. He was rescued by one of the other pilots who had, however, sustained injuries. When released from his aircraft, Deere managed to carry the wounded pilot to his sick quarters. On another occasion he collided head on with a Me109. The propeller of his aircraft was forced right back horizontally, yet he managed to glide his stricken plane back to the coast and landed in a field.

After the Battle, he was one of those pilots sent to America to lecture of his experiences. Subsequently, Deere had a very successful career in the RAF ending up as an Air Vice Marshal.

Comments

Kiwi Bloke: We have a flying Spitfire in NZ with Al Deere's unit markings. It belongs to his son Brendon Deere.

Tom Leathart: The extraordinary mission that is mentioned was flying cover with Johnnie Allen and escorting Prof. Leathart to Calais Marck airfield, who was I believe flying an unarmed Miles Master not a Magister. The mission is explained in detail by Al Deere in Douglas Bader's book *Fight for the Sky*, printed in the 70s. It suggests he only got one kill in that mission, but maintained probably the first sustained dogfight with an Me109, before running out of ammunition. Unfortunately Johnnie did not survive the war. Many will know that Al Deere's Spitfire markings were used for the original picture on the box of the very large scale Airfix model and the decals.

Day 9 – July 18 1940

Weather: continuing poor.

Fighter Command Serviceable Aircraft as at 09:00 hours:

- Blenheim – 62
- Spitfire – 232
- Hurricane – 323
- Defiant – 23
- **Total – 640**

The only major engagement was an attack by twenty-eight Me109s over the Straits of Dover which was met by Spitfires from 11 Group. The RAF lost three aircraft but failed to shoot down any of the enemy. Early that afternoon the coastguard station at St Margaret's Bay was bombed and the Goodwin Lightship was sunk. Four houses were destroyed during an afternoon attack on Gillingham.

266 Squadron Operational Record Book, 18 July

Average temperature, visibility very good. Flying 17 hours 25 minutes. B Flight at readiness. Ac Flight available. Practices included interception and attacks, target and cine gun practice. Spitfire aircraft N.3170 collided with tractor on aerodrome whilst taxiing and badly damaged. Pilot PO D.G. Ashton uninjured. Spitfire aircraft N.3244 force landed in a cornfield at Heckington, Lincs., owing to engine trouble. Pilot PO R.J.B. Roach uninjured.

Aircraft of the Battle
The Me109

Designed by Willy Messerschmitt, this was the aircraft which more than any other carried the colours of the Luftwaffe. The Me109 had entered service in the Spanish Civil War in 1937 and became the basic fighter of the German Air Force. It was fast, with a top speed of 357 mph, well armed with two cannons. The Me109 wasn't so much a beautiful aircraft as a very effective one. Powered by a Daimler Benz engine it had the advantage of direct fuel injection rather than a carburettor, which meant that in aerobatics the engine didn't cut out. The Spitfire, with its Merlin engine, suffered from the engine cutting out in certain aerobatics, meaning that the Me109 could out dive it. The Me109 had come into frontline service more than a year before the Spitfire and so had given German pilots the advantage of longer experience with this type of fighter. It was also hugely popular with pilots.

Comments

John Martin Bradley: No other aircraft has come close to the beauty of the Spitfire, but the Me109 was also a beautiful aircraft. And yes, the German pilots who flew it loved it, in spite of being able to see bugger all out of the badly designed canopy. General Günther Rall shot down a very large number of Russian aircraft in a 109. I also photographed Gunter Seeger and Theo Nau who inflicted terrible damage on the RAF and the USAAF in 109s. However, I was fascinated when Gunter told me he was terrified when set upon by a large flight of Beaufighters in the Med … and this is a man who shot down 28 Spitfires!

Ken Sinden: I understood that in the early stages of the battle the Me109E only had 2×7.62mm machine guns mounted in the wings. A single 20mm cannon located above the engine and firing through the propeller spinner was to be the main armament but was at that time unreliable and removed for modifications.

Day 10 – July 19 1940

Weather: improved with bright intervals.

Fighter Command Serviceable Aircraft as at 09:00 hours:

- Blenheim – 62
- Spitfire – 227
- Hurricane – 331
- Defiant – 22
- **Total – 642**

This was the day that the RAF fielded a force of Defiants. The Defiant was a single engined aircraft but with a very distinctive feature, namely a Boulton Paul power operated four gun turret complete with air gunner to operate it, situated behind the pilot and firing backwards. The aircraft had no forward firing guns. This odd design proved a disaster in combat. Nine of these aircraft, from 141 Squadron, had taken off from Hawkinge, near Folkestone, to patrol the Channel at 5000ft. They were almost immediately attacked by a force of twenty Me109s. In minutes, five Defiants had been shot down into the Channel and a sixth aircraft crash landed in fields around Dover. The remaining three were saved by the appearance of the Hurricanes of 111 Squadron. The Luftwaffe had lost one Me109 in this disastrous engagement. They subsequently claimed they had shot down twelve Defiants which was not far from the truth. Following this baptism of fire, 141 Squadron of Defiants was moved to Prestwick in Scotland. The other Defiant squadron, number 264, was sent to an airfield near Manchester. However, the squadron was, in due course, sent south again where a couple of days later it was in the thick of the fighting.

In the afternoon, radar reported a large body of aircraft forming up behind Calais. Three squadrons from 11 Group were vectored to intercept. Outnumbered nearly two to one they did not in the event achieve a score. The German aircraft, however, managed to destroy a boy's school near Fowey in Cornwall. RAF losses for the day were put at eleven aircraft downed. This compared with only four German aircraft shot down. This four to one ratio coincided with Hitler's speech to the Reichstag which included the famous 'last appeal to reason' overture to Britain. It was the German leader's most overt reference to a possible cessation of hostilities.

266 Squadron Operational Record Book, 19 July

Cool and squally. Slight rain showers during evening. Visibility moderate. Flying 14 hours 30 minutes. B Flight at readiness, Ac Flight available. Local flying, target practice – night flying circuits and landings.

Comments

Stan. Hurrell: Re. no forward firing guns on Defiants: The gun turret on Defiants was able to traverse through 360 degrees and when directed forward the guns were angled up a few degrees to clear the propeller arc. The pilot could then fire the guns forward via a reflector sight which was also angled up to correspond with the guns, and the conventional firing button on the control column. I doubt if they were ever used in this way though.

I later flew in Defiants with 278(A.S.R.) Squadron where they were used as escorts for Lysanders and Walruses.

Tony Rudd: I had a close personal friend, 'Rocky' Stone, who was an air gunner on a Defiant. They were shot down over Dunkirk and they had quite an adventure getting back.

The Squadrons

74 Squadron

I Fear No Man

74 Squadron was formed in July 1917 and served in France during the First World War. On returning to Britain, in February 1919, the squadron was disbanded. It was reformed from a number of detachments of other squadrons in 1935 whilst on board a troopship bound for Malta. The squadron was equipped with Spitfires in early 1939 and saw service in France covering the evacuation of the BEF in 1940. As part of 12 Group, the squadron was based at RAF Hornchurch during July and the early part of August 1940. The squadron moved north in mid-August and, having been rested for around two months, returned south to RAF Biggin Hill on 15 October.

The squadron was disbanded in September 2000.

Day 11 – July 20 1940

Weather: Thunderstorms in the Channel, patchy clouds over Dover.

Fighter Command Serviceable Aircraft as at 09:00 hours:

- Blenheim – 62
- Spitfire – 224
- Hurricane – 308
- Defiant – 11
- **Total – 605**

A large convoy was attacked opposite Dover. In a dogfight above this convoy, two Hurricanes were lost and four damaged. There was a major dogfight when 50 Me109s and Me110s clashed with some 24 Hurricanes and Spitfires. The RAF lost that day three aircraft against nine German aircraft destroyed which included five Me109s. The day's performance made up for the previous day's disappointing tally.

PO DH Wissler – Diary, 20 July

It was my evening off and Brigid managed to get a pass so we went out to the 'Red Lion' near Duxford and had dinner together in Flt Lt Quinn's car. A very nice evening.

(Reproduced with kind permission of the Imperial War Museum and Copyright holder)

The Airfields
RAF Kenley

Along with Biggin Hill, Kenley was built in the First World War, becoming operational in 1917. Its conversion into a peacetime RAF station dated from the 1920s. This began with a full scale reconstruction of the facilities there. It was a prime peacetime RAF station for squadrons flying in the Hendon air displays, a regular feature of the inter-war RAF.

Concrete runways were laid at Kenley in the years before the Second World War. Aircraft from this airfield played an active part in the Battle of France. In the Battle of Britain that followed squadrons from Kenley were in almost continuous action and became a prime target for the Luftwaffe. The race became intense in the latter part of August 1940. It was on 18 August that the greatest damage was done. Over 100 high explosive bombs were dropped and resulted in nine RAF personnel being killed. Nine aircraft were destroyed on the ground.

Kenley was to be linked to Croydon when the latter became available to the RAF. Croydon sometimes played host to squadrons from Kenley, particularly when damage to the latter was in danger of disrupting operations. Another airfield, Redhill to the south, acted in a similar manner in support of Kenley and became a satellite station. Redhill was readied for operations in case Kenley was actually put out of action by the German attacks.

Day 12 – July 21 1940

Weather: fine in the morning and fine in the evening but with cloud in the middle of the day.

Fighter Command Serviceable Aircraft as at 09:00 hours:

- Blenheim – 65
- Spitfire – 236
- Hurricane – 309
- Defiant – 21
- **Total – 620**

Three squadrons of 11 Group clashed with 50 Me109s and Me110s as well as a gruppe of Dorniers over a convoy threading its way through the Straits of Dover. An Me109 was shot down. Then a British fighter was shot down by an Me109 which in turn was shot down by a Spitfire. The RAF that day flew 571 sorties and lost six aircraft which was just less than the German losses of seven planes.

266 Squadron Operational Record Book, 21 July

Average temperature, bright and cloudy periods, visibility moderate. Flying 10 hours 20 minutes. B Flight at readiness, Ac Flight available. Practices included Beam attacks, formation, aerobatics, cine camera gun and local flying. Spitfire I aircraft R.6768 delivered to Squadron by Ferry Pool.

Comments

Caroline: Is anyone able to explain what is meant by B flight 'at readiness' and Ac flight 'available' in the squadron record books? What is the difference between these two?

Maurice: To my knowledge 'readiness' was when the crew sat waiting for the call and could be airborn in two or three minutes. 'Available' was the next in order when the crew needed more time to be ready to fly.

Captains and Commanders
Sir Keith Park

The original idea concerning an attack by the Luftwaffe on Britain was that it would come across the North Sea and hit mainly 12 Group under Trafford Leigh Mallory. But that idea had all been altered by the fall of France in June. Now, the German attack would be flying from airfields in northern France. It would be Park's 11 Group who would be in the front line.

Park was a tall, thin, wiry New Zealander who had started his First World War career at Gallipoli. Surviving this, he had then moved on to Britain, volunteered for flying duties, gained his pilot's wings and had become a fighter pilot on the Western Front. There, he had first won two MCs and a Croix de Guerre, while flying in the RFC, and followed this by a DFC, flying for the newly created RAF. Between the wars, he had climbed to seniority in the RAF and had now the responsibility for 11 Group as it became the front line of the RAF in the Battle.

Few men could have been better suited for the task. The battle resolved into a deadly game of chess between two commanders, Kesselring and Park. Park's job was to defend southern Britain against Kesselring's forces.

As he saw the daily plots created by the attackers unfold on the big map table in the control of his HQ in Uxbridge, Park had to assess which apparent raid was a feint and which the real thing. Get it wrong and lives would be lost. Doing this day after day must have been quite a strain. But Park was up for it. He was every inch the tough New Zealander. He believed in personally visiting the stations involved in the day to day fighting and flew his personal Hurricane around the group. Park became known to many of the pilots as a result of these visits.

Day 13 – July 22 1940

Weather: cloudy but with some bright intervals.

Fighter Command Serviceable Aircraft as at 09:00 hours:

- Blenheim – 63
- Spitfire – 228
- Hurricane – 357
- Defiant – 21
- **Total – 669**

That day enemy aircraft were elusive. Only one was shot down. Bombs were dropped in east Yorkshire and in Scotland on Leith. The day was also marked by Lord Halifax's dismissal of Hitler's last appeal to reason.

266 Squadron Operational Record Book, 22 July

Warm, visibility very good. Flying 5 hours 30 minutes. B Flight at readiness. Ac Flight available. Practices included cloud penetration, blind take offs and landings. Sector reconnaissance by night.

The People in Support
The WAAFs

The Dowding system of defence was an intricate machine in which the women of the Womens' Auxiliary Air Force, the WAAFs, played a vital role. There were several thousand young WAAFs in Fighter Command during that summer of 1940. They played a key role in helping to operate the radar system.

They were often to be found in the plotting rooms, on the telephones or peering into the radar screens. They were scrutinising the screens for the little blogs of light which indicated in coming aircraft. It was usually the WAAFs who transmitted a station's findings to another set of WAAFs sitting in Fighter Command's headquarters at Bentley Priory. It was also WAAFs who handled the business in the control rooms on their large scale plots. There, armed with their billiard cues, they would be pushing the tiny blocks of wood which represented the aircraft, with the Germans painted red and the RAF aircraft painted black. Watching the overall picture develop would be the controllers, on a platform, some 10ft above the plot.

Whilst in the Operations Rooms, the WAAFs were able to hear radio transmissions from both RAF and German pilots. This could be especially harrowing for those women who had formed romances with a pilot only to hear his agonising cries as he was shot down. Yet, the WAAFs had to, and did, remain composed and focused on their work.

It was also the WAAFs who managed the telephone exchanges. Moreover, it was three of them who, when Biggin Hill was suffering one of its worst raids from German aircraft, stayed at their posts despite the crashing masonry around them, helping to keep the station operational throughout the attack. Sgt Elisabeth Mortimer, Sgt Helen Turner and Cpl Elspeth Henderson were duly awarded the Military Medal for their bravery.

Day 14 – July 23 1940

Weather: another day of mixed weather in the Channel.

Fighter Command Serviceable Aircraft as at 09:00 hours:

- Blenheim – 62
- Spitfire – 243
- Hurricane – 282
- Defiant – 12
- **Total – 599**

A relatively quiet but successful day. Two enemy aircraft were shot down in combat over convoys but this was without loss to the RAF.

PO DH Wissler - Diary, 23 July

We went over to Martlesham and did a hell of a lot of flying. Two patrols one of 1.05hrs and one of 1.45hrs, at about 7pm we were told to take off for Debden, but having got half way home we were recalled and brought to readiness again. Eventually we were released at 9:15 and arrived to make a dusk landing. I shall sleep very well tonight, given half the chance. *(Reproduced with kind permission of the Imperial War Museum and Copyright holder)*

Week 2 Summary: The Problems of the First Phase

For the RAF, fighting the Kanalkampf wasn't what Fighter Command had really prepared for. The expectation had been that the enemy would be flying over the coast and trying to penetrate the mainland. The radar had been deployed so that enemy aircraft could be intercepted as they crossed the coast. The same applied to the Observer Corps, who were to detect their passage over land. But in this first phase of the Battle, enemy aircraft were being intercepted over the sea so that the convoys of coastal ships could be defended. The RAF hadn't invested in Air Sea Rescue Services, but the Germans had. This meant that when one of our pilots got shot up by an enemy fighter and had to bale out he was at serious risk of falling into the sea and drowning. Whereas, a German pilot in the same predicament would have been provided with, for example, a solid block of dye which, when chucked into the sea, would spread a large stain of vivid colour visible for miles, enabling the downed pilot to be found.

Secondly the pilot stood a good chance of being picked up by German sea planes, usually He59s which were deployed for the task. British pilots just had to rely on luck that they would be seen by a fishing vessel or a coast guard cutter if they were to be saved from drowning. Losing pilots who would have survived being shot down over land, but because they fell into the sea risked drowning, was a serious concern to Keith Park AOC of 11 Group. Eventually, in late July, he managed to obtain the use of a dozen Lysanders, a light aircraft used in army cooperation, to help rescue pilots in the war. But, it was not until the following year that a committee was set up in the Air Ministry to deal with the issue of air sea rescue; too late for the Battle which was then over.

Comments

Paul Handley: I'm very surprised that we didn't have effective air-sea rescue until 1941.

I'd always assumed this was something we had been rather good at in Battle of Britain.

David LaJuett: With the obvious benefit of hindsight, it seems almost criminal that nothing was done about organizing air-sea rescue in 1940. I wonder just how many British pilots drowned/went missing during the Battle? It does not seem to fit with the careful and exacting planning of Dowding, either. A strange oversight, specially given what we know was Dowding's concern about pilot losses, by early-mid August 1940.

Day 15 – July 24 1940

Weather: cloudy with rain over much of the Channel.

Fighter Command Serviceable Aircraft as at 09:00 hours:

- Blenheim – 56
- Spitfire – 238
- Hurricane – 294
- Defiant – 15
- **Total – 603**

In sustained fighting over two convoys, one over the Thames Estuary and the other off Dover, the RAF lost two aircraft whilst the Luftwaffe lost five aircraft. 561 sorties were flown. The day also saw Luftwaffe attacks on industrial targets in the Glasgow area.

54 Squadron Operational Record Book, 24 July, Rochford 08:12 hours

The biggest and most successful day since Dunkirk. Two early patrols were followed by a third in which B Flight distinguished themselves. Twelve Do 215s in two waves of six attempted to bomb a convoy off Dover. The first six reached, but missed their target. A determined attack by Green section under PO Gribble forced the e/a to jettison their bombs before reaching the target and to scurry home… This is the first instance in which coils of trailing wire (probably 50 ft in length) have been thrown out by enemy bombers as our planes pursued them.

11.25 hours

For over an hour the whole Squadron took part in the 'Battle of the Thames Estuary'. Eightenn Do 215s escorted by at least two squadrons of Me109s and an unknown number of He113s attacked a convoy in the estuary. In this, their biggest fight since the second day of Dunkirk and in the face of these considerable odds, the casualties inflicted on the enemy by the squadron (including three new pilots) can be considered eminently satisfactory and most encouraging:

2 destroyed confirmed (PO Gray and Sgt Collett)
4 destroyed unconfirmed (Flt Lt Deere, FO McMullen, PO Coleman, PO Turley-George)
8 probably destroyed (FO McMullen, Flt Lt Way (2), PO Gray, PO Gribble (2), FS Tew, PO Turley-George)
2 damaged (PO Coleman and PO Matthews)

Top Gun Gallery
Bob Doe

If there was a pilot who hid his light under a bushel, it was Bob Doe. Doe ended the Battle of Britain as the third most successful fighter pilot in the Battle, with fourteen victories to his credit. His extraordinary modesty and reticent nature inevitably meant that his name is less well known than some of the stars of the Battle.

Doe struggled to meet the requirements of a pre-war pilot. Initially he lacked confidence. He disliked aerobatics. His battle started on August 15 at Middle Wallop where he was flying a Spitfire on 234 Squadron. He wrote later that, on his first operational flight, he was filled with dread. But the fear of being a coward overcame that of being killed. He pressed on. On this, his first trip, he managed to score a victory over a Me110 near Swanage. On the following days he shot down several German aircraft including a Me109, a Ju88 and a Do18. By the end of the month he had destroyed five enemy aircraft.

On September 4, his Squadron intercepted a large group of Me109s. In the ensuing melee, Doe shot down no less than three of the German fighters. Still his record persisted.

A few days later he shot down several more enemy aircraft. The continuous fighting had, however, led to severe losses on the Squadron. Having started with fifteen pilots, there were only three of the original lot left by the middle of the month. Doe went on to join 238 Squadron as a Flight Commander. He managed to score several more victories before being shot down himself and being quite severely wounded. Parachuting from his stricken aircraft, he landed in a sewage plant which must, at least, have broken his fall.

Having recovered from his wounds, in January 1941, he was on a night flight, but suffered an engine failure. He succeeded in force landing his plane but he smashed his face when his harness broke. Doe had to endure a number of painful operations under the skilful surgeon Sir Harold Gillies. Having had his face rebuilt, he was rested.

However, subsequently he went out to India and formed a new squadron of the Indian Air Force. He flew as its Commanding Officer in the Burma campaign. For that he received the DSO, to add to his DFC and Bar.

Doe, the son of a gardener, had left school at the age of fourteen, when he had appeared to be a somewhat sickly boy. This extremely modest man ended up an outstanding leader of men and an amazingly brave and successful pilot. To top it all he was, apparently, a most agreeable character. He died a few months ago, in February 2010, at the age of 89.

Day 16 – July 25 1940

Weather: fine day.

Fighter Command Serviceable Aircraft as at 09:00 hours:

- Blenheim – 56
- Spitfire – 234
- Hurricane – 316
- Defiant – 25
- Gladiator – 8 (1 Flight only)
- **Total – 639**

This was a very active day. The RAF flew 641 sorties. In a number of sporadic attacks along the south coast sixteen aircraft were shot down with a loss of seven RAF fighters. However, the enemy succeeded in sinking five ships and damaging five more. The aerial attacks were coordinated with aggression by nine E Boats who were fought off by two destroyers – one of which had to be towed into Dover following an attack by a Ju88 bomber.

PO DH Wissler – Diary, 25 July

I went over to Martlesham to relieve one of the pilots and then did two patrols of 1.40 and 1.50 hours. The pilots in blue section did 6 hours while we in green did 4 ½ all told. God were we tired this evening. I was so sore around the back and backside. I hear that I and PO Pittman are doing the big social act tomorrow.

(Reproduced with kind permission of the Imperial War Museum and Copyright holder)

54 Squadron Operational Record Book, 25 July, Hornchurch

14:30 hours

Black Thursday. The squadron on two occasions bore the brunt of heavy enemy attacks on convoys between Deal and Dover. The loss of Flt Lt Way (missing) in this action was a great tragedy. That he accounted for an enemy aircraft before meeting his unknown fate is typical of his keenness and great courage in the face of odds large or small.

74 Squadron Operational Record Book, 25 July

Red Leader investigated a group of aircraft flying towards Calais and Red Leader, Flt Lt Malan, identified them as Me109s; attacked one at 150 yds and saw ammunition entering fuselage. Squadron returned to base without loss.

Comments

John Blake: Diaries, reports provide haunting immediacy. To think that world of dragonflies and buzzing wasps 'grappling in the central blue' is seventy years past! Yet tales of these bone-weary fighters, selfless and so very brave, do make us wonder– in such a deadly crunch, would we have risen to do battle as determined, even indomitable, as did these few, these very few, this band of brothers in their Finest Hour?

Andrew D. Bird: I would welcome anyone reading these blogs who has documentation or photographs on the Coastal Command Blenheim fighters' effort during the Battle – as these young men got clobbered too. Let's embrace the heroes we have left behind.

Aircraft of the Battle
The Hurricane

More than twice as many Hurricanes compared with Spitfires were on squadron service when the war began. The Hurricane was the product of Hawker's head designer, Sydney Camm. He had designed a whole series of bi-plane fighters for the RAF. The Hurricane was the direct descendent of the last of these. It was to replace the Hawker Fury bi-plane which had been standard on many RAF squadrons, and entered squadron service in January 1938.

The Hurricane's construction followed the same pattern as its antecedents. The body and the wing of the Hurricane were covered in fabric. The aeroplane was slightly larger than the Spitfire and in comparison it was slightly slower, having a top speed of 328mph, but it was a thoroughly reliable gun platform. Moreover, pilots who flew it swore by its performance. The aircraft was considered highly manoeuvrable: it could turn more tightly than both the Me109 and Spitfire. The aircraft had the advantage of being relatively simple to service. It also had the major advantage of being able to take a great deal of punishment from enemy fire. It was more simple and straightforward to manufacture than the Spitfire.

Comments

Peter Millist: I have always thought that the Hurricane got the raw deal on prestige and accolades for its role in the Battle of Britain. Basically, if we didn't have the Hurricane, the Battle of Britain would have been lost. So let's hear it for the Hurricane!

Mark: I fully agree. My brother Stanley Andrew was with 46 Squadron which operated Hurricanes and flew with them in Norway taking off from the flight deck of HMS Glorious. This episode, especially when ten flew back and landed with sandbags fixed to the tailplanes to hold down on landing with no arrester gear, must be one of the most famous but unknown episodes in the war. Sad loss of two pilots killed in action in Norway and eight when Glorious was sunk. At this year's 46 Squadron reunion I was a guest and they certainly remember those days at Digby, Norway, Digby and then Stapleford Tawney flying Hurricanes.

Day 17 – July 26 1940

Weather: heavy cloud and poor visibility.

Fighter Command Serviceable Aircraft as at 09:00 hours:

- Blenheim – 61
- Spitfire – 242
- Hurricane – 318
- Defiant – 26
- Gladiator – 8 (1 Flight only)
- **Total – 655**

Shipping near the Isle of Wight was attacked. The German aircraft were, however, intercepted by 601 Squadron fighters, with a later raid being met by 238 Squadron. One of the German aircraft was shot down with the loss of two RAF fighters. However, a further two German aircraft were lost later on that day. 581 sorties were flown. In widespread sporadic raids on Hastings, Essex, Monmouth and Gloucestershire minor damage was caused.

On this day, the Admiralty stopped further daylight shipping from passing through the Straits of Dover.

PO DH Wissler - Diary, 26 July

PO Pittman and I went to Lord and Lady Fitzgerald's for the day and night, we had a very quiet time, but it was a rest although very much without action. We had a fine night and a late breakfast.

(Reproduced with kind permission of the Imperial War Museum and Copyright holder)

The Squadrons

19 Squadron

Possunt quia posse videntur – They can because they think they can

19 Squadron was formed in 1915 at Castle Bromwich, and was sent to France the following year where it carried out patrols over the Western Front. The Squadron was disbanded in late 1919 only to be reformed several years later, in the early 1920s, at RAF Duxford. In 1938 the squadron became the first to receive Spitfires. In May and June 1940 the squadron flew patrols over Dunkirk as part of the support for the evacuation of the BEF. As part of 12 Group the squadron was based at RAF Duxford and Fowlmere during the Battle of Britain.

The squadron continues to operate as 19 (Reserve) Squadron based at RAF Valley.

Day 18 – July 27 1940

Weather: mixed, cloudy with some rain.

Fighter Command Serviceable Aircraft as at 09:00 hours:

- Blenheim – 63
- Spitfire – 242
- Hurricane – 331
- Defiant – 24
- Gladiator – 8 (1 Flight only)
- **Total – 668**

German operations that day started with an attack on convoys off Portland and Swanage. A little later that day two convoys off Harwich were attacked. In the course of this confrontation two Royal Navy destroyers were sunk, one of which was HMS Wren. Dover harbour also came under attack and yet another RN destroyer, HMS Codrington, was damaged and destroyed. In response, the Admiralty decided to close Dover as an advance base for destroyers. The RAF was consequently left to assume major responsibility for the defense of the Channel. That day the RAF flew 496 sorties, lost one aircraft, but destroyed four enemy planes.

266 Squadron Operational Record Book, 27 July

Average temperature, heavy rain showers during the day. Visibility poor, improving to good early evening. Flying 19 hours. Ac Flight at readiness, B Flight available. Practices included cine camera gun, interception with aircraft of no. 23 (Blenheim) Squadron and no. 229 (Hurricane) Squadron, Night Flying Patrol. 2 raid investigations carried out during day. PO H.M.T. Heron attached to St Athan for Fighter 3 weeks Navigation Instructors Course.

Comments

David Morgan: The book - *Gloucestershire Airfields in the Second World War* under Aston Down – 4 miles south of Stroud – states that this airfield was an OTU and on 27 Jul 1940 a Ju88 was shot down by an OTU Spitfire that had been armed as a contingency against random attacks. The four crew of the Ju88 baled out. One was killed when his parachute failed to open. Three were taken prisoner. The RAF pilot is not named.

In a recent edition of *Stroud Life* (July 21 2010), an article states that a Ju88 collided with a Hurricane P3271 on July 25. This is probably a typo because it was a Sunday. Three crew members of the Ju88 were captured and one was seen by the (now) 81 year old Mr. Bond, parachuting down from his school window (not on a Sunday!!). The pilot of the Hurricane – PO Alec Bird was killed. Mr. Bond has a photograph with the widow at Bird's grave in Leeds c. 2000. PO Alec Bird does not seem to appear on any Battle of Britain roll of honour.

The Airfields
RAF Manston

Manston was originally built as an airfield for use by the Royal Navy in the First World War. Its strategic location right on the coast of Kent, facing the North Sea, led to German Gotha bombers being intercepted on their way to attack London.

Its strategic location also meant that it was inevitably to play a major part in the Battle of Britain in 1940. However, its vulnerability on the sea coast of Kent led it to become a target of convenience for the Luftwaffe which bombed and strafed it mercilessly. Many of the raids which it suffered in August and September were carried out not only by Luftwaffe twin-engined bombers, but often involved Me109s making surprise attacks. The defenders often had no warning of enemy aircraft which were able to come in across the sea and then strafed Manston.

Manston was to see some of the most intense fighting of the Battle. Attacks on it did much damage. A particularly serious attack occurred on 24 August when seven RAF personnel were killed. It was the scene of some remarkable episodes particularly when enemy ground level attacks occurred when flights of Spitfires were actually taking off. Manston's importance was recognised when the Prime Minister, Winston Churchill, paid it a personal visit on 28 August 1940. He saw such a scene of destruction that he called for the Air Ministry to pay more attention to the urgent need for an organised system to be set up to handle the repairs required both here at Manston and elsewhere in Fighter Command.

Day 19 – July 28 1940

Weather: fair but cloudy in the evening.

Fighter Command Serviceable Aircraft as at 09:00 hours:

- Blenheim – 66
- Spitfire – 245
- Hurricane – 328
- Defiant – 26
- **Total – 665**

In the morning, a number of bombers attacked targets in Cornwall, Cardiff and Newport. At midday, a substantial Luftwaffe formation approached Dover but turned back without dropping any bombs and then dispersed. In the early afternoon, a large force of bombers accompanied by Me109s, around fifty of each, approached Dover. 74, 41, 11 and 257 Squadrons engaged them. Fighter Command that day flew 758 sorties with a loss of two Spitfires and three Me109s were shot down.

266 Squadron Operational Record Book, 28 July

Warm, visibility very good. Flying 18 hours 10 minutes. B Flight at readiness. Ac Flight available. Practices included tactical exercise in conjunction with aircraft of no. 23 (Blenheim) Squadron and aircraft of no. 229 (Hurricane) Squadron. Night flying tests and patrol.

Captains and Commanders
Albert Kesselring

With regards to the Battle, the most important of the German air fleets was Luftflotte 2 which was under the command of Kesselring. He had started his military career in the Army and thus lacked experience in the air but proved to be a very able man and a capable leader. Kesselring was to end up in the latter part of the war as the senior German commander of all forces in Italy.

Being in Command of Luftflotte 2 meant he had the central position handling Adler Tag, the Luftwaffe attack on Britain. The opening phase of the Battle, the Kanalkampf, was fought out on his doorstep, over the Channel, at its narrowest point. Aircraft from his command only had to fly under 100 miles to get into the action. Both at the beginning of the Battle and at its end, Luftflotte 2 acted as the spearhead of the action.

Kesselring was also the key player when it came to the many conferences that were held under Goering's command. He had earlier supported Erhard Milch's somewhat adventurous plan to launch an attack on specific British airfields almost immediately after Dunkirk.

Day 20 – July 29 1940

Weather: fair.

Fighter Command Serviceable Aircraft as at 09:00 hours:

- Blenheim – 66
- Spitfire – 241
- Hurricane – 328
- Defiant – 20
- **Total – 639**

The Air Ministry issued a statement saying that German Red Cross sea planes would not be granted immunity unless they were clearly engaged in rescuing downed pilots. Meanwhile, a raid of forty-eight Stukas and eighty covering Me109s approached Dover. They were intercepted by 41 and 501 Squadrons. A second raid occurred in the afternoon which was similar in character. Altogether, in the fighting that day, the Luftwaffe lost six aircraft and Fighter Command lost three. 758 sorties were flown by the RAF.

17 Squadron Operational Record Book, 29 July, Debden

Convoy protection patrols were maintained throughout the day, and while on patrol at 15:10 hours Blue Section was ordered to intercept raid. A He111 was sighted at 14,000 feet below cloud and the Section gave chase in line a stern. Flt Lt Bayne, the Blue Leader, delivered a frontal attack out of the sun, followed by a no. 1 attack, firing all his ammunition. The enemy aircraft dropped its undercarriage and jettisoned its bombs, pieces being seen to fall away from it and smoke pouring from both engines. FO Bird-Wilson (Blue 2) and PO Wissler (Blue 3) followed the Blue Leader with frontal and no. 1 attacks, Blue 3 experiencing some fire from the rear gunner but sustaining no hits. After further attack the enemy aircraft crashed into the sea and three of the crew were seen to climb into a rubber boat.

Comments

Stuart Bird-Wilson: My father was 'Birdy' FO HAC Bird-Wilson who was shot down by Galland on September 24. The Hurricane YBW in the Battle of Britain Memorial Flight is dedicated to him as he went on to have a long and unique history in the RAF, primarily in fighter development. I am enjoying putting together a Power Point on his life from photos and pages from the many books that include his history, some 210 slides so far. It enables me to remember much of my own life through that of a great aviator and father who unselfishly led the cutting edge of RAF flying. I was proud to see the Hurricane, depicted in a painting on the cover of Fly Past a special issue for the 70th Anniversary of the Battle of Britain. Thanks for your contribution to the history of these brave folks.

The People in Support
Royal Observer Corps

Enemy aircraft approaching Britain were picked up by the radar until they crossed the coast. Then they became the responsibility of the Royal Observer Corps. Radar could only pick up enemy aircraft over the sea. It didn't operate over land. There, it had to be the job of human eyes and a system linked to that. The Observer Corps consisted of a large number of personnel dotted around the countryside. Each post consisted of three essential positions, one using binoculars to watch, a second to operate the log and the third reporting what had been observed to the Observer Corps Headquarters in Horsham. Most of those involved were middle aged but there were also one or two youngsters on the post making themselves useful and in particular making the tea.

The Observer Corps played a vital part in the Battle. It was manned entirely by volunteers who were drawn to their task by patriotism and comradeship. There were some 30,000 during the Battle, including 4,000 women. They were the RAF equivalent of Captain Mainwaring and his faithful platoon. The Observer Corps obtained its title of 'Royal' in 1941 in response to official recognition of the valuable part it had played in the Battle.

The Observer Corps relied on a key figure in their midst to enable them to perform their job efficiently, he was the 'Aircraft Recognition Expert' who taught them to recognise the silhouettes of the aircraft they were observing. The silhouettes were on cards. The experts used an epidiascope which, with a small screen, was set up to rehearse the men with the binoculars in the art of aircraft recognition. He trained them to tell which aircraft was which. He was particularly keen to get them to recognise the difference between Spitfires, Hurricanes and Me109s. It was all part of increasing their effectiveness.

Day 21 – July 30 1940

Weather: unsettled with poor visibility.

Fighter Command Serviceable Aircraft as at 09:00 hours:

- Blenheim – 74
- Spitfire – 232
- Hurricane – 333
- Defiant – 23
- Gladiator – 8 (1 Flight only)
- **Total – 662**

Fighter Command flew 688 sorties and succeeded in shooting down two German aircraft with no loss to themselves. Barry docks were attacked that night.

266 Squadron Operational Record Book, 30 July

Average temperature, sky overcast, visibility poor. Flying three hours. B Flight at readiness, Ac Flight available. Practices included Air Fighting tactics and sector reconnaissance. Raid investigation by one aircraft of Ac Flight.

Comments

Paul Handley: I'm also following the day by day reports being published by the Daily Telegraph from their archives. It's very interesting to compare their reports of actions and enemy numbers shot down, with this factual information. Obviously, the numbers claimed were far more than actual, and there was a great need for morale boosting.

Week 3 Summary: Trouble with the Enemy's Seaplanes

The German Red Cross seaplanes were, unfortunately, to become an issue with the RAF. They bore civilian markings with a big red cross painted on the side of the fuselage. The trouble was that these aircraft, usually Heinkel 59s, carried an air gunner. The suspicion was that RAF fighters who took these seaplanes as bent on a mercy mission could fall into the trap of being shot down by the air gunner. It was also thought likely that these sea planes could be shadowing the British convoys and feeding back information about their location, thus putting them at an increased risk.

The powers that be, in the Air Ministry, were getting worried about these sea planes. Eventually, the decision was taken that they should be attacked, particularly if at the time it looked as though they were shadowing the convoys. It was to be a contentious matter. Some of our pilots did subsequently shoot down these seaplanes. Others did not. Goebbels the German Propaganda Minister complained of RAF barbarism. On July 14, Fighter Command issued a statement to pilots saying that these so-called rescue planes could not be guaranteed immunity unless it was clear that they were engaged in rescue efforts. On July 29, the Air Ministry issued a statement to the same effect.

Day 22 – July 31 1940

Weather: fair everywhere.

Fighter Command Serviceable Aircraft as at 09:00 hours:

- Blenheim – 63
- Spitfire – 239
- Hurricane – 348
- Defiant – 25
- **Total – 675**

Scattered raiders flew over the south coast. Then, late in the afternoon fifteen Me109s approached Dover. Several squadrons intercepted and a considerable fight followed. The RAF flew 395 sorties and 11 Group shot down five German aircraft for a loss of three RAF fighters.

Thus ended July. The Luftwaffe in the month had sunk eighteen coastal vessels and also sunk four destroyers. They had destroyed 77 RAF planes for the loss of 216 German aircraft.

74 Squadron Operational Record Book, 31 July

Total casualties to date (enemy) 30 confirmed, 19 unconfirmed. Our casualties – seven pilots missing – two known to be POWs in Germany, one sgt pilot in military hospital, Dover, slightly wounded.

Reported Casualties (RAF Campaign Diary):

*   Enemy: Fighters – 1 confirmed; Bombers – 2 unconfirmed.
*   Own: 2 Spitfires (both 74 Squadron)

Top Gun Gallery
'Sailor' Malan

Malan was a South African who had received an early training as a Sea Cadet at the South African Merchant Navy Academy before the war. He was to join the Union Castle Line. However, as war loomed, he joined the RAF and came to England where he got his flying training.

By December 1936, he had got his wings and joined 74 Squadron, which was the only squadron he was to serve on. He made it famous.

Apart from his extremely strong character, which gave him great leadership potential, he was a first class shot, considered the best in the whole of Fighter Command. He was also a very determined pilot. He duly became Commanding Officer of 74 Squadron which he led with confidence and élan.

He was to set out ten golden rules to be followed by the RAF fighter pilot.

Malan's first taste of action was over Dunkirk, during which, in combat, he succeeded in shooting down no less than three enemy aircraft and sharing in the destruction of six more. He was subsequently awarded the DFC. This was followed by continuous action as the Battle of Britain developed. After several moves, including periods at Hornchurch and Wittering, 74 Squadron ended up at Biggin Hill where, under Malan's leadership, it went from strength to strength. He ended his flying career in Britain with thirty-two victories, together with a number of instances where he had contributed to a kill.

He was a not untypical South African, with all the strength and conviction of the young men of the Dominion. After the Battle he had an extremely successful flying career. He ended the war as a Group Captain.

After the war, he became a leading light amongst those ex-servicemen in South Africa who fought against Apartheid. He was not always the easiest character to get on with. He had a very high standard when flying and expected his fellow pilots to achieve the same.

Day 23 – August 1 1940

Weather: fair.

Fighter Command Serviceable Aircraft as at 09:00 hours:

- Blenheim – 57
- Spitfire – 245
- Hurricane – 341
- Defiant – 21
- **Total – 664**

German raiders attacked a convoy off Hastings with considerable air fighting following. In the afternoon raiders attacked Norwich with a timber yard being destroyed. The Boulton Paul factory was also hit and suffered extensive damage. That same afternoon Luftwaffe planes dropped German propaganda leaflets over the West Country and East Anglia. This consisted of Hitler's 'last appeal to reason' speech. Some leaflets were collected up by enterprising civilians and sold the next day with the proceeds going to charity. It was that day that Hitler issued his Directive 17 which authorised the stepping up of the campaign to destroy the RAF. The RAF destroyed five enemy aircraft that day to the loss of one fighter. The RAF flew 659 sorties.

266 Squadron Operational Record Book, 1 August

Warm, cloudless, visibility excellent. 'B' Flight at readiness. 'A' Flight available. Raid investigation by two aircraft of 'B' Flight. FO N.W. Burnett posted to no. 46 Squadron for Flight Commander duties.

Reported Casualties (RAF Campaign Diary):

* Enemy: Fighters – None; Bombers – 1 confirmed, 2 unconfirmed; Reconnaissance -1 unconfirmed.

* Own: 1 Hurricane (No 145 Squadron)

Aircraft of the Battle
The Me110

This was the stable mate of the Me109. It came from the hands of the same aircraft designer and first flew in May 1936. It was meant to be the long range version of the single engine fighter that could take on offensive and defensive roles. The problem turned out to be that the Me110 just did not have anything like the performance of a single engine fighter, despite a top speed of 349mph. It couldn't hold its own in combat, particularly against the Spitfire and Hurricane. In dogfights it was the case that pilots of the Me110 often resorted to flying in a defensive circle which, it was thought, would give their rear gunners the best chance of keeping off British fighters.

In the end the Me110 became more of a fighter-bomber, than just a fighter. It even needed the protection of the Me109 flying cover for them. The conclusion has to be that certainly as a fighter the Me110 was just not a success.

Day 24 – August 2 1940

Weather: Cloudy in the Channel and along the East coast.

Fighter Command Serviceable Aircraft as at 09:00 hours:

- Blenheim – 63
- Spitfire – 238
- Hurricane – 352
- Defiant – 22
- **Total – 675**

The Luftwaffe attacked a convoy off the East coast and sank a trawler. Fighter Command intercepted several raiders and flew 477 sorties. No victories were claimed but several enemy aircraft were damaged. No RAF planes were lost but one Spitfire was burnt out.

That night Swansea was bombed and residential properties were damaged.

PO DH Wissler – Diary, 2 August

Returned off leave at 1:30 but the flight was forward at Martlesham so I did nothing all day. FO Count Czernin has been shooting up a grand line in the Daily Sketch about his dog, and the number of enemy he has shot down, it is treated with dirision [sic] up here, and his flight wrote to the 'Talk of the Town' section and said it was eighteen enemy not eight that he had shot down, and it was printed today.

(Reproduced with kind permission of the Imperial War Museum and Copyright holder)

Reported Casualties (RAF Campaign Diary):

* Enemy: Nil.
* Own: Nil.

The Squadrons
92 Squadron
Aut pugna aut morere – Either fight or die

92 Squadron was formed on 1 September 1917 and was sent to France where it operated on the Western Front, including the Somme offensive of 1918. Following the end of the First World War the Squadron was disbanded in 1919.

On 10 October 1939 the Squadron was reformed at Tangmere and equipped with Blenheims. These were replaced with Spitfires in early 1940. The Squadron flew patrols over Dunkirk during the evacuation of the BEF in May 1940. Following this the Squadron was rested for several months before returing to action in September at Biggin Hill where it was thrown into the midst of fierce fighting. Later in the war 92 Squadron served in Malta and Italy.

The Squadron served in Britain and Germany during the Cold War before changing to a training squadron in the 1990s. It was disbanded on 1 October 1994.

Day 25 – August 3 1940

Weather: foggy in the south with bright intervals.

Fighter Command Serviceable Aircraft as at 09:00 hours:

- Blenheim – 61
- Spitfire – 244
- Hurricane – 365
- Defiant – 24
- **Total – 694**

Sporadic German attacks occurred along the south coast and there were also a few minor bombing raids in the west. The Luftwaffe also dropped more propaganda leaflets. 415 sorties were flown with four German planes being shot down at no cost to 11 Group.

266 Squadron Operational Record Book, 3 August

Warm, cloudless, visibility excellent. 'B' Flight at readiness. 'A' Flight available. Practices included Fighter attacks – Formation Flying – Target practice and sector reconnaissance. Raid investigation by two aircraft of 'B' Flight. Flt Lt D.W. Balden and Sgt Pilot H.W. Ayre ceased to be attached to no. 418 Flight for temporary duty and posted to no. 261 Flight. PO D.L. Armitage appointed to acting rank of Flt Lt (unpaid) and takes over duties of Flight Commander of "A" Flight.

Reported Casualties (RAF Campaign Diary):

* Enemy: Nil. * Own: Nil.

The Airfields
RAF Debden

Opened in April 1937, Debden aerodrome was built as a fighter base as part of the RAF's reconstruction in the '30s. It was the only airfield that was originally constructed for fighters even though it served other purposes throughout its life. The airfield was grass covered when it opened and featured three large 'C' shaped hangers that would accommodate the three squadrons that were stationed there. Until the end of 1938, these revolved around normal flight training. As war loomed in Europe, fighter combat tactics were practised.

Debden was first attacked on July 10, 1940 when a single Do17 dropped more than twenty HE bombs causing no serious damage. The first big raid was on August 26, when a German formation dropped 100 HE and incendiary bombs. Five people were killed in addition to several buildings being destroyed and water and power lines fractured. Five days later on August 31, there was another raid on Debden. Once again, several buildings on the site were hit with three people killed and twelve injured. After this attack, the operations centre was relocated in a clay pit until a nearby grammar school was available for use. After these two major attacks, there were further raids but none of them caused serious damage and most of them were the result of less accurate, night bombing operations.

RAF Debden was home to the Debden Sector Operations Room and Staff, and the following Squadrons during the Battle:
• No 85 Squadron from 22 May 1940
• No 17 Squadron from 19 June 1940
• No 257 Squadron from 15 August 1940
• No 601 Squadron from 19 August 1940
• No 111 Squadron from 19 August 1940
• No 17 Squadron from 2 September 1940
• No 25 Squadron from 8 October 1940

Comments

Mark Surridge: Because of the Luftwaffe activity over RAF Debden (mentioned above) 85 Squadron, made up of Hurricanes under Squadron Leader Peter Townsend, were relocated to a grass track airfield in nearby Castle Camps.

85 Squadron had returned to Debden licking its wounds from northern France on 23 May 1940. Squadron Leader Peter Townsend said of their recall, 'So swift had been the German advance in France that 85 Squadron had had to leave many of its Hurricanes behind. The pilots arrived at Debden by dribs and drabs, some in Hurricanes they had managed to save, some in trainer aircraft, others by train or private car.'

Day 26 – August 4 1940

Weather: foggy, clearing in the evening.

Fighter Command Serviceable Aircraft as at 09:00 hours:

- Blenheim – 66
- Spitfire – 249
- Hurricane – 375
- Defiant – 21
- **Total – 711**

There was relatively little activity this day. A few reconnaissance sorties were flown over the Channel, otherwise there was little to report except for some bombing raids in the north and over Wales that evening and further propaganda leaflet drops. 261 sorties were flown during which neither side suffered any losses.

266 Squadron Operational Record Book, 4 August

Warm, cloudless, visibility excellent. 'B' Flight at readiness. 'A' Flight available. Practices included Fighter Attacks – tactical exercises with no. 23 (Blenheim) Squadron and no. 229 (Hurricane) Squadron.

Reported Casualties (RAF Campaign Diary):

* Enemy: Nil.
* Own: Nil.

Comments

Tjpalmquist: The Battle took place a couple of years before I was born, however it is still hard to wrap my head around the courage and determination of the British military to overcome a superior (supposedly) force. You have my most gratifying and never ending respect, along with the American forces, that were motivated by your accomplishments.

A Vietnam Era Vet.

Captains and Commanders
Hugo Sperrle

Sperrle was the man in charge of Luftflotte 3 flying from the Cotentin Peninsula. Physically, he was a huge bear of a man. But it wasn't all brawn; he had brains too. His early career had been in the Army and he had flown during the First World War before returning to the Army after 1918. He had been Commander in Chief of the Condor Legion in 1937 when a substantial contingent of the Luftwaffe had contributed to Franco's victory in the Spanish Civil War.

Sperrle may have been and indeed was a very commanding physical figure, as well as being a determined leader. When it came to Goering's conferences, he usually attended alongside Kesselring. He was a key player in the fortunes of the Luftwaffe in the Second World War.

Day 27 – August 5 1940

Weather: slight haze in the Channel otherwise fine.

Fighter Command Serviceable Aircraft as at 09:00 hours:

- Blenheim – 63
- Spitfire – 257
- Hurricane – 373
- Defiant – 26
- **Total – 719**

Early that morning, Spitfires patrolling over the Straits of Dover ran into a group of Me109s, as a result of which one Me109 was shot down into the sea and one of the Spitfire pilots was shot down and killed. Later that day, a Squadron of Hurricanes was similarly engaged with Me109s and Ju88s and further enemy losses were inflicted. 402 sorties were flown.

266 Squadron Operational Record Book, 5 August

Warm and close – sky overcast – visibility moderate. 'B' Flight at readiness. 'A' Flight available. Practices included Fighter Attacks and affiliation exercise with Blenheim aircraft of no. 110 Squadron from West Raynham.

Reported Casualties (RAF Campaign Diary):

* Enemy: 4 confirmed (2 by No 65 Squadron, 1 each by Nos. 64 and 151 Squadrons), 2 unconfirmed (1 each by Nos. 64 and 65 Squadrons); Bombers – nil.
* Own: 1 Spitfire (No 64 Squadron)

Comments

John Blake: Day by day, this reads like a thriller, as indeed it is. Are there any charts available that track daily and cumulative RAF losses vs.

Luftwaffe? Wonder how British aircraft production kept pace with incremental drain of capability.

Might emphasize role of newly-invented radar, plus UK's network of theatre communications with local controllers functioning as nodes. From 1938, Bletchley Park's cryptographers were active as 'Captain Ridley's shooting party'... any input there?

Heather: There has often been speculation that Dowding was privy to the top secret Ultra decoded material, but I think that's pretty much been denied.

The People in Support
The Controllers

For the pilots flying their fighters that summer, the most important voice they were to hear was that of the Controller responsible for guiding them in the right direction around the sky so that they would intercept the enemy. Behind the controller and contributing to his instructions were the WAAFs monitoring the blips on their radar sets and then the WAAFs pushing their billiard cues around the plot laid out at Bentley Priory. Then, at 11 Group, it was the Controller who gave the pilots their course to steer. All were part of an integrated team.

Comments

Andrew McCrorie: Fighter Command's control system gave it an edge and helped make it a complete air defense system, something that not even the Luftwaffe had at the time.

The only part that was not fully integrated was 12 Group due the failure of its leadership (and the failure of the RAF to correct it).

Tony Rudd: I believe 12 Group was integrated into the air defense system. However, it was a case of its commanders, such as Bader, ignoring the instructions given them by their controllers – basically swanning around the sky looking for the enemy. Every now and then they were lucky and very effective.

Andrew McCrorie: 12 Group were lucky sometimes but compared to other groups, 12 Group squadrons had a low interception rate. When they did intercept they over claimed (more than other squadrons) due to the confusion inherent in a big wing.

Historical analysis has shown that 12 Group were on the whole ineffective in the Battle of Britain, not due to the efforts of its pilots and crew, but due to poor leadership. Many 11 Group airfields were bombed when 12 Group should have turned up to protect them.

Day 28 – August 6 1940

Weather: cloudy.

Fighter Command Serviceable Aircraft as at 09:00 hours:

- Blenheim – 67
- Spitfire – 257
- Hurricane – 370
- Defiant – 23
- **Total – 717**

A quieter day with minimal activity. Three Spitfires from 616 Squadron were damaged as a result of return fire from Ju88s which they were attacking off the north east coast near Flamborough. The score was one all.

249 Squadron Operational Record Book, 6 August, Church Fenton

During the last few days a considerable amount of practice flying has been carried out and much attention paid to beam attacks and dog fighting practice. There seems to be very little activity in the North now, but things are boiling up in the South of England and attacks are being carried out by large numbers of e/a on convoys and South Coast ports. We are all hoping to get a move South.

William Joyce (Lord Haw-Haw) speaking on German Radio, August 6 1940

'I make no apology for saying again that invasion is certainly coming soon, but what I want to impress upon you is that while you must feverishly take every conceivable precaution, nothing that you or the government can do is really of the slightest use. Don't be deceived by this lull before the storm, because, although there is still the chance of peace, Hitler is aware of the political and economic confusion in England, and is only waiting for the right moment. Then, when his moment comes, he will strike, and strike hard.'

Reported Casualties (RAF Campaign Diary):

* Enemy: Fighter – nil; Bombers – 1 Do17 confirmed (by No 85 Squadron)
 * Own: Nil.

Comments

M B Bingham: Re Lord Haw Haw's traitorous utterances. As a young child I recall listening to ITMA on Thursday evenings when he was admirably de-bunked by using a spoof 'Herr Funf' character whose diatribe always began 'Dis ist Funf speaking…' Tommy Handley soon demolished it with a topical joke – to tumultuous studio audience applause! With sterling stuff like that to bolster the nation, defeat never entered our minds.

Week 4 Summary: Pilots from Overseas – 'He Died for England'

Statistical summary, Week 4:

- *Total Fighter Command Establishment: 1558 planes*
- *Strength: 1434 planes*
- *Balance: under strength 124 planes*
- *Losses: 4 Hurricanes, 4 Spitfires, 0 damaged*
- *Aircraft Production: 3 Beaufighters, 13 Defiants, 68 Hurricanes, 48 Spitfires*

Of the near 3000 pilots who flew in the Battle of Britain, roughly a fifth came from overseas to help the RAF win this encounter. Of these, about half came from British Dominions, of what was then the British Empire.

The largest contingent came from New Zealand, but the man who turned out to be the best shot in Fighter Command came from South Africa. He was called 'Sailor' Malan.

The rest of the contingents of overseas pilots came from countries already overrun by Hitler's legions. Of these, the largest number came from Poland.

Meanwhile, it is worth noting an all-important fact. This is that the contribution of so many nationalities to the RAF's efforts that summer led to the feeling that this was not just a battle, but a crusade, not just a purely national struggle, but something much more significant. The pilots who flew in this battle had come from half way round the globe. A pilot who typifies what might be called the 'chivalry' involved, was a young American, Billy Fiske.

America was not yet a participant in the war. That country was very much in the neutral camp. Furthermore, the American Ambassador in London, Joe Kennedy, father of John F. Kennedy the future President, was deeply sceptical about Britain's chances of survival. Nevertheless, Fiske threw in his lot as a participant in the fight. He paid with his life in doing so.

Billy Fiske came from a banking family and was, in fact, a banker himself working for Dillon Read. He had made his name heading the US bobsleigh team in the 30s representing his country in the Olympics. He was apparently a superb pilot. He was also very charming and had become an extremely popular member of 601 Squadron, nicknamed the 'Millionaires Squadron'. Additionally, he was the owner of a 4.5 litre open racing Bentley. In action, flying his Hurricane on August 16 from Tangmere, he took a hit from an Me 109 while chasing a pack of Stukas, a number of which were shot down. Instead of bailing out, he nursed his damaged plane back to his airfield and despite a substantial wound and burnt ankles and hands, landed his plane safely. But he had to be helped out of his cockpit and taken to hospital when he landed.

Later that day, when the Adjutant of the squadron visited him in hospital he appeared in great form, but the next day he died from surgical shock. There is a memorial plaque to him in the crypt of St. Paul's Cathedral which reads 'An American Citizen who died that England might live'. He tombstone in the graveyard of a small English country church reads simply 'He died for England'.

There weren't many Americans who flew in the Battle of Britain that summer – ten in all. On the other hand, the selfless sacrifice by this very attractive young man typified the spirit of the many young men who came from far and wide to join in the Battle.

Comments

John Morris Bush: Fiske is buried at Boxgrove Sussex, which is just across to A27 from Tangmere. My wife is a Fiske and has researched the family, which originated from Suffolk. The first one she has found is a Symond Fiske going back to the 13th century.

Jane Nissen: inspiring story for any Anglo-American. I would love to know about the other nine American pilots.

Day 29 – August 7 1940

Weather: cloudy with some bright intervals.

Fighter Command Serviceable Aircraft as at 09:00 hours:

- Blenheim – 66
- Spitfire – 256
- Hurricane – 368
- Defiant – 24
- **Total – 714**

Enemy activity was largely confined to convoy reconnaissance. Preparations by the Luftwaffe for Adlertag were accelerating. In raids by Bomber Command on Haamstede Aerodrome several Me109s on the ground were damaged. Fighter Command flew 393 sorties at no cost to themselves.

266 Squadron Operational Record Book, 7 August

Warm – bright and cloudy intervals – visibility good. 'B' Flight at readiness. 'A' Flight available. Practices included sector tactical exercise – affiliation exercise with Blenheim aircraft of no.110 Squadron from West Raynham. Night Flying Tests.

Reported Casualties (RAF Campaign Diary):

* Enemy: – nil.
* Own: – nil.

Top Gun Gallery
James 'Ginger' Lacey

Ginger Lacey was one of the highest scoring NCO pilots flying in the Battle. Like other successful fighter pilots, he was blessed with natural talent and a great deal of luck. He survived many incidents which might just have easily resulted in his being killed.

His first operational experience was in France where his Squadron had been sent on May 10. He achieved a number of kills in the subsequent fighting. Back in England he resumed his extremely successful record during the Battle of Britain. During the Battle he was credited with no less than twenty-eight kills, becoming the second highest scorer of any RAF pilot in the Battle.

On 13 September, he shot down a He111 which had just bombed Buckingham Palace. But in this encounter, his aircraft had received a lethal hit. Then, on 15 September, one of the heaviest days of the Battle, he had an outstanding day shooting down no less than three Me109s. But then on 17 September, he was himself shot down by a Me109, but managed to bale out uninjured.

He continued to notch up successes during the rest of the month and into October. Lacey during the Battle was shot down or forced to crash land no less than nine times.

Lacey went on with his flying career over the next two years when he was commissioned. But before that, he had won the DFM and Bar. He ended up being posted to India where he became Commanding Officer of 17 Squadron, operating in the Burma Campaign. After the war, he obtained a permanent commission and remained in the air force until retirement in 1967. There remains a memorial tablet dedicated to this extremely successful fighter pilot in the Parish Church of Bridlington in Yorkshire.

Comments

Adrian Frais: Enjoyed reading about Ginger Lacey. I had the privilege of meeting him in 1961 at RAF Dishforth when on a visit with school cadets. He looked after our party.

Day 30 – August 8 1940

Weather: showers and bright intervals.

Fighter Command Serviceable Aircraft as at 09:00 hours:

- Blenheim – 66
- Spitfire – 257
- Hurricane – 370
- Defiant – 20
- **Total – 713**

On the previous evening a substantial convoy, code named Peewit, had set out from the Thames. As it passed through the Straits of Dover it was picked up by the newly installed Freya radar on the French coast. The Germans saw that the convoy consisted of more than twenty ships. It was soon attacked by several E-boats which sank three ships in the convoy and damaged several others.

A second raid was then launched on this convoy by a force of Ju87 dive bombers accompanied by fighters. They attacked the ships off the Isle of Wight. They had orders to sink the whole convoy. Despite resistance from a number of squadrons of RAF fighters, further casualties were inflicted on the ships.

Nevertheless, a third attack, this time also from Cherbourg was launched. These enemy aircraft were intercepted near Swanage by seven squadrons from 10 and 11 Groups. In an intensive and prolonged series of engagements, with some squadrons flying as many as three sorties, substantial numbers of aircraft, particularly the Ju87s, were shot down. The remains of the convoy finally made Portsmouth Harbour with only four out of the twenty-one ships undamaged. It proved to be the most intensive attack on a convoy during that summer. The RAF lost nineteen aircraft as against thirty-one German aircraft destroyed. Churchill duly sent a congratulatory note on the day's performance to the Secretary of State for Air.

54 Squadron Operational Record Book, 8 August, Hornchurch

No enemy aircraft seen – very quiet day.

74 Squadron Operational Record Book, 8 August

Flt Lt A G Malan DFC appointed to the rank of Acting Squadron Leader and assumes command of no. 74 Squadron. Malan awarded bar to DFC.

Reported Casualties (RAF Campaign Diary):

* Enemy: 52 confirmed, 14 unconfirmed
* Own: 13 Hurricanes, 4 Spitfires, 1 Blenheim

Aircraft of the Battle
Ju87 Stuka

The Ju87 Stuka acted as the aerial artillery of the Luftwaffe. In battle, when the Luftwaffe had won control of the air, it was a hugely effective weapon. It was at its best against ground targets which it attacked with phenomenal accuracy. The technique of the dive-bomber saw to that. It involved the pilot putting the aircraft into a vertical dive from anything up to 10,000 ft. The pilot selected his target and dived directly at it, releasing his bomb a few hundred feet from the aiming point, allowing the bomb to continue on its trajectory while the pilot pulled the aircraft out from the dive at the last minute.

Stuka pilots were experts in the manoeuvre. To add to the effect, the aircraft was fitted with a siren which gave off a very audible scream that played its part in demoralising those on the ground who were being attacked.

When the Stuka was used in the Spanish Civil War and the early stages of the Second World War, it seemed to be a very effective weapon. But in the Battle of Britain this impression didn't last. The fact was the aircraft was terribly vulnerable when having to perform amongst enemy fighters such as the Spitfire and Hurricane. It was in these circumstances that the Stuka was a veritable sitting duck. The Stuka only had a top speed of a little over 200 mph. It had the disadvantage of a fixed non-retractable undercarriage. As the Battle wore on, the Germans had to ensure that the Stukas, when deployed, were accompanied by large formations of Me109s. If caught without this protection, disaster followed.

By the end of August, it became necessary for the Luftwaffe to withdraw them from operations. Too many were being lost. They were to be held in reserve, save for a few isolated raids during the Blitz, henceforward awaiting the day that the Luftwaffe had cleared the skies of British fighters. That day never arrived. The Stukas had to wait for the Russian Campaign before they could resume their role.

Day 31 – August 9 1940

Weather: cloudy with bright intervals.

Fighter Command Serviceable Aircraft as at 09:00 hours:

- Blenheim – 64
- Spitfire – 228
- Hurricane – 370
- Defiant – 23
- Gladiator – 2
- **Total – 687**

Sporadic raids were undertaken against suitable targets, for example the remains of the convoy attacked on the 7/8 August was targeted by a Ju88 which was subsequently shot down by 234 and 601 Squadrons. One RAF aircraft was lost and one of the enemy was shot down. The RAF flew 409 sorties. That night Wiltshire was bombed and the landing ground was hit at the Marston Aircraft Factory.

The Germans had spent much of the day planning for Adler Tag which was due to be launched on the following day. However, by the evening this had to be cancelled because of bad weather.

249 Squadron Operational Record Book, 9 August

Friday morning boredom relieved at the sound of shots being discharged during the pay parade in the Squadron hangar, as a result of which no. 566614 Cpl Parry Jones of B Flight grasped his side and fell to the ground. He was found to have been wounded by a bullet and was taken to York Military Hospital by Ambulance. On subsequent investigation, it was found that a Hurricane aircraft of no. 73 Squadron was being loaded whilst in the flying position, pointing towards our hangar and two rounds had inadvertently been fired. This incident did a lot towards fostering the already excellent competitive spirit between the two squadrons on the station.

Reported Casualties (RAF Campaign Diary):

* Enemy: Enemy: Fighters – nil, Bombers – 1 He111 confirmed (by No 79 Squadron).
* Own: – nil

Comments

Ben Piscitelli: Tony, my late father served with the USAAF at Mount Farm near Oxford from 1943 to the end of the war. He was a crew chief with the 714th photo squadron which consisted of P-38s and Spitfires mounted with cameras, but no guns to maximize speed for reconnaisance missions. He'd told me that one of his planes, I believe the name was Spook Foof or something similar, was one of the few Spitfires that survived the Battle of Britain before it was converted to a recon plane. It had been badly shot up. I've heard these stories since childhood and have always regarded the RAF's veterans of this battle as real life members of the Knights of the Round Table. Thanks for keeping the memories of these great men alive. Ben Piscitelli, Columbus, Ohio

The Squadrons
257 Squadron
Thay myay gyee shin shwe hti – Death or Glory

257 Squadron was formed on 18 August 1918 at Dundee and flew anti-submarine patrols along the east coast of Scotland. The squadron was disbanded on 30 June 1919.

On 17 May 1940, 257 Squadron was re-formed at Hendon. The Squadron was initially equipped with Spifires but was re-equipped with Hurricanes a few weeks later. It served throughout the Battle of Britain and was based at a number of airfields in the south, including Debden, Matlesham and

North Weald. In 1944 the Squadron was part of 2nd Tactical Air Force which provided air support during the D-Day landings in northern France.

The Squadron was disbanded on 31 December 1963.

Comments

Geoff Nutter: I understand that my brother was one of the first two RAFVR pilots to join 257 when Stanford Tuck took over in May 1940. He flew as a Sgt Pilot throughout 1940 before being posted in Feb 1941, as a flight instructor, to the Empire training Scheme in Canada. He returned to England (Feb 1944), converted to Typhoons (175 Squadron and 245 Squadron) and saw action as part of the 2nd Tactical Air force supporting the landings and campaign to liberate Europe. After demobilization he and his Canadian wife and boy returned to Canada. She was disappointed at not being able to go to the Palace for the presentation of his DFC which took place in Canada.

At one time he wondered if he would ever celebrate his 21st birthday – he did. If fact he celebrated his 89th birthday in January of this year.

Of those who flew with Stanford Tuck he and one other pilot are still alive, both in Canada!

Day 32 – August 10 1940

Weather: Unsettled with some bright intervals.

Fighter Command Serviceable Aircraft as at 09:00 hours:

- Blenheim – 60
- Spitfire – 245
- Hurricane – 382
- Defiant – 22
- Gladiator – 2
- **Total – 711**

German reconnaissance aircraft were active. There were also some sporadic raids including an attack on West Malling. 116 patrols were flown but no contact was made.

There were no losses on either side.

PO DH Wissler Diary, 10 August

I had the day off today but what a day! I attended PO Britton's funeral at 1:30 and this was the most harrowing affair I have ever come upon. Having finished with this I flew Flt Lt Bayne to Wittering and returned in a Magister. I had a good time in the evening when I went to Cambridge to see a flick and then went to an Indian restaurant and had a fine curry, getting back to Debden at 12:30 approx.

(Reproduced with kind permission of the Imperial War Museum and Copyright holder)

Reported Casualties (RAF Campaign Diary):

* Enemy: – nil.
* Own: – nil

The Airfields
RAF Tangmere

Tangmere aerodrome was first founded in 1917 as a training base for the Royal Flying Corps. The following year, it was turned into a training ground for the American Air Force and remained that way until the end of World War One. Afterwards the airfield was abandoned. It reopened in 1925 to serve the RAF's Fleet Air Arm and became operational in 1926. In 1939 Tangmere's airfield was enlarged in order to defend the south coast against attacks by the Germans.

The first raid at Tangmere was also the worst. On August 16, 1940, 100 Ju87 'Stuka' dive bombers and fighters damaged and destroyed numerous buildings and aircraft on the base. In addition, the power, water and sanitation systems were put out of commission. Fourteen servicemen and six civilians were killed and another twenty were injured in the attack. Yet, even after the devastation of the attack, the station remained open and returned to full operation. It was not a complete German victory though, as Hurricanes and Spitfires destroyed nine enemy dive-bombers in addition to severely damaging seven others.

Two days later, both sides suffered heavy losses as Tangmere squadrons attacked more Stuka planes in defense of RAF Thorney Island, Ford and Poling RDF Station. This caused the Luftwaffe to scale back these kinds of operation over England. As the Luffwaffe was entering its third phase, Tangmere's Hurricanes and Spitfires were involved in intercepting many raids on other RAF airfields and aircraft factories in southern England.

RAF Tangmere was home to the Tangmere Sector Operations Room and Staff, and the following Squadrons during the Battle:
• No 145 Squadron from 10 May 1940
• No 43 Squadron from 31 May 1940
• No 601 Squadron from 17 June 1940
• No 1 Squadron from 23 June 1940

- No 266 Squadron from 9 August 1940
- No 17 Squadron from 19 August 1940
- No 607 Squadron from 1 September 1940
- No 601 Squadron from 2 September 1940
- No 213 Squadron from 7 September 1940
- No 145 Squadron from 9 October 1940

Day 33 – August 11 1940

Weather: mainly cloudy.

Fighter Command Serviceable Aircraft as at 09:00 hours:

- Blenheim – 60
- Spitfire – 247
- Hurricane – 373
- Defiant – 24
- Gladiator – 2
- **Total – 706**

The day began with a feint in the east with the real attack coming in over the west country. A substantial raid developed on Portland and Weymouth with well over 100 aircraft involved. Several squadrons intercepted. Dogfights ensued. Over 70 bombs were dropped and damage was done to property and the railway line. This was the biggest battle so far during the Battle of Britain.

Meanwhile, in the east, there was continuous activity around Dover and the Straits. 74 Squadron flew no less than four sorties from Manston. Several more squadrons were engaged before hostilities ended. It was indeed a busy day for Manston. Losses were heavy on both sides. Over thirty German aircraft were shot down in return for losses to the RAF of twenty-seven aircraft. There had been much fighter to fighter combat, hence the losses.

Adler Tag had now been set for August 13.

19 Squadron Operational Record Book – 11 August

New Spitfire equipped with two cannon and four Browning Guns delivered today. Is slightly overweight but in the general opinion is a step in the right direction. Possibly another step in the same direction would be the re-equipping with the old eight-gun machines.

Reported Casualties (RAF Campaign Diary):

* Enemy: 37 confirmed, 47 unconfirmed.
* Own: 20 Hurricanes, 5 Spitfires

Captains and Commanders
Sir Christopher Quintin Brand

Air Vice Marshal Sir Christopher Quintin Brand was a South African who headed 10 Group during the Battle of Britain. After serving with the South African Air Force, Brand joined the RFC with whom he saw active service during the First World War. In May 1918 he was credited with bringing down a German Gotha bomber near Faversham. He was subsequently awarded the DSO. After the First World War, Brand continued his flying career with the RAF. In 1920 he and a fellow South African aviator, Pierrie van Ryneveld, made a pioneering flight from Brooklands to Cape Town. Leaving England in February 1920, the pair arrived in Cape Town on 20 March having spent 109 hours flying. Brand and van Ryneveld were knighted in recognition of their achievement.

Brand formed a close and effective relationship with Keith Park, commander of 11 Group. When Park's resources were stretched to the limit, Brand was always available to help out by seconding squadrons to assist 11 Group.

Moreover, Brand was another adherent to the tactics adopted by Park of putting up squadrons, if necessary, singly to react immediately to the enemy's attacks. He paid for this, of course, when the 'Big Wing' enthusiasts got their way and took over Fighter Command. Brand was, in the late autumn of 1940, relieved of his command and sent off to Training Command to cool his heels.

During the Battle itself, Brand turned out to be a very effective commander. His group in the west of England fought against the attacks from Luftflotte 3, coming across the Channel from the Cotentin Peninsula.

Brand retired from the RAF in 1943.

Day 34 – August 12 1940

Weather: fine.

Fighter Command Serviceable Aircraft as at 09:00 hours:

- Blenheim – 60
- Spitfire – 248
- Hurricane – 363
- Defiant – 24
- Gladiator – 4
- **Total – 699**

Operations began in the morning over Dover as usual. Then followed attacks on radar stations in the vicinity of Dover. Despite a number of bombs being dropped, no serious damage was done. The radar station by Dover itself was slightly damaged, but that at Rye suffered considerable damage as did the station at Pevensey. However, Rye was back on air by noon. The radar station at Pevensey took longer to repair.

An hour later, an attack by Ju87 dive bombers took place on a convoy in the Thames Estuary followed by a heavy raid on Portsmouth which resulted in the destruction of the pier and damage to the railway station. While this was occurring a serious raid was launched on the radar station at Ventnor on the east coast of the Isle of Wight. Numerous direct hits were scored on Ventnor which put it out of action for three days.

At lunchtime, switching back to the east coast, a heavy attack was launched by a large force of Dorniers on the airfield at Manston. Over one hundred bombs were dropped on the airfield, but happily without heavy casualties being caused. Hawkinge was also attacked and a considerable amount of damage done. The station was, however, serviceable the next day. Lympne airfield, also in the south east, which had been the subject of an attack that morning, was once again visited with a number of bombs being dropped. Most fell on the airfield but some also fell in surrounding fields. Small raids by German bombers that evening attacked Hastings and Dover.

Back in Germany, the day's raids were assessed as having been very successful. Wildly exaggerated estimates were made of the number of planes destroyed on the ground. A number of the airfields visited that day were duly crossed off as irreparably damaged. However, there was more realism concerning the radar stations. The Head of Signals reported that attacks had not put the radar stations out of action for long. It was all part of the process by which the Luftwaffe, within the next few weeks, estimated they had virtually wiped out Fighter Command. Nothing could have been more disappointing to the German fighter pilots, who on their raids over Britain, went on being met by an undiminished number of Spitfires and Hurricanes. German losses that day totaled thirty-one as against the RAF losses of twenty-two.

54 Squadron Operational Record Book, 12 August

The squadron engaged the enemy twice during the day – once in the morning and again in the evening when Flt Lt Deere added still further to his personal score with one Me109 and one Me110 both destroyed. One of our Polish Sergeants (Sgt Klozensky) vented his wrath on the Hun to the extent of one certain Me109 and one probable Me109.

Reported Casualties (RAF Campaign Diary):

* Enemy: 62 planes confirmed destroyed, 36 probable, 39 damaged
* Own: 9 Hurricanes, 6 Spitfires

Comments

Stan: I am surprised to see that four Gladiators were at readiness. Where were they stationed and did they ever go into action? I imagine they would have been sitting ducks against the Luftwaffe.

The only Gladiators I can remember going into action were *Faith, Hope* and *Charity* on the island of Malta.

Heather: Malta is the best known action where Gladiators were used, I think. You'll find the type served admirably, even in the Battle of Britain.

Brett: One of my favourite curiosities of the Battle — the Gladiators in question were from 247 Squadron, based at Roborough near Plymouth (Devon). They did make at least one interception of a German bomber force, on 25 September, but were not quite fast enough to make an attack.

The People in Support
The Air Transport Auxiliary

The Air Transport Auxiliary (ATA) was the brainchild of a British Overseas Airways Corporation director, Gerald d'Erlanger. D'Erlanger approached the Air Ministry with proposals for a pool of civilian pilots, and when the Air Ministry decided that it was not viable to use RAF pilots to ferry aircraft, it was agreed to appoint d'Erlanger as administrator of the newly formed ferry organisation, the ATA. Aircraft were a precious commodity, and the ATA needed to ensure that its pilots were of the highest standard in order to minimise any potential losses. Therefore, the ATA cast its net wide when recruiting pilots, and in August 1940 a concerted effort was made to get skilled American pilots to join. This was not without success, and American pilots were the largest percentage of foreign pilots in the ATA.

The ATA provided a crucial service in ferrying planes from factories to maintenance units and then onto squadrons. Male pilots delivered much needed Fairey Battles to the Advanced Air Striking Force in France, and in May 1940, ATA pilots were used to bring some of the RAF's planes back to Britain. During the Battle of Britain, male ATA pilots were responsible for delivering Hurricanes and Spitfires to squadrons – a vital contribution to the Battle. There were twenty-six female pilots in the ATA in 1940 – including the famous aviatrix Amy Johnson – and whilst they were not allowed to fly Spitfires and Hurricanes until 1941, they delivered training aircraft such as Tiger Moths and Avro Ansons which were an important part of helping to keep a supply of trained RAF pilots. The ATA pilots were highly skilled and had to adapt to many different types of aircraft, none of which were armed during the ferry flights. Keeping the squadrons and training schools supplied with aircraft during the Battle was crucial to Britain's survival, and the ATA provided a vital service.

Pilots and groundcrew with their trophy

Sqdn Ldr Peter Townsend

Censored photo of Czech pilots of no. 310 Squadron and their British flight commanders grouped in front of a Hawker Hurricane Mk. I at Duxford, Cambs.

19 Squadron debrief after a sortie at RAF Fowlmere; (L-R) Flt Lt WJ 'Farmer' Lawson, Sqdn Ldr BJE 'Sandy' Lane (Commanding Officer) and FSGC 'Grumpy' Unwin

Squadron Leader Douglas Bader with some Canadian pilots

*Flt Lt Nicholson
receiving his VC*

Censored photo of a squadron scoreboard

Flt Lt JH 'Ginger' Lacey

Hugh Dundas

*Gp Cpt A G 'Sailor'
Malan*

Wg Cdr Alan Deere with Sqdn Ldr Denis Crowley-Milling

Adler Angriff
August 13 – September 6 1940

Adler Angriff
August 13 – September 6 1940

Day 35 – August 13 1940

Adler Tag (Eagle Day)

Weather: Fine; some patchy cloud over Channel.

Adolf Hitler, Directive No. 17 (1 August, 1940)

The Luftwaffe will use all the forces at its disposal to destroy the British air force as quickly as possible. August 5 is the first day on which this intensified air war may begin, but the exact date is to be left to the Luftwaffe and will depend on how soon its preparations are complete, and on the weather situation.

Fighter Command Serviceable Aircraft as at 09:00 hours:

- Blenheim – 71
- Spitfire – 226
- Hurricane – 353
- Defiant – 26
- Gladiator – 2
- **Total – 678**

There was some mist at first but this later cleared. Early in the morning, a large force of Do17s had taken off under the leadership of Commander Johannes Fink. But the fighters who were meant to accompany the bomber stream had turned back. Goering, back in Karinhall, had been told that the weather wasn't, after all, all that good. He decided to postpone the opening of the new campaign that had been scheduled for today, codenamed 'Adler Tag', or 'Eagle Day'. He personally ordered those aircraft, which had already taken off, to be recalled. The recall signal reached the fighters, but not the bombers. The former turned for home, leaving the bombers to forge on alone.

However, the bombers' target was an RAF station in Kent, Eastchurch. This wasn't a Fighter Command station at all, as it belonged to Coastal Command, although 266 Squadron Spitfires were there having just been moved down from the Midlands. No fighters were permanently stationed there. The raid on Eastchurch turned out to be very damaging and destructive, wrecking a number of aircraft, killing several personnel, and it gave the impression to Fink and his men that they had completely destroyed a fighter command station, together with ten Spitfires. In fact, only one Spitfire was destroyed, although sixteen ground crew were killed and five Blenheims were destroyed. Despite this damage, the station was back in service the next day.

On the way home, flying across Kent, five Do17s of Fink's group were shot down with several more being damaged by 111 and 151 Squadrons. On return to base Fink was furious. What had happened to his fighter escort?

Yet the most serious error made that day was mistaking Eastchurch, a Coastal Command station for a Fighter Command one.

A second German group had not received details of Eagle Day's postponement and a sizeable force of Ju88s was heading for Odiham and the research establishment at Farnborough. But they were intercepted by 601 Squadron and forced to return to their base.

In the afternoon came a series of raids from Luftflotte 3 from the Cherbourg peninsula which were aimed at Portland and other south coast ports including Southampton. Several interceptions were made by RAF squadrons on this latest incursion. However, several German aircraft managed to get through to Southampton and did serious damage.

At the same time, Luftflotte 2 was also in action. Detling was hit and the Commanding Officer was killed. The day had given Fighter Command a taste of the much more intensive battle which was about to take place over the next few weeks. Cumulatively, it was to put the Command under severe strain. The RAF lost thirteen aircraft with the Germans losing forty-five.

That night the Nuffield works near Birmingham were hit.

54 Squadron Operational Record Book, 13 August

A respite with only one patrol over Hornchurch for an hour early in the morning.

19 Squadron Operational Record Book – 13 August – Eastchurch

Eastchurch Aerodrome (and 'B' Flight) most thoroughly bombed. Approximately 220 bombs dropped in twenty minutes. The personnel were also machine-gunned by low-flying enemy aircraft. Fortunately 'B' Flight sustained no damage or injuries. The dispersal of the aircraft would help considerably to this end.

Reported Casualties (RAF Campaign Diary):

* Enemy: 78 aircraft destroyed, 33 probable, 49 damaged.
* Own: 11 Hurricanes, 2 Spitfires

Week 5 Summary – Adler Tag is Launched

Statistical summary, Week 5:

- *Total Fighter Command Establishment:* 1558 *planes*
- *Strength:* 1396 *planes*
- *Balance:* *under strength 162 planes*
- *Losses:* 33 *Hurricanes (+ 3 damaged), 12 Spitfires (+10 damaged), 3 Blenheims*
- *Aircraft Production:* 5 *Beaufighters, 10 Defiants, 64 Hurricanes, 37 Spitfires*

By early August, the German attitude to Britain had hardened. After the fall of France, most of the world had expected Britain one way or the other to fall out of the war, either because it was pushed out or it opted out. This is certainly what Hitler had hoped for. But when that didn't happen, Hitler had to think again. On July 19, in a speech to his assembled top brass, who were there to receive their decorations and promotions, following the French campaign, Hitler made what was to be called his 'last appeal to reason'. What he said was that he'd never wanted to make war on the British Empire. He urged London to reconsider its attitude.

A few days later, when Halifax made it quite clear that Britain wasn't in the least interested in falling into line with Hitler's policies, Hitler set in motion a new strategy. He decided to unleash attack from the air.

Britain was surrounded by sea. This meant that the only way to force Britain to accept a German settlement was by attacking it from the air. The RAF had to be neutralised. This is where Goering came in. He was delighted that 'his' Luftwaffe had been chosen as the instrument to bring Britain to terms. So the orders were given. Adler Tag, Eagle Day, was to be fixed very shortly with the exact day to be decided according to the weather. After a postponement from the original date, August 8, it was finally launched on August 13 – though not without some confusion, as our previous post examines.

The following weeks were to see an intense and concentrated effort to smash the RAF.

Comments

Cherry East-Rigby: This time must have been full of trepidation for government then and why does it take such an extreme situation to bring out the best in the British people? It was a time of great sacrifice for all but how well it turned out! Respect to all always.

Day 36 – August 14 1940

Weather: cloudy.

Fighter Command Serviceable Aircraft as at 09:00 hours:

- Blenheim – 59
- Spitfire – 219
- Hurricane – 342
- Defiant – 25
- Gladiator – 2
- **Total – 647**

At midday a substantial force was detected by radar building up over Calais. Escorted by a large number of fighters, bombers advanced on Dover and on airfields in Kent. Groups of Me109s and Me110 fighters flew above cloud, endeavouring to attract RAF fighters into combat. 32, 65 and 610 Squadrons were sent up and were involved in heavy fighting. The Goodwin Lightship was destroyed. Another group of aircraft took the opportunity, as usual, to attack Manston.

Luftflotte 3 sent over a number of small pockets of aircraft. Middle Wallop airfield was attacked, killing three men.

Eight RAF fighters were lost and nineteen German aircraft were destroyed.

54 Squadron Operational Record Book, 14 August

A day of absolute inactivity as far as the squadron was concerned.

Reported Casualties (RAF Campaign Diary):

* Enemy: 30 confirmed, 8 unconfirmed; 9 damaged.
* Own: 5 Hurricanes, 3 Spitfires, 3 Blenheims

Comments

Mike Arthur: I'd be interested to see more background / a picture of how German air operations were opposed in totality (e.g. including RAF fighter & bomber operations over German held airfields). I am fairly familiar with the Battle of Britain story (my father was an RAF Bomber Command ground engineer in World War Two; he retired from the RAF in 1973), but these daily reports raise a number of questions:

1) I'd not appreciated how quiet many of the days were, nor how quiet many of the squadrons on otherwise intense days, e.g. Aug 14 report 54 Squadron: 'a day of absolute inactivity'. Where were they (which Group)? In retrospect, did the groups co-operate as well as they could have? Flying time would have allowed squadrons from other groups to provide cover over engaged stations, leapfrogging cover and re-location for a day from even as far as Scotland. How much was this done on a day-by-day basis?

2) Some of the reports have carried numbers of new-build aircraft: a) generally, new-build seems to have comfortably exceeded casualty aircraft, yet the number in service in squadrons seems to remain almost constant, even after days of no aircraft or pilot casualties. Why? Insufficient pilots? Where did the new-builds go to – reserve (St Athan?)?

b) Why did they persevere in building the Defiant – almost useless as a day-fighter? Were the Defiants even used in day fighting after Dunkirk?

c) New-build Beaufighters are reported, but no Blenheims, but Fighter Command is shown as having Blenheims, but no Beaufighters. Are these facts correct? Who was getting the Beaufighters (Coastal Command?). Were any of the Beaufighters (or Blenheims) yet being equipped with airborne radar and then employed as night-fighters?

3) What was the armament and crew (presumably pilot & top gunner, like Me110) of Blenheim day fighters? Were they any use as day fighters?

Otherwise, what did the Blenheims reported as fighters (I thought they were only bombers) do? Were any (or Beaufighters) employed on fighter-intruder operations over the German airfields at this time?

4) What was done in the way of bombing (Battles (if still so employed), Hampdens, Blenheims, Wellingtons, etc) the German airfields?

5) At this stage German night operations were not large, yet existed, and these reports show night fighting training for the Spitfire and Hurricane squadrons, but no reports of actual night operations by them. Were any night defensive operations carried out by the RAF fighters at this time? If so, which types?

Tony Rudd: Generally, I think the answer to many of the questions in this comment just have to be seen as part of the intricate nature of the operations that summer. For instance, night radar was in its infancy at this stage of the battle and was still in essence being developed. The Blenheim was not really a fighter but when introduced had had to assume this role. In the Battle itself it hardly figured and was on its way out. The Defiant was, of course, a failure, but I assume that it took some while for this to filter back to High Command who was sometimes reluctant to accept unpleasant facts. As for the Beaufighter, I was under the impression that it was only introduced into Fighter Command in September and probably later in the month.

Top Gun Gallery
Paddy Finucane

Finucane was the eldest son of Irish republican parents who had emigrated to this country in 1936, his father having been a veteran of the 1916 Uprising. Despite this Republican background, Finucane joined the RAF in 1938. After gaining his Wings, he joined 65 Squadron at Hornchurch. He won his first victory in the Battle on August 12 shooting down an Me109. His Squadron was withdrawn from frontline operations at the end of August and did not return to operations until November that year. By then Finucane had shot down four Me109s and one Me110.

Finucane went on the next year to become the youngest Wing Commander in the RAF, credited with twenty-six kills in all. He finally perished on 15 July 1942. His Spitfire had been disabled by ground fire and crashed into the sea at low level. His last words were a laconic message, 'this is it chaps'. A few seconds later he was dead. He was only twenty-one.

Day 37 – August 15 1940

Weather: fine.

Fighter Command Serviceable Aircraft as at 09:00 hours:

- Blenheim – 61
- Spitfire – 233
- Hurricane – 351
- Defiant – 25
- Gladiator – 2
- **Total – 672**

The fine weather was what Goering had been waiting for. Earlier that morning the three Luftflotten were busily preparing for a major coordinated attack on the RAF. The intention was to hit as many RAF airfields as possible and to bring up as many British fighters as they could which could then be shot down.

The first attack came from airfields in northern France where hundreds of German aircraft were detected as they came across the Channel. They were divided very roughly between Ju87 dive bombers and protecting Me109s. They were aiming at Lympne which suffered considerable damage. The airfield was put out of action for two days. Hawkinge was also attacked but much less damage was done. The radar stations at Rye, Dover and Foreness were hit by the Ju87s and subsequently had to be shut down.

The next phase of the day's battle saw a major attack by German aircraft from Luftflotte 5 from its bases in Denmark and Norway. This attack was the brainchild of German Intelligence. They were presuming that the Luftwaffe's continued attacks on southern England would have led Dowding to concentrate all his fighter resources on protecting the area south of London. He would have drained away all fighter protection from the north of England. They therefore concluded that targets in the North would now be undefended. How wrong they were.

An attack by several groups of bombers, He111s and Ju88s, as well as some He115s duly came in from across the North Sea to the Northumberland coast whilst a second wave of bombers headed south. But they had been picked up by the local radar. They were intercepted by squadrons of Hurricanes and Spitfires. Many German bombs were dropped into the sea. Some German aircraft immediately turned for home. As these interceptions proceeded, the whole Luftflotte 5 attack proved to be a costly failure.

In the south of England, Manston suffered heavy damage that afternoon. Sixteen men were killed and two Spitfires were destroyed on the ground.

At 3:15pm a force of Me109s, led by Rubensdoerffer, attacked Martlesham Heath causing fairly widespread damage and leaving the airfield out of action. Repair work continued for the next 2 days.

At the same time, two large concentrations of German aircraft were observed crossing the coast at Deal and at Folkestone, each wave consisted of over 100 aircraft. The aircraft then broke up to attack individual targets including factories in Surrey working on Short Stirling bombers near Rochester, where approximately 300 bombs were dropped. The other targets included the radar stations at Dover, Bawdsey, and Foreness.

In the early evening, there were further attacks by Luftflotte 3 flying over from Brittany. 100 aircraft attacked airfields including Middle Wallop. More action was to follow. Another 70 plus German aircraft were now proceeding from the area behind Calais. But this attack was intercepted by RAF squadrons and was broken up leaving the German aircraft to seek individual targets. Attacks were delivered on airfields at West Malling and at Croydon. The latter had been mistaken for Kenley. The attackers' bad luck continued with Rubensdoerffer, their famous Commander, being shot down and killed. The final action of the day was when a mixed force of Me109s and Me110s, which were looking for targets amongst the suburbs south of London, were caught by two RAF squadrons when on their way home. Four German aircraft were shot down.

After what had been a hugely busy day, the RAF announced that they had shot down 182 enemy aircraft. Subsequently, this was paired down to a more accurate figure of 75 German losses from 974 sorties flown. This compared with thirty RAF losses. The outcome for the day nevertheless represented a considerable success for the RAF, particularly their performance in the north of England.

As it was, the day put Luftflotte 5 out of the battle. It was also clear that the Me110 and the hitherto invincible Stuka dive bomber could only operate effectively given massive fighter cover.

Back in Karinhall, Goering was lecturing his commanders that day. He ordered that Stukas should be given protection by Me109 fighters in front, above, and behind the dive bombers. Goering had also come to the conclusion that the Luftwaffe's attacks on radar installations were just not paying dividends and should be abandoned. The Reichsmarschall never quite got his head round the part played by radar in the British defences.

For his part, Churchill congratulated Dowding on his 'generalship' in his success in eliminating the attack by Luftflotte 5 in the north of England.

54 Squadron Operational Record Book – 15 August

Four patrols during the day resulted in two clashes with the enemy. By now the order 'patrol behind Dover and engage enemy fighters' is becoming as familiar as the old convoy patrols. Flt Lt Deere claiming a Me109 destroyed (11:18 hours).

18:28 hours: Flt Lt Deere two He 113s. 1 probable was gained for the loss of Flt Lt Deere's machine when he was shot down in Kent after a flight which has taken him (unwittingly) over Calais Marck! He suffered only a sprained wrist after a parachute jump at 15,000 feet.

17 Squadron Operational Record Book – 15 August

The Squadron carried out convoy patrols from 05:25 to 16:00 hours. At 15:10 hours the aerodrome was attacked by Ju87s and Me110s and was dive bombed. About eighteen bombs fell on the aerodrome causing damage, but none of our personnel or aircraft suffered. Meanwhile Flt Lt Harper, Sgt Griffiths and PO Pittman had taken off to intercept and climbed to attack Me109s at 20,000 feet over aerodrome. Flt Lt Harper was seen to go down with smoke pouring from his engine, but was later reported to have force-landed near Felixstowe, wounded in the leg and face. He is in Felixstowe Hospital and claims one Me109 confirmed. FO Hanson and PO Pittman took off during the raid. Convoy patrols were continued until 18:10 hours.

610 Squadron Operational Record Book – 15 August, 18:43 hours

Eight aircraft ordered to intercept e/a approaching Biggin Hill, about ten miles to the SE, they met about twenty-five Do215s escorted by many Me109s. The bombers flying at 14,000 feet and the fighters at 16,000 feet. Flt Lt Warner attacked a Me109, gave it three long bursts, smoke came from the fuselage and it dived down vertically. Sgt Arnfield fired several bursts at a Me109 which began to smoke badly. PO Cox fired three short bursts at a Me109 which went into a vertical dive with engine on fire. Sgt Corfe fired three short bursts at a Me109, the tracer appeared to hit him about the rear of the fuselage and wings.

Enemy casualties: 1 Me109 destroyed, 1 Me109 probable, 2 Me109s damaged.

73 Squadron Unofficial War Diary – 15 August 1940

Today the Squadron drew its first blood in England. 'A' Flight who were at Leconfield at the time were ordered off towards Flamborough Head at 19,000 feet. The enemy were encountered and being unescorted in wide formation. 'A' Flight 'went to it'. PO Carter got two Ju88s and a possible third. Others were shot down by Sgt Griffin, Sgt McNay, PO Scott and Flt Lt Lovett. Sqdn Ldr Robinson shot up everything within sight and it is thought he must have accounted for at least three of the enemy. 'B' Flight are now eagerly awaiting an opportunity to come to grips again but as the days pass it seems as if this is unlikely as long as the Squadron remains at Church Fenton.

Reported Casualties (RAF Campaign Diary):

* Enemy: 161 confirmed, 61 probable, 58 damaged
* Own: 34 destroyed, 18 pilots killed or missing

Comments

John Blake: Fascinating– reads like a thriller. Hadn't realized that Luftwaffe targeted RAF airfields to this extent, but note on radar as a Goering blind spot and marks his seminal misapprehension.

Fortunate indeed that British forces were not diverted south towards London and environs, but maintained substantial defenses far up north. In context, a note on popular reaction, including King and Churchill, Parliament would be of interest in this, Britain's 'finest hour'.

Battleofbritaintv: 5 August 1940 – the day the Battle comes to the North East

Flying from Denmark and Norway, a Luftwaffe force of more than 60 bombers with a thirty-four-strong fighter escort was making for the

RAF's fighter bases in north-east England. With two other Spitfire squadrons, and one Hurricane Squadron, No 72 raced to intercept them.

72 Squadron Operational Record Book

15 August 1940, 12:15 Squadron patrol Acklington 25,000 ft. Investigate raid coming inland from Farne islands. E/A variously reported as from twenty-four to fifty. At 13:00 hours all aircraft down, refuelled and rearmed. Estimated E/A casualties eleven – three probable – one damaged.

The hero of the day was Australian, Flt Lt Desmond Sheen DFCL

Sheen accounted for two Me110 fighters, one of which almost did for him. 'Flames and smoke appeared near the inside of the port engine,' he said. 'The enemy aircraft, either with the pilot shot or in a deliberate attempt to ram me, approached head on left wing low'. Sheen took evasive action and saved his neck.

The Spitfires of No 72 Squadron from Acklington were led by Flight-Lieutenant Edward Graham, who thus stepped into the place of honour in one of the most spectacularly successful air combats of the war.

The Luftwaffe Armada was so vast in comparison with Graham's little force that he hesitated for a moment, uncertain at what point and from what direction to attack it. Apparently unable to bear the suspense, one of his pilots asked whether he had seen the enemy. With a slight stutter which was habitual, he replied 'Of course I've seen the b-b-b-bastards, I'm trying to w-w-w-work out what to do'. The reply became famous through-out Fighter Command.

The Me110s turned and fled from the wing of Spitfire and Hurricane squadrons, leaving the Bombers to fend for themselves.

The attack was startlingly effective and caused widespread panic among the German planes whose pilots had been told not to expect that much opposition. Jettisoning their external tanks, some of the Me110s formed a defensive circle, while others dived almost to sea level and were last seen heading east. The bombers, less an indeterminate number destroyed by Graham's squadron, then split into two formations, each accompanied by some of the remaining fighters. One formation headed for Tyneside, apparently with the intention of bombing the sector station at Usworth; the rest turned South-East towards two aerodromes at Linton on Ouse and Dishforth which they had been ordered to attack. Some of them jettisoned their bombs and headed back to Norway, leaving several of their number in the sea.

In the words of writer Robert Dixon, 'The Luftwaffe launched an attack on the northern counties of Northumberland, Durham and Yorkshire. The Luftwaffe received heavy losses with the RAF losing none, the only day in the Battle of Britain that the Luftwaffe was decisively beaten'.

David LaJuett: In the description of the Luftflotte 5 bombers' northern attack on August 15, it was not actually mentioned that it was due to the great flight distance that no covering Bf 109 fighters escorted the 65 He111s of KG 26, the 'Lion' Geschwader. Furthermore, the twenty-one Bf 110s that did accompany the Heinkels did not even have their rear gunners on board; they were left behind to save weight! Such was the Luftwaffe overconfidence.

72 Squadron from Acklington scrambled first to meet them. They passed 3,000 feet above and flew on, to turn and attack out of the sun. 'Haven't you seen them?' asked one of the pilots, to which the leader famously replied as mentioned. Fifteen German aircraft were promptly shot down for the loss of one RAF fighter that had got too close.

It might be noted also that the He115s were floatplanes, and were a feint from the north, trying to draw off 13 Group's fighters. But, by a careless navigation error, the bombers' track almost overlapped that of the 115s, thus radar indicated a very large formation. Every squadron from Catterick to Drem, east of Edinburgh, was scrambled.

The fifty Ju88s were met by squadrons from 12 Group. Ten Ju88s were downed.

Finally, I would note that the southern attack on Croydon, a mistake, resulted in random bombs falling on some southern suburbs of London, killing over 70 civilians. As a result, 'the Fuhrer, when informed of this, was appalled and enraged'. He had reserved the decision of if and when to bomb the London area for himself.

Aircraft of the Battle
Boulton Paul Defiant

This RAF aircraft turned out to be a real lemon. It had a strange configuration. In outline, the aircraft resembled a slightly oversized Hurricane but its feature was a Boulton Paul power operated turret with four Browning machine guns operated by an air gunner and the whole thing situated just behind the pilot. The aircraft had no forward firing armament at all, except for the turret which could be aligned to fire forward over the pilot's head, an arrangement which was never actually to be used in combat.

In combat the aircraft proved a death trap. It could not hold its own against German fighters. It first saw service over the beaches of Dunkirk during the evacuation of the BEF. It had one initial day of success. This was before German pilots had recognised the aircraft's features. The rear-firing gun came as a surprise. But the Luftwaffe was ready for it the next time it appeared. When its initial element of surprise had worn off concerning its peculiar configuration, it was the equivalent of a dead duck.

It was never a popular machine with Dowding; Fighter Command only had two squadrons equipped with them: 141 and 264. They were withdrawn from frontline service by day early in August, and relegated to a role as night fighters.

Day 38 – August 16 1940

Weather: fine with occasional mist.

Fighter Command Serviceable Aircraft as at 09:00 hours:

- Blenheim – 64
- Spitfire – 216
- Hurricane – 345
- Defiant – 24
- Gladiator – 4
- **Total – 653**

German raids began mid-morning with yet another attack on West Malling which succeeded in putting the place out of action until the 20 August.

At noon, three further raids developed comprising of over 350 aircraft. Two waves of aircraft were headed for the Thames Estuary and Dover. A third wave was coming across from Cherbourg and making its way towards Portsmouth and Southampton aiming in particular for Tangmere. Many of the bombers managed to avoid contact with the RAF fighters sent up to intercept them and pressed on to their targets. A number of London suburbs were hit. Established airfields such Harwell and Farnborough were attacked. Meanwhile, the aircraft from Cherbourg had reached the south coast and headed in separate directions towards targets such as Tangmere, Lee-on-Solent and Gosport. Tangmere was badly damaged and twenty people lost their lives and several aircraft on the ground were destroyed. Ventnor was once again a target, this time by five Ju87s which made a pinpoint bombing attack. This attack put Ventnor out of action until 23 August.

However, numerically, the most damaging attack that afternoon was on a training command airfield, Brize Norton. Over 50 aircraft were destroyed, several hangars were completely obliterated and a number of casualties were caused. This damage was the work of two Ju88s.

The Luftwaffe that day put up just over 1700 sorties for the loss of forty-fiveaircraft. The RAF lost twenty-two planes and a large number of aircraft destroyed on the ground which included over ten Hurricanes. Although the Luftwaffe had hit eight airfields, their intelligence had been inaccurate as only three of them were Fighter Command airfields.

54 Squadron Operational Record Book – 16 August

Another engagement with the enemy when a large formation of Do215s escorted by He113s and Me109s was encountered very near Hornchurch. Two Me109s (by Colin Gray in celebration of his DFC) and one He113 (FO McMullen) all destroyed and two bombers and a fighter damaged for no loss on our part was a most satisfactory hour's work.

249 Squadron Operational Record Book – 16 August, Boscombe Down

A formation of Me109s were seen and Red Section, Flt Lt Nicholson, PO MA King, Sqdn Ldr King were ordered to investigate. Red Section unfortunately bought it, being heavily attacked by fighters. Flt Lt Nicholson, Red 1 was hit by a cannon shell and his aircraft caught fire. Flt Lt Nicholson remained in the cockpit in order to get a burst at a Messerschmitt 110 which appeared in front of him. He was then forced to abandon aircraft owing to the heat. He made a successful descent, but when about forty feet from the ground he was fired at by a member of the LDV. He was very badly burnt and taken to Royal Southampton Hospital. PO MA King, Red 2 was attacked at the same time, and also abandoned his aircraft. His parachute had been severely damaged however by a cannon shell, and collapsed during the descent. Pilot Officer King was killed. Sqdn Ldr King's aircraft was hit in several places but he was able to return to base.

Note – Flt Lt Nicholson was subsequently awarded the VC – the only member of Fighter Command to receive this honour.

Reported Casualties (RAF Campaign Diary):

* Enemy: 75 confirmed, 29 probable, 41 damaged
* Own: 22 aircraft of which 14 pilots are safe

Comments

Mark: Flt Lt Nicholson was sadly lost over the Indian Ocean when a passenger on a flight that did not return. His name is on the Singapore Memorial. But, as he attended Tonbridge School they have a wonderful memorial to him, and as a member of the Battle of Britain Historical Society I organised our Society Memorial Plaque at Tonbridge.

On returning home by train I read the sad story that his wife was having to sell memorabilia items she had retained. She was then living in Tadcaster Yorkshire. Photographs exist of them when he was based at nearby Church Fenton

Alfred W Thorne: Flt Lt Nicolson shot up a Bf109, I was witness to the dogfight and can confirm this, as I saw the plane descend and make a wheels up landing in a cow field at the Leigh Rd / Oakmount Rd junction in Eastleigh, Hants. I was on the scene shortly after and was able to free a piece that hung down from the wing. It was what I now know to have been - the starboard aileron balance weight strut, which had snagged the cattle fence. The plane was removed under cover of darkness, and I am led to believe that it was taken to Eastleigh Airport, where it was repaired and flown for evaluation purposes. I was 76 in January.

Scott: When was Flt Lt Nicholson, VC, lost over the Indian Ocean? Did he recover from the burns and fight on in the Battle?

Mark: Nicholson was moved to RAF Hospital Halton and in November was convalescing at Torquay so was not in the Battle of Britain again. He was posted to India early 1942. On August 4 1943 he took command of 27 Squadron. On August 11 1944 he was posted to HQ TAF Bengal awarded DFC as Wing Commander. In April 1945 he joined the staff at HQ Burma. On May 2 1945 he went as Observer on a Liberator from Salbani and was 100 miles south of Calcutta when one engine caught fire. The Liberator crashed into the sea, only two NCOs survived.

David LaJuett: Also on this day– the crash landing at Tangmere of a Hurricane flown by Pilot Officer W.M. 'Billy' Fiske, after a fight with the Ju87s. Fiske, a 'dashing, wealthy former captain of the US bobsled team at the Winter Olympics of 1928 and 1932, died of burns two days later. He was the first American killed in action during the war.

The Squadrons
249 Squadron

249 Squadron was formed on 18 August 1918 at Dundee as a seaplane squadron flying anti-submarine patrols along the east coast of Scotland. The Squadron was disbanded on 8 October 1919.

On 16 May 1940 the Squadron was reformed at RAF Church Fenton. Initially equipped with Spitfires, a month later the Squadron was re-equipped with Hurricanes. The Squadron was based at Boscombe Down during the initial part of the Battle of Britain, but in September 1940 it was moved forward to North Weald. Following the end of the Battle of Britain the Squadron went on to serve in Malta in 1941 and Italy in 1943. After the war the Squadron served in the Middle East during the Suez crisis. It was disbanded on 24 February 1969.

Comments

Gerald Broadhead: Patrick Bishop in his book Fighter Boys told of PO Richard Barclay of 249 Squadron chasing down a Me109 which then tried to crash land near Manston. A Sergeant Pilot shot at the E/A causing it to crash in flames, at a time when Polish pilots fought bitterly against the Germans. On returning, Canadian Flight Lieutenant Robert 'Butch' Barton tore a terrific strip off the Sergeant about his unsportsmanship, but after the bombing of Coventry in the winter of 1940, British sensibilities hardened. I was a National Service PO personnel officer to Wg Cdr. Barton OBE DFC & Bar Station Commander at RAF Acklington, but he never spoke to me of his over eleven enemy planes destroyed, or the Battle of Britain, or the Squadron's part in the defense of Malta, or being wounded with second-degree burns. Testament to the courage, bravery and modest humility of the great men and women who fought in World War Two. I believe Wing Commander Barton lived into his nineties.

Flight Lieutenant R A Barton of 249 Squadron was shot down and wounded in his Hurricane 1 (V6625) over Shellhaven Essex, on the 5 September 1940 at 15:30 hrs by a Messerschmitt Bf109.

On one day in late September, 249 Squadron destroyed twenty enemy aircraft.

Day 39 – August 17 1940

Weather: fine.

Fighter Command Serviceable Aircraft as at 09:00 hours:

- Blenheim – 50
- Spitfire – 208
- Hurricane – 345
- Defiant – 28
- Gladiator – 0
- **Total – 631**

A much quieter day with the Luftwaffe recovering from its exertions over the previous two days. As for the RAF, these recent very active days were leading to a growing shortage of pilots. However, volunteers were successfully sought from other commands. This helped to fill some of the gaps at least.

That night Liverpool and Coventry were bombed and a number of civilians were killed.

54 Squadron Operational Record Book – 17 August

Probably the lull before the storm. No enemy activity until the late afternoon.

Reported Casualties (RAF Campaign Diary):

* Enemy: 2 confirmed
* Own: nil

The Airfields
RAF Warmwell

RAF Warmwell in Dorset, just five miles from the coast, was operational from 1937 to 1946. It was a 10 Group sector airfield and housed a flight from 609 Squadron (main base at Middle Wallop) flying Spitfires, as well as no. 152 Squadron from 12 July 1940, and was Dorset's only RAF airfield. It came with the heavy responsibility of protecting the nearby naval base of Portland, which often came under attack in the early days of the battle, most notably from Stuka dive bombers.

It was attacked by the Luftwaffe on several occasions in August 1940.

Day 40 – August 18 1940

The Hardest Day

Weather: fine to begin with but cloudy later.

Fighter Command Serviceable Aircraft as at 09:00 hours:

- Blenheim – 50
- Spitfire – 228
- Hurricane – 396
- Defiant – 27
- Gladiator – 5
- **Total – 706**

Early that afternoon saw a return to heavier attacks. These were aimed at airfields south of London, Biggin Hill, Kenley and West Malling. The raid on Kenley was especially damaging. It was delivered simultaneously by enemy aircraft flying at several thousand feet with others attacking at a height of less than 100ft. A number of aircraft were destroyed on the ground. Several hangars and other buildings were also hit and there were casualties. Twelve people were killed in a direct hit on a shelter. The operations room had to be relocated to a butcher's shop nearby. The damage, though severe, was made good in a couple of days. Squadrons had to be temporarily diverted. Croydon was also bombed and further damage done. Biggin Hill was another target for the dual level attack, one from enemy aircraft flying at 5000ft and the other from Do17s flying at a 100ft. The latter ran into heavy trouble, losing over half their number. The damage was, however, considerable.

Later that afternoon there were a series of raids from aircraft of Luftflotte 3 which hit Thorney Island on the coast doing considerable damage and destroying a number of aircraft on the ground and on the airfield of Ford, also on the coast, which was heavily damaged.

The final raids of the day were on Croydon and also on Manston where twelve Me109s once more beat up the airfield destroying aircraft on the ground and causing more casualties. Fighter Command flew 760 sorties and destroyed seventy-one German aircraft against a loss for the RAF of thirty-nine aircraft with ten pilots killed.

The week had seen the virtual end of operations by Ju87 dive bombers. They were proving just too vulnerable. As for the RAF, it was becoming evident that the sighting of vital functions such as control rooms should not have been on airfields themselves. They should instead have been widely dispersed. The most dangerous attacks during the week had been those at low level. These had been almost impossible to guard against. But from the German point of view they had been hugely costly. They were to be replaced by raids at medium height of several thousand feet.

54 Squadron Operational Record Book – 18 August

A great day! In four sorties the squadron bore the brunt of the station's thrust against the enemy. A twenty minute 'warming up' over Manston was followed by the leisurely shooting down of a Me110 which descended from 31,000 feet to sea level rather more rapidly than it could have originally intended.

12:40 hours – first big attack of the day. Ten destroyed, probable and damaged – no loss to squadron (plane or pilot).

16:45 hours – second wave of bombers and their escorts – this time about 300 strong – came north and south of the Thames. It looked as if a pincer movement was being evolved with Hornchurch the objective! Once again the squadron dealt faithfully with the enemy – being able to include some damage of the main formation, which might have made things very unpleasant for the station:

14 destroyed, damaged and probables. No loss to squadron.

Total for day: 8 destroyed, 6 probable, 11 damaged.

Reported Casualties (RAF Campaign Diary):

* Enemy: 139 confirmed, 26 probable, 45 damaged
* Own: 22 aircraft with 12 pilots safe.

Captains and Commanders
Richard Saul

Air Vice Marshal Richard Saul was the Commander of 13 Group covering the north of England and Scotland. He, like Trafford Leigh Mallory, commander of 12 Group, was very much the product of the RAF peacetime strength. He had served as an observer during the First World War during which time he was awarded a DFC. In the inter war years he had been Senior Air Staff Officer at Fighter Command HQ and had been active in organizing the structure of Fighter Command.

Saul's career was notable for his performance as an athlete. He played rugger and hockey for the RAF. He was also an outstanding tennis player.

During the Battle, 13 Group was seen as providing a quiet period for squadrons which had been run ragged by the pressures of fighting in 11 Group south of London. However, Saul's group came out trumps when attacked in strength by Luftlotte 5 flying from Norway and Denmark. Expecting no fighter opposition, the German attackers were intercepted by the fighters of 13 Group and dealt a very nasty blow. This ended operations by Luftflotte 5 against Britain.

After the Battle, Saul continued to serve in the RAF, taking command of 12 Group in the winter of 1940. He retired from the RAF in 1944.

Day 41 – August 19 1940

Weather: cloudy with occasional showers.

Fighter Command Serviceable Aircraft as at 09:00 hours:

- Blenheim – 49
- Spitfire – 219
- Hurricane – 388
- Defiant – 27
- Gladiator – 6
- **Total – 689**

This day saw another stock taking exercise by Goering at Karinhall. The Reichsmarschall was far from satisfied with recent results from the battle. He had attributed the perceived lack of success to a failure on the part of his fighter pilots to support the bombers with sufficient vigour. He duly replaced some of his older pilots with younger aces like Galland and Mölders. By this move, Goering was aiming to sharpen up the attack of his fighter groups.

Meanwhile, at Uxbridge, Keith Park and Dowding were also reviewing the recent fighting. The main thrust of the Luftwaffe had moved from the attacks on convoys to mainland targets, particularly RAF airfields. Park issued instructions to controllers to avoid vectoring squadrons over the sea. Pilots' safety had to be considered and they were losing too many from drowning.

The afternoon saw desultory attacks by several large formations of enemy aircraft. The Command flew 383 sorties, losing three fighters but destroying six German aircraft.

At night attacks took place over the Midlands, in particular Coventry, and northern England.

266 Squadron Operational Record Book – 19 August – Hornchurch

Very warm, sky overcast – visibility moderate. Squadron at readiness at advanced base from 13:30 hours until dusk. Two Spitfire aircraft delivered from no. 6 Maintenance Unit.

Reported Casualties (RAF Campaign Diary):

* Enemy: 6 confirmed, 1 probable, 1 damaged
* Own: 3 aircraft of which two pilots are safe.

The People in Support
Balloon Command

A feature of the skies around key targets that summer were the balloon barrages. They were a fine sight, those hundreds of balloons. Each balloon looked like a silver sausage some 29 ft long and around 25 ft wide. They were filled with hydrogen and flew at some 2 to 5,000 ft up. They were secured by a steel hauser which was tethered, at ground level, to a winch. They usually flew in a large group, several hundred feet apart.

Their purpose was to prevent attacking aircraft swooping low over a target. The point is that enemy aircraft tended to avoid them. Occasionally, a balloon was responsible for bringing a fighter down. But one thing was for certain, their very visible presence gave a reassurance to those below. They were all part of the deterrent effect of the counter measures that summer.

Comments

Mark: On August 19 it was reported that a Hurricane of 1 Squadron, Tangmere P3684 'blundered' into a London Barrage Balloon during a night patrol, crashed and burnt out near Finsbury Park, PO C N Birch who baled out landed on the roof of 28 Gillespie Road. It was reported that it took him a long time to convince the locals he was British.

Day 42 – August 20 1940

Weather: rain in the north, scattered showers in the south.

Fighter Command Serviceable Aircraft as at 09:00 hours:

- Blenheim – 53
- Spitfire – 240
- Hurricane – 396
- Defiant – 22
- Gladiator – 7
- **Total – 718**

The weather restricted activity this day. Nevertheless there were small raids on Oxford and Southwold. There were also reconnaissance flights over Hatfield and Northolt airfields.

Later bombs were dropped on oil installations on Pembroke Docks. In the afternoon there were small raids on Manston and Eastchurch. There were also raids on a convoy off East Anglia.

Due to the difficult weather, 11 Group Squadrons had limited success during their interceptions. The RAF flew 450 sorties and lost two aircraft but shot down six German aircraft. Amongst these latter was the first success by one of the Polish squadrons, 302(P), which shot down a Ju88.

That day Churchill visited RAF Uxbridge, on returning to his car he said to General 'Pug' Ismay 'don't speak to me, I have never been so moved'. After a few moments he said 'never in the field of human conflict has so much been owed by so many to so few.' Four days later the phrase formed the centrepiece of his famous speech in the Commons.

54 Squadron Operational Record Book – 20 August

Score to date – 69 destroyed, 41 probable, 27 damaged.

PO DH Wissler Diary – 20 August

I took off from Debden at about 10:15 and flew to Tangmere. I navigated my way ok but being on the coast this wasn't very hard. Tangmere is in a shocking state the buildings being in an awful shambles several 1000lb bombs having fallen. We were put to thirty mins at 1, and did nothing for the rest of the day. The dispersal hut is most cozy and puts ours at Debden to shame.

(Reproduced by kind permission of the Imperial War Museum and Copyright holder)

Reported Casualties (RAF Campaign Diary):

* Enemy: 7 confirmed, 4 probable, 5 damaged.
* Own: 3 aircraft of which two pilots are safe.

Week 6 Summary – Crystal Trouble

Statistical summary: week 6:

* **Total Fighter Command Establishment:** *1558 planes*
* **Strength:** *1379 planes*
* **Balance:** *under strength 179 planes*
* **Losses:** *29 Hurricanes (+ 5 damaged), 10 Spitfires (+8 damaged), 76 unidentified (not categorised in the reporting)*
* **Aircraft Production:** *5 Beaufighters, 11 Defiants, 43 Hurricanes, 31 Spitfires*

When the great assault which it was hoped would bring Britain to its knees began, it was beset by a very un-German dose of 'finger trouble'. There are two theories about why this happened. The bombing force that day, August 12, consisted of dozens of Dornier 17s and was led by a senior officer, Johannes Fink. He had been appointed Commander of the Kanalkampf. Fink had set up his headquarters in a bus on the cliffs of Cap Gris Nez where he could actually see through his binoculars the defenses of Dover.

This day he had deserted his bus for a pilot's seat in the lead bomber. His fleet of Dornier 17s were to be accompanied by an equally large armada of Me109s. The trouble that day was that his radio broke down. One explanation is that the wavelength had been altered. But his radio had not been fitted with the new crystals required. Either that or his radio communications just didn't work.

However, the accompanying fighters had radios which were fully operational. The problem was that the weather that day turned out to be less good than expected. Goering, back in Karinhall, his comic opera pile south of Berlin, got the disappointing news about the weather and duly cancelled the operation.

By then, the massive group of Fink's air armada was on its way. The cancellation was radioed to them. The fighters received the message and turned back. Fink didn't get it and pressed on. One of the fighter pilots saw what was happening. His group had turned back. Why hadn't Fink done so too? On his own initiative he flew just ahead of Fink's armada gesticulating, trying to send some kind of signal to them, that the operation had been postponed. But to no avail. Fink's group pressed on. They duly bombed their target in Kent.

But as they turned for home, the inevitable happened. Spitfires and Hurricanes intercepted them. Undefended, they immediately lost five of their number shot down. The mistake had proved costly. When he landed, Fink was so furious that he rang Kesselring, the Commander of Luftflotte 2 in Brussels to complain. Fink was extremely angry. One thing the Germans had was an unrivalled expertise on staff work. But this day had been a disaster.

Comments

Paul Handley: Why were Defiants still being produced if they had proved to be inadequate?

Tony Rudd: I think the issue may have been that once you had got an aircraft into service, it took a lot of effort to take it out. Besides which there would always be some who would be supporters of an aircraft even when it proved inadequate in one role.

Day 43 – August 21 1940

Weather: cloudy with some rain.

Fighter Command Serviceable Aircraft as at 09:00 hours:

- Blenheim – 58
- Spitfire – 239
- Hurricane – 400
- Defiant – 25
- Gladiator – 7
- **Total – 729**

The bad weather led to the Luftwaffe adopting harassing tactics using small groups or even single aircraft. Attacks took place on the Scilly Isles which were bombed and strafed by machine gun fire.

Fighter Command flew 599 sorties. However, thirteen German aircraft were destroyed and only one RAF fighter shot down. Four Blenheims on the ground were destroyed.

19 Squadron Operational Record Book – 21 August

POs Dolezal and Huadil, Sgts. Plzaxk and Marek of 310 Squadron attached to us today. All Czechs and very keen and eager to have a crack.

Reported Casualties (RAF Campaign Diary):

* Enemy: 13 confirmed, 2 probable, 2 damaged
* Own: 1 Hurricane

Comments

Mark: RAF Leconfield, PO F S J Chalupa who escaped from Poland having been credited with one German aircraft destroyed, was with the French Air force with great success. He joined 302 Squadron at

Leconfield Yorkshire on July 23 1940. In action off Bridlington he claimed a Ju88 in Hurricane P3934 and made a forced landing near base with engine trouble. Aircraft was damaged but repairable. He had an interesting career and later retired to Canada.

Top Gun Gallery
Douglas Bader

Bader joined the RAF in 1928. An enthusiastic pilot from the start, he had the misfortune of crashing during an attempted slow roll at minimum altitude. In this accident, he lost both his legs, one amputated below the knee, and the other above. However, by dint of extreme determination, he learnt to walk unaided despite his injury.

But his flying career had been cut short. However, on the outbreak of war, he succeeded in re-enlisting and had no difficulty in flying despite his legless state.

During the Battle of Britain, he became Commanding Officer of the mostly Canadian 242 Squadron at Coltishall in 12 Group. This was after Bader had had several successes during operations over Dunkirk in the previous month of May. As CO of 242 Squadron, Bader achieved two further kills, shooting down two Dornier 17s.

As the Battle proceeded, Bader continued to achieve more successes shooting down half a dozen enemy aircraft. However, by then Bader's name was securely linked to the Big Wing theory. He had become the leading exponent of this tactic in aerial warfare as distinct from the methods used by Keith Park in 11 Group which favoured immediate interception by one or two squadrons.

After the Battle, Bader was promoted to Wing Commander and took over a wing flying from Tangmere. During the Summer of 1941, leading one of these attacking operations over northern France, he was shot down and became a prisoner of war for the rest of hostilities. After several attempts to escape he was taken to Colditz Castle. By then he had racked up a total score of twenty-two victories and had been awarded a DSO and Bar and a DFC and Bar.

After the end of the war, having achieved the rank of Group Captain, he left the RAF for a peace time existence. He died in 1982.

Comments

Andrew McCrorie: Douglas Bader's contribution to the Battle of Britain is very controversial due to his involvement in the Big Wing and the subsequent debacle where the key Battle leaders were sidelined by inferior officers.

Day 44 – August 22 1940

Weather: dull day with some rain.

Fighter Command Serviceable Aircraft as at 09:00 hours:

- Blenheim – 58
- Spitfire – 219
- Hurricane – 412
- Defiant – 26
- Gladiator – 6
- **Total – 721**

In the morning, a major convoy heading westwards was attacked as it passed through the Straits of Dover. At first the attack was by shells fired from France. When this proved unsuccessful, the Luftwaffe sent up aircraft to bomb the convoy. 54 and 610 Squadrons intercepted this attack which led to some fierce fighting. There were further attacks on the Scilly Isles and Manston was targeted in the early evening. Unusually, five RAF fighters were lost as against two German fighters shot down.

54 Squadron Operational Record Book – 22 August

Signs that the enemy was collecting his forces near Calais and so the squadron patrolled Manston. No results.

Reported Casualties (RAF Campaign Diary):

* Enemy: 6 confirmed, 4 probable.
 * Own: 5 aircraft (2 pilots lost).

Comments

Mark: There were three Yorkshire born pilots involved in action that day. Flying from Kenley in 616 Auxiliary Squadron, formed in Doncaster, were Hugh Dundas and Lionel Casson. Dundas was born in Doncaster and educated first at Aysgarth Prep School, Bedale, Yorkshire where his name appears on the Battle of Britain Historical Society School Memorial Plaque. Whilst flying Spitfire R6926 he was attacked by Bf109s and baled out, admitted to Kent & Canterbury Hospital with arm and leg wounds.

Casson was born in Sheffield and after being attacked by Bf109s returned to base with damage by 20mm cannon shell.

At Warmwell PO Walter Beaumont from Mytholmroyd, Nr Halifax was shot at by fire from a Ju88 and made forced landing near Bedford in Spitfire R6829. He was unhurt, aircraft repairable. Walter is remembered in two local schools, Scout Road Primary and Calder High, Mytholmroyd and his name will be on a new housing development in Halifax as a 70th anniversary record

Aircraft of the Battle
Dornier 17

This aircraft was one of three designs of twin-engined light bombers to be seen over the skies of Britain during the Battle. It had been designed in the mid-thirties, initially as a commercial aircraft carrying a few passengers. Not achieving much success in that role, it was taken over by the Luftwaffe as a potential light bomber and saw service during the Spanish Civil War. In this role, it was to have a fair success.

The feature of this aircraft was its long rather slim fuselage, which led it to be dubbed a flying pencil. Equipped with 4 to 8 machine guns, it was especially good at accurate low-level attacks. The usual bomb load of the Do17 was some half dozen 250 kg bombs.

The aircraft did much damage that summer to Britain, particularly hitting the airfields of 11 Group.

Day 45 – August 23 1940

Weather: dull but with some bright intervals.

Fighter Command Serviceable Aircraft as at 09:00 hours:

- Blenheim – 55
- Spitfire – 236
- Hurricane – 410
- Defiant – 26
- Gladiator – 6
- **Total – 733**

The deteriorating weather that day led to a repetition of the Luftwaffe hit and run tactics, often by individual Me109s. 580 sorties were flown by the RAF with two German aircraft being shot down without loss to the RAF. A wide variety of targets were attacked from St Eval in the west to Biggin Hill south of London.

At night, there were widespread bombing raids over South Wales, Bristol, Birmingham and the North. In Bridlington, a café was hit trapping the people inside.

266 Squadron Operational Record Book – 23 August – Wittering

Cold. Sky overcast – visibility moderate. Rear party arrived from Hornchurch. Move of Squadron completed.

Reported Casualties (RAF Campaign Diary):

* Enemy: 3 confirmed
* Own: nil

The Squadrons
303 Squadron

303 Squadron accounted for the most enemy kills during the Battle of Britain. Formed on 22 July 1940 at RAF Northolt, the Squadron was made up of Polish airman who had escaped to Britain following the invasion of their country in 1939. Equipped with Hurricanes, 303 Squadron flew in the Battle until mid-October when it was sent to Yorkshire for a much needed rest. The Squadron served for the duration of the war, when it was re-equipped with Spitfires. In 1944 the Squadron was part of 2nd Tactical Air Force which supported the D-Day landings and was then moved to East Anglia to serve as fighter escorts for Bomber Command. The Squadron was disbanded on 11 December 1946.

Comments

Nathan Richmond: Well done the Poles!! As their country had already been overrun they were given an opportunity to hit back at the enemy through 303 Squadron. To the Poles it probably felt it was only a tiny response compared to what had happened to them but they were given some solace, and their revenge must have felt sweet indeed, in proving to be the top-scoring Squadron. This is a fact for which we are all grateful and admire.

Tony Rudd: I myself served with some fine Poles on 305 Squadron flying Mosquitoes based at Epinoy in 1945, and I have a Polish Airforce medal from my time with them. We took over this airfield from the Germans, and when we arrived we found crates of French wine specially 'bottled for the German Forces' which we drank with gusto.

Day 46 – August 24 1940

Weather: fine.

Fighter Command Serviceable Aircraft as at 09:00 hours:

- Blenheim – 63
- Spitfire – 238
- Hurricane – 408
- Defiant – 23
- Gladiator – 8
- **Total – 740**

This day was to see the end of the days of bad weather and the start of a fine spell lasting some two weeks. These next two weeks were to be the period of greatest strain on Fighter Command. The period ushered in the major effort by the Luftwaffe to finish off the fight against the RAF. The enemy was to concentrate on attacking the airfields surrounding London and at the same time for it to try and bring the remaining RAF fighters up into the air where they could shoot them down.

To strengthen the attack, the bulk of the Me109s, on the strength of Luftflotte 3 on the Cherbourg peninsula, were flown across to the airfields of Luftflotte 2. A similar move of these Me109 fighters was made from Luftflotte 5 in Denmark and Norway. This would enable the protective fighters flown by the Luftwaffe, when accompanying their bombers on their operations, to be strengthened. The Germans also bowed to the inevitable in withdrawing much of the Ju87 strength from the battle. They were to be held in reserve against the time when German fighters had at last wrested control of the air over England from the RAF. It would be then that they would come into their own and punish British installations on the ground.

Meanwhile, Park and Dowding readied themselves for the renewed onslaught which this fresh period of fine weather would bring in its wake. The one problem which they could not overcome was the growing shortage of pilots. They were never short of new planes, but pilots were a different matter. It took months to train them. Looking forward to the next month or two, the prospect of a growing pilot shortage was a nightmare to the two Commanders.

Furthermore, the new phase of the Battle, which was to start on 24 August saw Fighter Command squadrons suffering from sheer exhaustion. The pilots were often desperately short of sleep. Moreover, their nerves were often shot to pieces. They needed rest and recuperation. Instead, they were being asked to fight on all day and every day. The ground crew who serviced the planes were exhausted too. They had been working round the clock as well. They had got to an amazing pitch of efficiency. They were able to refuel, rearm and check over a squadron of Spitfires in ten minutes of their landing. Yet the whole command was operating whilst being bombed and strafed throughout daylight hours. Telephone lines were continually being cut, reconnected and the next day cut again. Death and injury were never far away. Unexploded bombs littered the average airfield. Operating in this manner, the question was beginning to be asked, how long could they continue like this. As they looked at the weeks to come, doubts were beginning to enter the minds of some who had been so confident at the beginning of the Battle. It couldn't go on forever.

Nevertheless, on 24 August the Battle got going again. The weather was fine, at last. It was perfect for a resumption of the campaign. The day started with a large raid which had built up behind Calais of over 100 aircraft. As it advanced on Dover, RAF squadrons were sent up to intercept. The mass raid was indeed broken up. Smaller sections made for individual targets. These began with Manston. The raid was intercepted but substantial damage was done nevertheless, with three Defiants of 264

Squadron being shot down. These same raiders also bombed Ramsgate, firing their machine guns on ARP personnel. More attacks were to develop on Manston. The largest one of over 100 aircraft came in from the Le Havre area. As a result of the further damage, the decision was taken at Fighter Command to evacuate Manston altogether. It was to be closed to all but emergency use. The attacks went on that day on airfields further north such as North Weald which was also heavily damaged by a force of another 50 Do17s and He111s. Air raid warnings were now being sounded in London as the raids approached the metropolis.

Meanwhile, Portsmouth and Southampton had become targets for a massive raid from a fresh group of aircraft from airfields near to the Somme. The raid was intercepted with the result that many of the bombers jettisoned their bombs at random over Portsmouth causing more than 100 fatalities. That day Fighter Command flew no less than 936 sorties losing twenty-two fighters but shooting down thirty-eight German fighters and bombers.

The day finished with a misdirected attack on the City of London. The bombs had been meant to fall on oil storage facilities in the docks but ended up falling on built up areas of London. Over 100 people in Bethnal Green were made homeless.

54 Squadron Operational Record Book – 24 August

Hornchurch bombed and squadron in action twice. In the afternoon came the raid on the Aerodrome…in spite of over 100 bomb craters in the vicinity very little damage was done except to the SW corner of the drome where dispersal pens and the concreted road were hit.

249 Squadron Operational Record Book – 24 August

Two aircraft of Blue Section ordered to intercept e/a over Bristol at 30,000 feet. No further information was given them by R/T, and no interception was made. It is worthy of note here that the controllers at

Middle Wallop appear to be working under very difficult circumstances with untrained personnel and lack of equipment. On many of the patrols so far carried out, no information other than the original telephoned order and the order to land has been received.

56 Squadron Operational Record Book – 24 August- North Weald

The Squadron went up twice in the morning on X raids, without result. The Squadron flew to Rochford, there carrying out various patrols. On one of these they engaged a number of Heinkel 111s with fighter escort. PO Wicks destroyed a Me109, the pilot balling out and being captured. Sqdn Ldr Manton destroyed a Me109 and Flt Lt Weaver sent a Heinkel 111 into the sea, seeing two of the crew bale out. The Squadron returned to North Weald late in the evening, while they were away the aerodrome had been bombed, considerable material damage (none of it vital) being caused, there being ten soldiers killed from a direct hit on a shelter trench.

Reported Casualties (RAF Campaign Diary):

* Enemy: 41 confirmed, 13 probable, 19 damaged
* Own: 20 aircraft with 6 pilots and 4 air gunners lost or missing.

Comments

Stephan: This is an excellent resource....colleagues and I follow it avidly. As an amateur military historian I'm intrigued to know how much there is still to be researched about the battle?

Andrew Bird: 24 August 1940 – No Line on the Horizon.

Three Blenheim fighters of 235 Squadron, scrambled to protect Portsmouth and the aerodrome at 16:30 hours – took off, ahead black flecks painted the sky. Drawing near Portsmouth at 16:45 the three Blenheims were engaged by 1 RCAF Squadron five miles off Thorney Island, mistakenly thought to be enemy bombers having not recognised the colours of the day being fired by the gunners. The three desperately tried to get out of their line of fire. 0.303 rounds scythed through the aircrafts' skin shattering instrument panels, and other engines were hit and one motor stopped. It was like being in a hail storm as the young novice Canadian Hurricane pilots picked out their targets. Two Blenheims managed to crash-land back at Thorney Island whilst T1804 crashed in flames near Bracklesham Bay. Unfortunately both crew members were killed. PO Woodger's body was never recovered and Sgt Wright was found and laid to rest at St Ann's Churchyard, Chasetown, Staffordshire.

The untold battle of 24 August 1940.

Day 47 – 25 August 1940

Weather: fine but cloudy later.

Fighter Command Serviceable Aircraft as at 09:00 hours:

- Blenheim – 54
- Spitfire – 233
- Hurricane – 416
- Defiant – 18
- Gladiator – 6
- **Total – 727**

There was little activity until late afternoon when a massive force of over 200 aircraft built up over Cherbourg and then headed towards Weymouth and Warmwell nearby. The Scilly Isles and Croydon were also bombed by day. In the early evening in the east of the country a force of over 100 aircraft approached Dover. This force was attacked by 32 and 54 Squadrons. The day's tally was sixteen RAF aircraft lost with twenty-two German aircraft shot down. At night Plymouth and Coventry were bombed.

However, an important development occurred that night. As a reprisal for the attack on London which had happened the previous day, 81 twin engine RAF bombers were heading for Berlin. This escalation was to have a profound effect on the outcome of the Battle.

54 Squadron Operational Record Book – 25 August

Al Deere awarded Bar to his DFC – the first member of the squadron to achieve this distinction. He has shot down eleven enemy machines, shared in the destruction of another three and probably destroyed another three. Heartiest congratulations.

Squadron to date: 78 destroyed, 42 probable, 28 damaged.

PO DH Wissler Diary – 25 August

This was our hard day being at 15mins and readiness the day long. At about half past seven we had a hell of a scrap over Portland, in which about 100 a/e were engaged. Flt Lt Bayne made an attack below and astern quarter. The Me110 whipped up in a stall turn and I gave him a long burst while he was in a stalled condition, it fell over and went down. I then went on my own and made a Me110 brake [sic] formation, I gave it another burst and it went down towards the sea. Flt Lt Bayne shot down but ok. Sqdn Ldr Williams lost, wing shot off.

(Reproduced by kind permission of the Imperial War Museum and Copyright holder)

73 Squadron Unofficial War Diary – 25 August

During the early hours of the morning, Sgt Lang was shot down by our own AA guns while chasing a Hun. After a further attempt to reach the aerodrome he decided to bail out having come down to 4,000 feet with his aircraft on fire. Fortunately he landed safely in the middle of Beverley High Street when he was promptly arrested by the Home Guard. AA officers are not popular in the mess these days!

Reported Casualties (RAF Campaign Diary):

* Enemy: 53 confirmed, 15 probable, 16 damaged
* Own: 16 aircraft with 10 pilots killed or missing

Captains and Commanders

Oberst Josef 'Beppo' Schmid

Schmid was the head of Luftwaffe intelligence. He played a large part in the formation of the Germans' official view of the RAF in their attempt to wipe out Fighter Command in the summer of 1940.

It was on July 16, the day that Hitler issued his Directive No. 16 promising the ultimate invasion of Britain, that Schmid delivered an assessment of the RAF and the likely tenor of the battle which was about to begin. His conclusions were that the RAF was inferior to the Luftwaffe in almost every department with regard to the fighting qualities of the Hurricane and Spitfire. Both, he asserted, were inferior to the Me109, particularly the Hurricane. Many of these assertions were included in order to please Goering. With regard to the numbers he was not far out, crediting the RAF with a fighter strength of 900 aircraft, of which 675 were fit for operations.

The yawning gap in Schmid's assessment was the failure to take account of the innovative system of control adopted by Fighter Command. He completely underestimated the effectiveness of this radar based system. This was the most serious omission of his intelligence assessment. But above all else, in July the Luftwaffe was suffering from a massive overdose of confidence bred from its impressive performance up until that time. That summer, the RAF, in German eyes, was just another enemy, which, like Poland, Norway and France, was there to be overwhelmed. The only question was how long it would take. Goering wondered whether it would be one or two or even three weeks. For Goering, the outcome was never in doubt.

In truth, the fact was that the German High Command never had a clear or proper appreciation of the RAF's real strength. Schmid's prolific output of work, which was often based on what the commanders wanted to hear, did nothing to dispel the idea that the Luftwaffe was vastly superior to the RAF.

Day 48 – 26 August 1940

Weather: cloudy with some bright intervals.

Fighter Command Serviceable Aircraft as at 09:00 hours:

- Blenheim – 56
- Spitfire – 240
- Hurricane – 408
- Defiant – 18
- Gladiator – 6
- **Total – 728**

This was to be a day of heavy attacks on Fighter Command. The day began with an attack aimed first at Dover and Folkestone which was bombed, but with the main targets being Biggin Hill and Kenley, the airfields just south of London. The raiders had come over from Lille and St Omer. In the afternoon a second large 100 plus raid came in. They appeared to be aiming at airfields in 12 Group. Hawkinge and Debden were bombed. At Debden, three people were killed and there was a direct hit on a hangar. This was followed in the late afternoon by further raids by Luftflotte 3 on Portsmouth. 43, 615 and 602 Squadrons were involved in the fighting with He111s, Me109s and Me110s. This last attack was contested by RAF squadrons in the area. This led to a bitter fight. No less than twenty-six RAF fighters were lost that day. This was against a figure of forty-one casualties inflicted on the enemy. Fighter Command flew 787 sorties that day. The RAF's loss of pilots seemed to be increasing each day. The trend was ominous.

That night bombs were dropped over West Hartlepool, Sunderland, Lincolnshire, Plymouth and Birmingham. Ten people were killed in the raid on Birmingham.

73 Squadron Unofficial War Diary – 26 August

The Squadron had its first dawn scramble today with great enthusiasm. 'B' Flight set off and carried out a successful interception only to discover that the incoming 'raid' was our own bomber boys on their way back from Berlin. The Flight returned feeling somewhat peeved at having been disturbed at such an ungodly hour for a wild goose chase.

Reported Casualties (RAF Campaign Diary):

* Enemy: 46 confirmed, 7 probable, 19 damaged
* Own: 28 aircraft with 4 pilots and 2 air gunners killed or missing.

The People in Support
The AA Batteries

Anti aircraft fire was the first line of defense against the German bombers. The guns were a 3.7 inch calibre. They fired a substantial shell, fused to explode at a given height. The Ack-Ack barrages around London did succeed, occasionally, in downing a German aircraft. But they proved to be relatively inefficient. However, one of their primary achievements was the boost civilian morale. The din they made at night was terrific.

The Anti Aircraft Command was part of the army, but the General who was in command, Sir Frederick Pile, had his headquarters bang next door to Dowding's at Bentley Priory. Pile played a useful part in the Battle of Britain by becoming a close friend and confidant of Dowding. The latter would often, in the evening, expound for an hour or more his thoughts on the Battle. Pile was a very good listener and didn't interrupt. It was a great help to Dowding to let off steam in this way.

Day 49 – 27 August 1940

Weather: dull and cloudy.

Fighter Command Serviceable Aircraft as at 09:00 hours:

- Blenheim – 55
- Spitfire – 228
- Hurricane – 420
- Defiant – 18
- Gladiator – 7
- **Total – 728**

This day the Luftwaffe flew scattered attacks and also flew a considerable number of photographic reconnaissance flights aimed at establishing what damage had been done during recent days.

It was on this day that Park let his dissatisfaction surface with regard to the lack of cooperation he was getting from the neighbouring group to the north, no 12. In a well distributed signal he contrasted the cooperation his group had been receiving from 10 Group to the west , with what he was getting from 12 Group. On two occasions, he had apparently asked for reinforcements from 12 Group to patrol airfields, including Debden, while its squadrons were fighting further south. The cooperation requested had not materialised and Debden was heavily bombed. Park was getting seriously frustrated. In his signal, he told his controllers that when they needed assistance from 12 Group they should put their request through Fighter Command at Bentley Priory. It was the start of a dispute which was to escalate into a full scale row. To start with the AOC of 12 Group, Leigh Mallory disliked Dowding and had told Park about it. He thought he should have got Park's job when the latter had been selected as the new AOC of 11 Group. It was clearly a plum job and he thought he should have got the plum. Finally, he was jealous of the opportunity that Park had been given. 11 Group was clearly the frontline of the Battle. He resented the primacy given to Park as a result.

Furthermore, there was another problem hatching in those weeks. Douglas Bader, the famous legless pilot, was, in his way, similarly put out by the prominence being given to 11 Group pilots. Moreover, Bader had his own idea of how the battle should be fought. The airmen he modelled himself on were the aces of the First World War, men like Ball and McCudden who had taken the lead in the battles they had fought. But here he was being asked to play second fiddle to 11 Group squadrons and being ordered about the sky by disembodied voices. What he wanted to do was to meet the enemy with superior force. This meant forming a wing of several squadrons, three or even five, led, of course, by him. Park was to find this suggestion impractical. There was too little time to assemble such a force given the imminent attacks from which 11 Group squadrons were suffering. All this was to build up ahead of steam over the next few weeks.

That day, 27 August, was to be one of the last in which Luftflotte 3 was to participate. Their part in the day time battle was shortly to end. Their role then became the leader of the night time campaign by the Luftwaffe which followed the day time Battle of Britain.

54 Squadron Operational Record Book – 27 August

A day of rest. Our new squadron leader – of international fame –Sqdn Ldr Donald Finlay, arrived at Hornchurch.

74 Squadron Operational Record Book – 27 August, Kirton Lindsey

Mr Mansbridge RA who has been appointed by the Air Ministry to paint portraits of famous fighter pilots arrived and painted portrait of Sqdn Ldr Malan DFC (bar).

Reported Casualties (RAF Campaign Diary):

* Enemy: 4 confirmed, 1 probable, 1 damaged
* Own: 1 aircraft

Comments

Rod Sanders: The more I have read over the years the more I am convinced that Park was right and Leigh-Mallory wrong. The treatment of both Dowding and Park was a national disgrace. Any other country would have promoted or given higher commands to them not kicked them out. It is worth pointing out that Park is the only man in history to win a defensive air battle. (In fact, two if you include Malta). He should have at least that empty plinth in Trafalgar square.

Week 7 Summary – Flawed Intelligence

Statistical summary, Week 7:

* ***Total Fighter Command Establishment:*** *1558 planes*
* ***Strength:*** *1377 planes*
* ***Balance:*** *under strength 181 planes*
* ***Losses:*** *20 Hurricanes (+ 1 damaged), 23 Spitfire, 4 Defiants*
* ***Aircraft Production:*** *5 Beaufighters, 8 Defiants, 64 Hurricanes, 44 Spitfires*

Good intelligence relies on the capacity to understand what is going on in the head of the enemy. During the Battle of Britain, the Germans were not good at this. The Germans had a number of intelligence agencies, each of which jealously guarded their own information. This rivalry, coupled with the intelligence officers providing the leadership with the figures that they wanted to hear, meant that German intelligence could be notoriously inaccurate .

The Luftwaffe had convinced itself that in every way it was more effective than any other air force that existed including the RAF. The trouble was that the Luftwaffe completely failed to appreciate the potential advantage which the new control system of defense, based on radar, gave the RAF. This system was after all the very core of the way the British fought the Battle. The underestimation by the Luftwaffe of the importance of radar to the British can be seen from the way that Goering, in the middle of August, countermanded the orders to attack radar installations. This was because, very shortly after being attacked, they were once again transmitting their signals. The explanation for this was that the Germans thought that the workings were buried beneath concrete reinforcements, which was just not the case. Being above ground, once damaged they could be put back together again very quickly.

The teams responsible for repairing bomb damage were extremely efficient. The only concrete reinforcements were to be found at Fighter Command Headquarters at Bentley Priory and at 11 Group where the control room was protected in this way. All the rest of the radar installations were housed in flimsy huts, easily damaged but easily reconstructed. It also seems as though the Luftwaffe had no system for identifying which airfield being attacked actually belonged to Fighter Command. Consequently, they attacked airfields belonging to Coastal and to Training Command. Indeed, the most apparently successful attack by the Luftwaffe during the Battle was when a couple of Ju88s succeeded in destroying over fifty aircraft at Brize Norton airfield. In fact these had been training aircraft. It was a brilliant attack but had no effect on Fighter Command. The result was a continuing overestimation by the Luftwaffe of how, in the light of the rate of destruction, Fighter Command was being damaged. It all contributed to the feeling that they were much nearer achieving the complete elimination of Fighter Command than in reality was the case.

Day 50 – 28 August 1940

Weather: fine but cloudy in the Channel.

Fighter Command Serviceable Aircraft as at 09:00 hours:

- Blenheim – 55
- Spitfire – 225
- Hurricane – 413
- Defiant – 23
- Gladiator – 7
- **Total – 723**

German attacks that day came in three phases. The first in the morning consisted of around 100 aircraft, made up of slightly more fighters than bombers. Once across the Channel, one section headed for Eastchurch while another flew to Rochford. The RAF made desperate attempts to break through the fighter screen and get at the bombers but without success. Losses were heavy. Four Defiants from 264 Squadron were shot down. In consequence, Eastchurch suffered yet another attack with some aircraft destroyed on the ground and a number of craters in the runway.

The second attack fell on Rochford near Southend. Again the RAF had tried to get at the bombers but the defensive screen had been too strong. However, little damage was done but during the fighting Al Deere was shot down.

In the afternoon the third attack consisted of a large scale visitation of Me109s over Kent looking for targets.

That afternoon the Prime Minister visited Manston and the south coast to see the damage for himself.

The score for the day had taken a toll of 11 Group fighters, namely twenty shot down. This compared with thirty-one enemy aircraft destroyed. The problem was that Park's policy of avoiding fighter to fighter combat and preference given to only attacking the bombers had not been followed. This was partly because of the increased proportion of fighters now being flown by the Germans. This was the last time Defiants were used as day fighters.

That night Coventry and London were bombed and there was a major attack on Liverpool.

54 Squadron Operational Record Book – 28 August 12:13 hours

Patrol over Manston. Flt Lt Deere got a probable Me109…later in combat Flt Lt Deere had to bale out; this is an art in which he is rapidly becoming expert!!

Reported Casualties (RAF Campaign Diary):

* Enemy: 28 confirmed, 14 probable, 10 damaged
* Own: 20 aircraft. Seven pilots and three air gunners killed or missing.

Top Gun Gallery
Richard Hillary

Hillary was a fine pilot who came from the young generation who started their flying career in one of the university air squadrons. In his case, the Oxford University Air Squadron. He became famous during the war, having written a memoir describing what it was like to join the RAF, become a fighter pilot, to shoot down enemy aircraft and finally to be shot down himself, in the course of which being terribly burnt. The book was called The Last Enemy and it became a best seller during the war. It gave an insight to the general public of what the experience was really like. It is still an amazing read.

Hillary was an extremely good looking young man. He was an athlete and a fine oars man. He served on 603 Squadron. He was credited with five kills. He was shot down in a dog-fight when, having disposed of an enemy fighter, he was shooting at a second target. Unfortunately by his own admission, he rather foolishly followed this second target down, exposing himself to a lethal burst of fire from another Me109. Like so many fighter pilots, when he tried to get out of his now blazing plane, he found the canopy very difficult to open. That was how he got so burnt. He then had many months as a patient of McIndoe's East Grinstead unit where they attempted to patch up his face and hands. He underwent dozens of operations. His problem was that he longed to get back to the companionship of the squadron and the flying. By pestering authority, he got their reluctant acquiescence. But, on 8 January 1943, he crashed on a practice flight, killing not only himself, but also his navigator. It was a sad end to a tragic life, but yet one which radiated a certain romantic warmth, mainly because he had written it all down in his remarkable book.

Day 51 – 29 August 1940

Weather: fine but with some cloud and rain.

Fighter Command Serviceable Aircraft as at 09:00 hours:

- Blenheim – 53
- Spitfire – 230
- Hurricane – 412
- Defiant – 18
- Gladiator – 7
- **Total – 720**

The morning was quiet but the afternoon produced massive fighter sweeps flown by the Luftwaffe. Over 500 Me109s, together with 100 Me110s, flew over Kent. They were hoping to attract the RAF into the air so that they could be destroyed. 11 Group had been expecting at least a small element of bombers in this group. So when they saw that the Luftwaffe was fielding a purely fighter formation, in accordance with Park's orders, they avoided combat. The Scilly Isles were once again bombed and machine gunned that afternoon and there were reports that the islanders wanted to be evacuated. The RAF lost nine aircraft that day, but this was against a score of seventeen enemy aircraft shot down.

That night Liverpool was hit once again.

501 Squadron Operational Record Book – 29 August

The Squadron was released until 12:00 hours. They left for Hawkinge at 12:55 and patrol carried out from 15:45 to 16:30. No interceptions were made. The Squadron again took off at 18:00 to patrol Gravesend at Angels 15 over Hawkinge. The Squadron were attacked by nine Me109s out of the sun. Flt Lt J A A Gibson baled out after his aircraft had been shot up, and Sgt Lacey shot down the Me109. Sgt Green also baled out and was picked up near Hawkinge. The Squadron's victories were 2 Me109s destroyed.

Cyril Shoesmith Diary – Aged 14, Bexhill on Sea – Thursday 29 August

Had two air raids today. In the firstt one, which was from 3:20-5 we watched a dog-fight in the air. There was [sic] about thirty planes. Machine gun fire could be heard. Saw three planes in 6:15-7:30 raid.

(Reproduced by kind permission of the Imperial War Museum and Copyright holder)

Reported Casualties (RAF Campaign Diary):

* Enemy: 9 confirmed, 10 probable, 5 damaged
* Own: 9 aircraft with 2 pilots killed or missing.

Aircraft of the Battle

Ju88

This was the third twin-engined bomber used by the Luftwaffe at the time. It was the pick of the bunch. It was a very well designed aircraft with smooth lines. It came into service in August 1939 but only a handful saw action in the Polish campaign. With a top speed of 286mph, it was the fastest of the bomber fleet and could carry a relatively large bomb load of 5510lbs. Capable of a formidable self-defense, it often operated alone or in relatively small groups and was a very accurate dive bomber, proving to be very successful during the Battle of Britain. It remained in service until the end of the war.

Day 52 – 30 August 1940

Weather: fair.

Fighter Command Serviceable Aircraft as at 09:00 hours:

- Blenheim – 52
- Spitfire – 234
- Hurricane – 410
- Defiant – 14
- Gladiator – 7
- **Total – 717**

On this occasion, the Luftwaffe returned to attacking a convoy. In fact, it was a feint. The real effort was an attack picked up by radar of a large formation coming in from the Pas de Calais. The enemy target turned out to be airfields south of London. A group of bombers flying at 20 000 ft struck Biggin Hill doing considerable damage to the area but not the aerodrome itself. A little later, a second group of aircraft attacked with a large segment aiming once again at Biggin Hill. To this was, however, added Shoreham and Tangmere. Later that afternoon, a third wave of attacks came over, including a third visitation for the day on Biggin Hill, together with a number of other airfields. The most damaging raid of the day was flown by a group of ten Ju88s which, aiming at Biggin Hill, flew north of that airfield, then turned round and came in from that direction. The bombing was extremely accurate. It left the airfield a virtual wreck. It also left thirty-nine dead and many of the buildings demolished. Detling and Kenley were also hit in this serious attack. Detling was out of action until the following day.

Finally another group got through to Luton where bombs hit the Vauxhall works and caused a large number of casualties.

At the end of a busy day, the RAF had lost twenty-five fighters compared with thirty-six German aircraft destroyed. However, fifteen RAF pilots had survived. 1050 sorties had been flown by the RAF. This was to be the highest number of sorties flown in a day during the Battle.

That night Liverpool suffered a third episode of heavy bombing.

242 Squadron Operational Record Book – 30 August

Squadron ordered to proceed to Duxford. Operations from Duxford. Enemy planes shot down north of London without any loss to Squadron. Four e/a attacked and probably shot down. Signal received from AOC 12 Group congratulating Squadron on its achievement. The above brings the Squadron's total bag for month to fourteen certainties and five probables. Signal received from AOC 12 Group read: 'heartiest congratulations on a first class show. Well done 242'. Signal received from Chief of the Air Staff which read: 'magnificent fighting. You are well on top of the enemy and obviously the fine Canadian traditions of the last war are safe in your hands'. Signal received from Under Secretary of State for Air congratulating Squadron.

253 Squadron Operational Record Book – 30 August

Fourteen Hurricanes took off Kenley 10:50 hours followed by five more at 11:25 hours when an attack on Croydon and Kenley appeared likely. The Squadron was first ordered to patrol Maidstone, but the flights were separated and were ordered back to orbit base where they were joined by the other five aircraft. They were then vectored off to the south, where at 18,000 feet near Redhill they saw three formations of nine bombers escorted by thirty fighters, Me110s and Me109s. B Flight at once attacked the bombers, which included He111, Do215 and possibly Ju88s, but observed no results with the exception of PO Nowak (Green 3) who probably destroyed a Do215 (this pilot maintained that this bomber was a Ju88) A Flight who were behind and below followed in to attack and Yellow 3 (PO Greenwood) fired all his ammunition into a Heinkel 111 which force landed, four of the crew being seen climbing out. A series of individual fights took place, chiefly with Me110s and Me109s which had come to the rescue of the bombers.

303 Squadron Operational Record Book – 30 August, Northolt

First operation. In the course of training interception with 6 Blenheims in the afternoon, B Flight contacted with some 60 German bombers, 60 fighters and British fighters having a running battle near Hatfield. FO Paszkiewicz brought down one Do17 (destroyed) while the rest of the fighters escorted the Blenheims safely back to Northolt.

Reported Casualties (RAF Campaign Diary):

* Enemy: 62 confirmed, 21 probable, 29 damaged
* Own: 25 aircraft (10 pilots killed or missing)

The Squadrons
310 Squadron
We fight to rebuild

310 Squadron was formed on 10 July 1940 at RAF Duxford and became operational just over a month later on 18 August. The Squadron was comprised of Czech airmen and was led by a British Squadron Leader, GDM Blackwood. 310 flew throughout September as part of Duxford's 'Big Wing'. The Squadron served for the duration of the war and was part of 2nd Tactical Air Force during the D-Day landings in 1944. The Squadron was disbanded on 15 February 1946.

Day 53 – 31 August 1940

Weather: fair.

Fighter Command Serviceable Aircraft as at 09:00 hours:

- Blenheim – 54
- Spitfire – 212
- Hurricane – 417
- Defiant – 13
- Gladiator – 4
- **Total – 700**

This day proved seriously expensive for the RAF. Airfields including North Weald, Duxford and Debden were attacked in the first wave. But this was followed by a second wave of enemy aircraft numbering roughly 100 and once again launched a very damaging attack on Biggin Hill and Croydon. The raid on Croydon caused a certain amount of damage to the hangars. The raid on Biggin Hill which was from high flying aircraft did further damage to this hard pressed RAF station. However, the Biggin Hill raiders were attacked, as they retreated, by 253 Squadron.

Another wave of raiders targeted Hornchurch. A group of 54 Squadron Spitfires were taking off just as the raiders started to release their bombs. Three of the Spitfires were caught by the blast just as they were leaving the ground. Two of the aircraft were tossed in the air and the third, which was being piloted by that eternal survivor, Alan Deere, skidded along upside down. By enormous luck, none of the three pilots were seriously hurt and were all flying the next day.

The last raid of the day was that afternoon and was targeted on Hornchurch and Biggin Hill which suffered more damage to hangars and telephone lines that were brought down. However, both Biggin Hill and Hornchurch were serviceable the next day.

This day proved seriously expensive for the RAF. The home team lost thirty-seven aircraft as against thirty-nine German shot down.

That night Liverpool suffered another heavy raid. A direct hit on a shelter killed twenty people.

Cyril Shoesmith Diary, Aged 14, Bexhill on Sea – Saturday 31 August

In first air raid, 8:50-9:30, I saw eleven planes. Nine of these were high up. Next air raid was from 5:40-7:30. Heard planes and explosions. Saw three planes, then five planes came over fighting. Heard machine gun fire, and later we found a bullet clip each. Three of the planes were German and two were Hurricanes.

(Reproduced by kind permission of the Imperial War Museum and Copyright holder)

PO DH Wissler Diary – 31 August

We did four patrols today ending up with one on which we intersepted [sic] about thirty Do17s and twenty- thirty Me109s. I got onto a Me09s tail, after an ineffectual attack on the bombers, and got in several long bursts at about 300yds, however nothing was observed in the way of damage. Another got on my tail and I had to break away. I succeeded in throwing him off in a steep turn but not before he had put an explosive bullet through my wing. Sgt Stewart was shot down, but was safe. I burst another tail wheel today.

(Reproduced by kind permission of the Imperial War Museum and Copyright holder)

54 Squadron Operational Record Book – 31 August

A really amazing day. Hornchurch bombed; the miraculous escape of three of our pilots who were bombed out of their planes; the station bombed a second time. The squadron was ordered off just as the first bombs were beginning to fall and eight of our machines safely cleared the ground; the remaining section, however, just became air borne as the bombs exploded. All three machines were wholly wrecked in the air. The survival of the pilots is a complete miracle.

56 Squadron Operational Record Book – 31 August

The Squadron went up to intercept enemy bombers approaching the aerodrome which they did near Colchester. They became involved with the fighter escort and Flt Lt Weaver was shot down and killed. He had been given the DFC this very day and he was a great loss to the Squadron. FO Westmacott and PO Mounsdon were also injured but not seriously, their a/c being lost. Sgt Whitehead was shot down by an unseen a/c. He baled out and was unhurt. Weather cloudless, wind westerly 10 to 15mph.

Reported Casualties (RAF Campaign Diary):

* Enemy: 85 confirmed, 34 probable, 33 damaged
* Own: 37 aircraft with 12 pilots killed or missing.

Comments

Allen Syms: 253 Squadron on the 31st August 1940 lost three COs that day, two of them being Sqdn Ldr H Starr and Sqdn Ldr T Gleave.

The Airfields
RAF Hornchurch

Before it was used as an airbase in World War Two, Hornchurch aerodrome was first used during World War One. Originally called Suttons Farm, it was the ninth aerodrome that was located around the perimeter of London. The location was so important that it was the base for the No. 39 Home Defense Unit and plans were made to accommodate several squadrons. Suttons Farms saw its share of activity throughout World War One yet when the war was over in 1919, the Air Ministry decided they no longer needed to use the area and restored the farm to original condition. In 1922 the Royal Air Force wanted to increase its force and Suttons Farm was an ideal location. A task force went back to the old airfield and it was found to be in a usable condition. The owner of the farm refused to turn over his land once again to the Air Ministry yet in 1926 they eventually acquired enough land to build an aerodrome after considerable negotiations.

The new aerodrome was officially opened on April 1, 1928 and the name changed in January, 1929 to Hornchurch. Several squadrons occupied the aerodrome between its opening and the outbreak of World War II, including the 111 and 65 Squadrons. In August 1939 all the buildings were ordered to be camouflaged and manned twenty-four hours a day as a war with Germany was approaching. These were the first stages of Hornchurch being a front line station during the Battle. Even though eight squadrons used Hornchurch in early 1940, none of them stayed permanently. Despite that, Hornchurch was gaining a reputation, with 128 victories by June and several distinguished guests visiting.

Before the Battle of Britain, Hornchurch was a high ranking Sector Station. The aerodrome was attacked twenty times during the Battle of Britain. The worst attack was on August 31 with two attacks in one day; one in the morning and one near 5:30 p.m. Although the damage was widespread, it was not severe and only one person died during the attacks. Eventually, things became too dangerous at Hornchurch and the main Operations Room was moved to Lambourne Hall, Romford on October 15, 1940. By June 1944, Hornchurch had lost its identity as a fighter station and became a transit station for British and American personnel to the battle fronts in France.

RAF Hornchurch was home to the Hornchurch Sector Operations Room and Staff, and the following Squadrons during the Battle:
• No 65 Squadron from 5 June 1940
• No 74 Squadron from 25 June 1940
• No 54 Squadron from 24 July 1940

- No 41 Squadron from 26 July 1940
- No 54 Squadron from 8 August 1940
- No 266 Squadron from 14 August 1940
- No 600 Squadron from 22 August 1940
- No 264 Squadron from 22 August 1940
- No 603 Squadron from 27 August 1940
- No 41 Squadron from 3 September 1940

Day 54 – 1 September 1940

Weather: fine morning, cloudy afternoon.

Fighter Command Serviceable Aircraft as at 09:00 hours:

- Blenheim – 57
- Spitfire – 208
- Hurricane – 405
- Defiant – 24
- Gladiator – 7
- **Total – 701**

This day four main attacks developed. No less than 450 aircraft of the Luftwaffe were involved. The first attack was by 100 plus aircraft which, once over the south coast of Britain, split up to launch their individual attacks. Fourteen and a half squadrons were sent up by the RAF to intercept. Once again it was Biggin Hill which was the first to be hit. Detling and Eastchurch were also targeted. A group of Do17 aircraft bombed the station and made it temporarily inoperable. 72 Squadron was relocated to Croydon. At around midday a second attack developed with 150 aircraft which, when they crossed the coast, aimed at exactly the same targets as the aircraft in the earlier attack.

There were two more major attacks that afternoon and early evening. They went for Hawkinge and Lympne. The fourth group also went for Detling. Finally a group of Do17s split off from this group and went for Biggin Hill yet again. It was what the long suffering airmen and WAAFs were becoming accustomed to, namely the six pm visit from the Luftwaffe. The Operations Room, on this last occasion, was wrecked. Most of the communication with the outside world was severed and much damage done. There was one bright spot however. The two WAAF telephonists, Corporal Elspeth Henderson and Sergeant Helen Turner, had refused to abandon their post and continued operating until the very last moment when they had flung themselves to the ground to avoid glass and shell splinters. For this, they both received a well merited Military Medal. The raid left a vast amount of urgent repair work to be done, mainly by GPO engineers, but by the next morning the Operations Room had been relocated to a local butcher's shop.

An order was issued by the German High Command stating that attacks should be made on the British aircraft industry. It was an attempt to holt the seemingly unstoppable flow of new fighters to the squadrons of the RAF.

This day 147 patrols were flown by the RAF which suffered fifteen losses, but, happily, nine of the pilots survived. The Luftwaffe lost fourteen aircraft.

Night raids took place in Kent, the Midlands, the Bristol Channel, South Wales and Tyne/Tees.

266 Squadron Operational Record Book: 1 September – Wittering
Very warm – visibility excellent. Practices included formation flying, sector reconnaissance – R/T test. Two raid investigations by aircraft of 'A' Flight.

Reported Casualties (RAF Campaign Diary):

* Enemy: 25 confirmed, 10 probable, 24 damaged
* Own: 15 aircraft with 6 pilots killed or missing.

Comments

Bshistorian: Elspeth Henderson's Military Medal is on display at the National Museum of Flight in East Lothian.

Captains and Commanders
Air Vice Marshal Trafford Leigh Mallory

Mallory was the AOC of 12 Group which covered the area north of London and on the east coast up to the Midlands. Leigh Mallory was a complete contrast to Park. Compared with Park, he was thick set and a complete Englishman. Affable, and on the plump side, he came from a well known family which included a brother who had conquered Everest but died on the way down (or the way up? – we shall never know).

His background was not as a fighter pilot. He had served with the Army in France during the First World War, and in 1916 transferred to the RFC. After flying training he returned to France where he flew on reconnaissance and Army co-operation missions. In the inter-war years, Leigh Mallory had postings in Geneva and Iraq before being appointed head of 12 Group in December 1937.

Leigh Mallory was not part of the Dowding/Park axis. He didn't like Dowding and he was jealous of Park. The latter had got the position which he would have liked at 11 Group. The fact was, he thought his group was being treated as a kind of reserve which from time to time was called upon to support Park in the south.

On the other hand, Leigh Mallory was an innovator and an enthusiast. The result was that when Douglas Bader, the legless ace, came to him with the idea of the Big Wing, meaning that instead of operating singly as squadrons, he should be allowed to form a wing of three squadrons or even perhaps five to give them an advantage of numbers when they met the enemy, Leigh Mallory fell for it. It seemed to him a great idea. It had its points. The fact was that 12 Group was ideally placed to support a large wing of squadrons which could descend on the Me109s as they turned for home. Unfortunately, Bader's scheme was misinterpreted as being the ultimate solution in the fight against the Luftwaffe. It was a deeply unfortunate misunderstanding.

In December 1940, Leigh Mallory replaced Park as CO of 11 Group, and in November 1942 he was appointed head of Fighter Command. In 1944 Lord Louis Mountbatten offered him a post as air commander in India. Leigh Mallory was en route to India on 14 November 1944 when his aircraft hit mountains near Grenoble, France and all passengers on board were killed.

Day 55 – 2 September 1940

Weather: fine.

Fighter Command Serviceable Aircraft as at 09:00 hours:

- Blenheim – 60
- Spitfire – 204
- Hurricane – 398
- Defiant – 21
- Gladiator – 7
- **Total – 690**

This day saw an acceleration of the Luftwaffe's attempt at wiping out the RAF's strength, particularly that of 11 Group, the airfields of which were under continuous attack.

Early that morning several groups of thirty plus aircraft were forming up behind Calais. These groups turned into one large formation of 100 aircraft, split roughly between fighters and bombers. They were soon flying across the Channel where they split up into small groups again going for individual targets. These turned out to be Eastchurch, Rochford, North Weald and Biggin Hill. 11 Group succeeded in getting five squadrons into position where they could intercept. Some attacks were from high flying aircraft while others were from low flying aircraft, the latter being very difficult to detect.

Early in the afternoon a group of some 250 aircraft crossed the south coast and then broke up into smaller groups. Amongst the targets which were attacked was Debden which was very heavily damaged.

In the mid afternoon a third group formed up over Calais, mounting to 250 aircraft. Once again being half bombers and half fighters. They then crossed the Channel and spread widely over Kent. Raids were sent yet again to Biggin Hill, Kenley and Brooklands. Damage was also caused to Eastchurch and Hornchurch. But at Hornchurch the interception by 11 Group squadrons was so successful that only some six bombs fell within the perimeter of the airfield. Maidstone was heavily bombed. Industrial targets were also hit namely the Vickers factory at Brooklands and the Short Brothers factory at Rochester.

Finally, a little after five pm the fourth raid of the day developed. This raid concentrated on Eastchurch and Detling. Eastchurch received two attacks where severe damage was done where some five aircraft were destroyed on the ground together with considerable damage being done to the airfield's communications. Eastchurch was made unusable.

That day Fighter Command had lost twenty-five aircraft to the Luftwaffe's thirty-five. Eight RAF pilots had been killed.

303 Squadron Operational Record Book: 2 September

17:30 hours

About ten Me 109s dived out of sun onto squadron near Dover at 19,000 ft…Sgt Frantiszek pursued one 109 over French coast. Enemy aircraft damaged in engine and fuselage, escaped smoking.

501 Squadron Operational Record Book: 2 September, Gravesend

At 07:50 bombs were dropped on the edges of the aerodrome but no material damage was done. The only casualties were two soldiers slightly injured. The Squadron was ordered to patrol Gravesend at 07:36 hours. Engagement took place but too late to prevent a few 40lb bombs being dropped across the lower part of the aerodrome. One pilot encountered fifteen Do17s at 10,000 feet and another pilot encountered nine He113s. Sgt Henn was injured in this engagement and PO Skalski force landed and was injured.

PO D.H. Wissler Diary - 2 September

We took off at about 6:30 for Debden and arrived about 45 mins later. We did two patrols over Thames Haven, the first time we saw hundreds of huns but they were fleeing back home. Our AA guns fired at us, and came much too close. We had one more flap, but ops had their fingers so far up that everything was messed up and we never saw a thing.

(Reproduced by kind permission of the Imperial War Museum and Copyright holder)

Reported Casualties (RAF Campaing Diary):

* Enemy: 41 confirmed, 18 probable, 32 damaged
* Own: 20 aircraft with 10 pilots killed or missing.

The People in Support
The Ministry of Aircraft Production

Amongst the early decisions taken by Churchill when he became Prime Minister was the setting up of the new Ministry of Aircraft Production. The RAF had started the war with two excellent fighters, the Hurricane and the Spitfire. The question was, however, whether the factories would be able to turn out sufficient of these aircraft to fill the gaps in the squadrons which would soon result from the German onslaught. Hence, the formation of the new Ministry.

Even more important, was the appointment of the new Minister. The new man was Lord Beaverbrook, newspaper proprietor and a great old chum of Churchill himself. Beaverbrook was an absolute firebrand and something of a bully. He had no respect for the average civil servant, or, indeed, managing director. He just pursued his task with demonic energy ensuring that, as the Battle developed, production of new aircraft spiralled upwards. The squadrons were never to be short of planes. Moreover, Beaverbrook soon formed a close and very friendly relationship with Dowding himself. He would ring Dowding every evening to discuss the latter's requirements. Churchill had made an inspired choice.

Day 56 – 3 September 1940

Weather: fine.

Fighter Command Serviceable Aircraft as at 09:00 hours:

- Blenheim – 53
- Spitfire – 221
- Hurricane – 400
- Defiant – 25
- Gladiator – 8
- **Total – 707**

The day began as before with a build up of mixed groups of bombers and fighters forming up behind Calais and appearing on British radar screens. The targets turned out to be North Weald, Hornchurch and Debden. However, interceptions made by 249 and 603 Squadrons were successful and were followed by confused dogfights. Out of this melée a force of some thirty Do17s reached North Weald. The bombing there led to substantial damage with two hangars set on fire and four RAF personnel killed. Communications were damaged and a number of other administrative buildings were wrecked including a direct hit on the ops room. As the bombers withdrew they were attacked by 303 and 46 Squadrons.

The afternoon featured a second phase of the attack which was aimed at the same area as the first attack. This was however successfully intercepted with the Czech squadron, 310, playing a major part and shooting down four Me110s. Significantly though, the tally of losses of the two sides was equal at sixteen for each force with the RAF losing eight pilots.

303 Squadron Operational Record Book – 3 September

14:15 hours

Patrol – Maidstone/Dover. Sgt Frantiszek, Green 2 rearguard, descended from 22,000 feet to investigate aircraft above cloud and found Spitfires, then below cloud saw solitary He113 over sea. He dived and closed to 100yds firing two seconds into cockpit. Enemy aircraft dived slowly and disappeared into sea mid channel from Dover.

249 Squadron Operational Record Book – 3 September, North Weald

09:00 hours Squadron ordered to patrol Chelmsford, Eastchurch, nothing seen, ordered to land by sections after one hour's patrol, and immediately after refuelling the Squadron was ordered off again to intercept a large formation of enemy aircraft approaching from the NE. Owing to being ordered off too late, the Squadron was unable to gain height in time to intercept this force, and we all had the most unsatisfactory experience of seeing North Weald being heavily bombed and being unable to do anything about it. The enemy carried out a pattern bombing attack from approx. 15,000 feet, which was very accurate, but it is interesting to record that although between 200 and 300 bombs were dropped on the buildings the damage to the buildings etc… did not in any way hinder the operation of the squadrons from North Weald. From the air, this attack appeared to have been far more effective than it actually was and no doubt the enemy pilots reported, quite justly, that they had knocked out North Weald. The Squadron brought to readiness during the afternoon, patrolled Eastchurch, Canterbury and Dover. Three Me109s were seen well above but they sheared off towards France. We were fired at by AA from the Dover guns and Sgt Rowell's aircraft was apparently hit. He was unaware of this however, until his aircraft caught fire just before he landed on return to North Weald. He was slightly concussed but otherwise uninjured.

PO D.H. Wissler Diary – 3 September

We did two patrols, on the first we intersepted [sic] about 100 e/a (Do215 and Me110). Flt Lt Bayne and I got on a Me110s tail and firing together sent it down in flames. We then attacked a Do215, PO Hearny finishing the attack and the bomber crashing in a field just north of the River Crouch. I collected a bullet in the radiator and got covered with glycol, force landing at Castle Camps. I collected a Hurricane of 111 Squadron, flew back to Debden and got my own plane back. We did one more patrol over the Thames. Then in the night I was aerodrome control pilot.

(Reproduced by kind permission of the Imperial War Museum and Copyright holder)

Reported Casualties (RAF Campaign Diary):

* Enemy: 25 confirmed, 11 probable, 10 damaged
* Own: 20 aircraft with 10 pilots killed or missing.

Week 8 Summary – The Churchillian Spell

Statistical summary, Week 8:

* *Total Fighter Command Establishment: 1558 planes*
* *Strength: 1422 planes*
* *Balance: understrength 136 planes*
* *Losses: 81 Hurricanes (+ 10 damaged), 47 Spitfires (+6 damaged), 7 Defiants*
* *Aircraft Production: 5 Beaufighters, 3 Defiants, 54 Hurricanes, 37 Spitfires*

No account of the Battle of Britain would be complete without mentioning the spell which Winston Churchill's personality had thrown over Britain that summer. The way the country accepted Churchill's 'Blood, Toil, Tears and Sweat' as their lot was the product of the Prime Minister's remarkable capacity to fire up the mood of the people of

Britain. Churchill's character had a great deal to do with it. He had become every inch the wartime leader to whom Britain would respond.

On the face of it, Dowding wasn't really the kind of character who Churchill naturally warmed to. But he had been quick to realise that Dowding was the supreme professional who was perfectly fitted to his role as head of Fighter Command. Churchill's response was generous indeed. It was after spending the day at 11 Group's headquarters at Uxbridge, on August 16, watching Keith Park and his team handling one of the busiest days of the Battle, that he told the General who was with him, when they left and got into their car, not to speak to him for a few minutes. He had been so moved by the experience, he said. He wanted a few minutes to reflect. He then spoke the sentence which will forever be associated with the Battle of Britain 'never in the field of human conflict has so much been owed by so many to so few'.

Churchill was to make many speeches during the war but none became more famous than this tribute to the fighter pilots as they fought the battle, which he made the centrepiece of his speech in the Commons on 20 August. It resonated heavily during the following weeks, just at the moment when the RAF's pilots faced the most intense effort yet by the Luftwaffe to smash them.

Comments

John Blake: As Churchill well knew, Leonidas' 300 Spartans at Thermopylae stood off massed Persian forces under Xerxes to save Western Civilization from the antique equivalent of Nazi Germany's rampaging Aryan hordes. We view Washington's depleted regiments at Valley Forge in the same light, if not strictly comparable.

Day 57 – 4 September 1940

Weather: fine.

Fighter Command Serviceable Aircraft as at 09:00 hours:

- Blenheim – 50
- Spitfire – 218
- Hurricane – 407
- Defiant – 21
- Gladiator – 8
- **Total – 704**

The first attack was on Eastchurch producing six craters on the runway but causing no casualties. In the early afternoon, a massive attack, several hundred aircraft strong, crossed the south coast. They were met by fourteen RAF squadrons and a large scale aerial combat ensued. However, twenty enemy aircraft managed to leave the fight and made their way up the railway line to Brooklands where Wellingtons were produced. The Me110s attacked from a very low level. Their bombing was extremely accurate. Much damage was done and there were heavy casualties, eighty-eight people were killed. Other pockets of enemy aircraft attacked Eastchurch, Rochester, Shoeburyness, Canterbury, Faversham and Reigate. The target at Rochester was the Short Brothers' factory.

Fighter Command flew 678 sorties losing seventeej aircraft but destroying twenty-five of the enemy.

73 Squadron Operational Record Book – 4 September – Church Fenton

Poles arrived at 14:30hrs and seem a very good crowd, their manners being apparently unimpeachable – an individual bow on entering the mess and salutes at every turn.

Reported Casualties (RAF Campaign Diary):

* Enemy: 52 confirmed, 19 probable, 22 damaged
* Own: 17 aircraft with 6 pilots killed or missing.

Comments

Mark: Also on this day – Sergeant J W ' Jack' Ramshaw

Jack Ramshaw from Beverley, Yorkshire was educated at Beverley Grammar School, where with Sgt Pidd, his name is on one of the first of the Battle of Britain Society Memorial Plaques presented. He is buried in the cemetery next to his school, in a family grave. Flying with 222 Squadron at Hornchurch he was shot down on September 4 in his Spitfire K9962 in combat with Bf 109s and crashed near Yalding, he was dead on arrival at West Kent Hospital

46 Squadron

9:00 the Squadron patrolled Rochford at 20,000 ft., but no enemy aircraft were seen.

12:45 A second patrol was carried out over Rochford and 'A' Flight was attacked from astern by Me109s which then escaped in the clouds. FO Plummer and PO Ambrose baled out in the vicinity of Southend, the former was detained in hospital at Rochford, the latter returned to his unit. PO Barber force landed at Maldon and sustained fractures of the neck and lower jaw bone.

Richard Pryor Plummer was born 1912 at Haywards Heath and joined 46 Squadron in 1938 so was one of the experienced pilots when the war started and took park in their first engagement over Spurn Head [Humber Mouth]:

21 October 1939, the Squadron was ordered to North Coates Fittes, and at about 14:15 hours 'A' Flight was ordered on patrol. This flight consisted of the following pilots:

Yellow Section

(1) PO R.M.J. Cowles

(2) PO R.P. Plummer

(3) PO P.W. Lefevre

The flight was controlled by radio telephony from the operations room at Digby, assisted by an R/T tender situated at North Coates. After various patrolling positions had been given, the Flight was in position over Spurn Head at 5000 feet at about 14:50 hours. At about 14:55 hours an order was received, 'Twelve enemy float planes approaching convoy from the South East at 1000 feet. Intercept'. The convoy at this time was about five miles east of Spurn Head and it was in sight.

After the main attack, the enemy formation broke up and just after seeing his target crash onto the water, the Squadron Leader noticed one of the enemy aircraft diving in a southerly direction. He followed it and fired the remainder of his ammunition, which was about one-third of his full amount, from a range of about 300 yards. The aircraft continued to fly and it was then attacked by three other Hurricanes, piloted by PO R.M.J. Cowles, FS E. Shackley, PO R.P. Plummer.

The Squadron Leader watched them attack and it appeared that they were firing from rather long range, so he called up on the R/T and told the last aircraft that he saw attacking to get closer. This he did, and after a repeated attack he saw the enemy aircraft crash and turn upside down in the water. This was PO R.P. Plummer.

He was with them in Norway in May – June 1940 but does not appear in any ORBs but this record was found:

Date: 29 May 1940
Flight B
Type of Enemy: He111
Time: 20:30 app
Place: 5 m south of Andebes Pt
Height of enemy: 12,000 app
Enemy Casualties: 1 a/c 3 prisoners

General
This aircraft was intercepted by FO Lydall in company with Sgt Andrew. FO Lydall successfully brought down his target and then brokeaway with Sgt Andrew after two Me110s which had apparantly been escorting the bombers. Sgt Andrew brought down his machine but FO Lydall did not return. He was last seen chasing the enemy aircraft and was later reported to be down.

signed R P Plummer.

After the action on September 4 FO Plummer baled out with severe burns and was admitted to Southend Hospital but when it was bombed he was transferred to St Lukes Bradford, Yorkshire, where he died on September 14 and was buried at Western Road Cemetery, Haywards Heath.

His name is on the Battle of Britain Historical Society Plaque I presented at Cranleigh School.

PO Charles F Ambrose survived the war and retired as Group Captain, made CBE and died 1986

PO Robert Hugh Barber was also admitted to hospital with serious injuries which prevented him flying again. He served until 1947 and retired to New Zealand.

As a pupil at Oakham School we are hoping to present them with a Memorial Plaque this year.

Rod Sanders: Reading the figures of servicable aircraft for each day does give the impression that Fighter Command was able to match numbers with the raiding Luftwaffe. It is well to remember that 11 group had barely half of the command's strength and could only rely on 10 Group for support, 12 Group 'doing their own thing' with big wings. Yes they really were 'The Few'.

Top Gun Gallery
Max Aitken

Max Aitken was the son of Lord Beaverbrook, who had been appointed by Churchill as the head of the new Ministry of Aircraft Production. In this position, his father played a very important part in cranking up the pace of aircraft production, particularly of Spitfires. Consequently, he forged a close relationship with Dowding. Both men had sons flying as fighter pilots in the Battle.

Max Aitken had learnt to fly in 1935 when he joined an auxiliary squadron in the RAF. When it came to war, Aitken had become CO of 601 Squadron. He led this with some distinction, being awarded the DFC in July 1940.

After the Battle was over, Aitken had a varied and successful career, being responsible for several more kills. Over the course of the war he was credited with sixteen victories He ended the war as a Group Captain. Aitken was a friend of Richard Hillary, and shared much of the life described by Hillary in his book. After the war, Aitken joined his father's

Express Group and briefly served as MP for Holborn having been elected in the 1945 election. He died in 1985.

Day 58 – 5 September 1940

Weather: fine.

Fighter Command Serviceable Aircraft as at 09:00 hours:

- Blenheim – 49
- Spitfire – 214
- Hurricane – 422
- Defiant – 25
- Gladiator – 9
- **Total – 719**

A mass of Me109s were lying in wait over the Channel. Part of the force headed towards North Weald, Eastchurch and Lympne. No fewer than fourteen RAF squadrons were involved in intercepting these attacks and heading them off. Later in the afternoon a very large attack was lined up over France heading towards Britain. Once over Britain, the attack broke up into separate onslaughts attacking Biggin Hill, Detling and oil storage facilities in the Thames estuary. Meanwhile, a large number of Me109 fighters were cruising around over the Channel positioning themselves to escort the bomber force home. The score during the day was ominously close, the RAF losing twenty aircraft against twenty-three for their adversary.

That night London was bombed.

266 Squadron Operational Record Book – 5 September

Very warm, bright sunshine all day. Visibility excellent. Practices included sector reconnaissance – Squadron formation flying – interception practice. Five Spitfire II aircraft delivered by Ferry pilots.

Reported Casualties (RAF Campaign Diary):

* Enemy: 37 confirmed, 22 probable, 18 damaged
* Own: 23 aircraft with 11 pilots killed or missing.

Aircraft of the Battle

Heinkel III

This was the second of the standard light-bombers of the Luftwaffe in service that year. The prototype flew in February 1935 and it went on to see service in Spain and Poland. This aircraft, together with the Do17 provided the backbone of the daylight bombing strength of the Luftwaffe. It was armed with four to eight machine guns and had a bomb load of 4410lbs. However, with a top speed of 270mph it was too slow against the fighters.

Day 59 – 6 September 1940

Weather: fine.

Fighter Command Serviceable Aircraft as at 09:00 hours:

*   Blenheim – 52
*   Spitfire – 200
*   Hurricane – 410
*   Defiant – 29
*   Gladiator – 9
*   **Total – 700**

Park realised the Luftwaffe was concentrating its attack on factories – particularly those producing aircraft. He therefore ensured that Brooklands where Hurricanes were manufactured and the Supermarine factory down near Southampton, which manufactured Spitfires, were both protected. The day proved he was right. Brooklands was the subject of a fierce attack but the squadrons were there to fend it off. No serious damage was done. Affording this protection was costly. During the day the RAF lost twenty-three aircraft from which twelve of the pilots were safe. A similar number of German aircraft were destroyed.

An intelligence report stated that a German soldier dressed in civilian clothes had been captured at Denton, Northamptonshire. He was carrying a wireless and had a British identity card.

73 Squadron Unofficial War Diary – 6 September, RAF Castle Camps

Another bright day and everyone looking forward to more hunting. About 07:55 all our serviceable machines, seven in all, took off on a 'scramble' to Gravesend. Contact was made near Maidstone. Blue Section, led by Mike Beytagh, waded into a pile of 109s. Chubby Eliot unfortunately was shot down, and is now in Twickenhurst Hospital after baling out, the nature of his injuries is not known. PO Marchand got a fairly definite Me109 and gave us a bit of heart flutter when he failed to return. He landed at Tunbridge and had a bath and a shave. 'Mike' also got a probable. Green Section did not make contact being too low.

Once again at 12:55 hrs nine machines, six from 'B' Flight and three from 'A' Flight. The order was to scramble Gravesend, and look for bandits at 36,000!! Then two other Squadrons were vectored on to 100 bandits. We did see a solitary EA but so high that white vapour was all we could make out.

No rest for the wicked! At 18:10 hrs nine machines scrambled for Chelmsford and were vectored out to sea. Nothing was seen, so Sgt. Webster is firmly convinced that there are no Hun aircraft left, he complains that he's been with us three months and hasn't seen an EA. Well, live and learn!! 'A' Flight have been released, and we all went to sample the night life in Castle Camps, Helions Bumpstead, the nearby villages.

Cyril Shoesmith, 14 years old, Bexhill-on-Sea, Diary – Friday 6 September

Had four air raids today. In the firstt which was from 8:40am-10, I saw nine planes. The second was at 12:50-2. During this three 'Spitfires' were seen and others heard. The siren sounded at 6:10pm and planes were heard. The 'all clear' went at 7:17. At 9:50pm-1:10 there was a fourth raid. Planes came over and there were several heavy explosions.

(Reproduced by kind permission of the Imperial War Museum and copyright holder).

Reported Casualties (RAF Campaign Diary):

* Enemy: 44 confirmed, 20 probable, 14 damaged
* Own: 22 aircraft with 7 pilots killed or missing.

The Squadrons
242 Squadron
Toujours prêt – Always ready

242 Squadron was formed in August 1918 at Newhaven as a seaplane squadron. For the last few months of the Fist World War the squadron flew anti-submarine patrols over the Channel. Following the end of the war it was disbanded in May 1919.

The squadron was reformed in October 1930 at Church Fenton. Initially equipped with Blenheims it received Hurricanes in January 1940. The squadron saw action during the spring of 1940 when a detachment was sent to France. During the Battle of Britain the squadron was mainly comprised of Canadian personnel. After the Battle the squadron went on to see service in North Africa and in the Italian campaign. Towards the end of the war the squadron was converted from a fighter squadron to a transport squadron.

242 squadron was disbanded on 30 September 1964.

George VI and the Queen with Sir Hugh Dowding

Sir Robert Alexander Watson Watt

Air Chief Marshal
Keith Park

Air Chief Marshal
Trafford Leigh Mallory

The Attack on London
September 7 – September 30 1940

The Attack on London
September 7 – September 30 1940

Day 60 – 7 September 1940

Weather: fair.

Fighter Command Serviceable Aircraft as at 09:00 hours:

- Blenheim – 44
- Spitfire – 223
- Hurricane – 398
- Defiant – 20
- Gladiator – 9
- **Total – 694**

A new phase of the Battle was to begin this day. There was a growing frustration, particularly in Luftflotte 2, at the resilience of the RAF under attack. Something had to be done to bring the remaining fighter force up into the sky where it could be overwhelmed by the stronger force of Me109s. How to do this? This meant a fully frontal attack on London itself. The decision was made. It was in a sense a desperate one. Just when the German attacks on RAF airfields close to London were beginning to show considerable results and when Fighter Command was being ground down and was being made less and less efficient by the repeated attacks on its airfields and was suffering serious trouble from the exhaustion of its personnel, especially its pilots, the entire weight of the Luftwaffe was switched to one target, London. Fighter Command was virtually saved at the expense of London itself.

The main reason behind this switch was tactical, but there was another. It was revenge. Hitler and top brass in Berlin had been needled by the nightly visits of British bombers to Berlin and other German cities. They hadn't been doing much damage but they irritated the hell out of Hitler. Bombing London by day was in his mind a fitting response. Still, the decision to go for London was not entirely Hitler's. At a meeting of Commanders held in The Hague on September 3 an argument had broken out between Kesselring and Sperrle about the remaining strength of the RAF fighter force. Kesselring had taken the optimistic view that the RAF was near the end of its tether. One more big air battle would finish it off. Attacking London would precipitate the Battle. Sperrle however was doubtful. He credited the RAF with a much greater strength. But Kesselring won. Preparations for the attack began. For it to actually happen required Hitler's approval. Hitler readily gave it. If Britain wanted to trade blows, he was happy to oblige.

So the switch of policy by the Luftwaffe could not have come too soon for Fighter Command. The RAF had been losing fighters faster than they could be replaced. 300 had been lost in August against a total replacement figure of 260. Worse still, between August 24 and September 6, 103 pilots had been killed. The outlook had seemed grim. So as the events of 7 September unfolded and the great armada of German aircraft rolled over southern England towards London, the realisation that miraculous deliverance had in truth arrived must have brought phenomenal relief. It must have been almost unbelievable.

What happened that day can only be explained by the completely different attitude to air warfare by the two countries which were at war. The idea that by an all out effort to bomb London, the British would be brought to their knees shows just how wrong the Germans were. First they underestimated the hold that Churchill had on the country. Secondly they underestimated the morale of Londoners. And thirdly they were putting their money on Kesselring's optimistic view of the RAF's strength, rather than on Sperrle's more conservative view. We shall never know whether if the Luftwaffe had gone on wearing down Fighter

Command's ability to fight on, they might have actually won the battle. What we do know is that the policy of switching their offensive to a strategic attack on London meant that they threw away the chance they might have had of winning the contest.

Goering was never the man to miss the opportunity of exploiting what he saw as the drama of a great victory in battle. He had arrived in northern France to take personal command of what he clearly saw as a truly Wagnerian episode, travelling in his magnificent personal train with its many luxurious appointments. Furthermore he had dressed in a magnificent new uniform. The day had begun with an inspection of fighter pilots at a major Luftwaffe base at St Omer. There he did what he really liked, joking and chatting with the young pilots, having been one of them himself. Then it was off to Cap Gris Nez where a large concentration of top brass had assembled. Refreshments with champagne, of course, were served as they watched no less than 300 bombers, accompanied by 600 Me109s, thundering overhead on their way to the systematic demolition of London.

The Luftwaffe that day certainly had the advantage of surprise. They unloaded a huge tonnage of bombs mixed with incendiaries on London's docklands. Warehouses full of food went up in flames. Incandescent sugar flowed down the streets. Rows of cheaply constructed Victorian houses collapsed in ruins. There were hundreds of casualties. Keith Park flew in his personal Hurricane over the scene. It was a terrible sight. But what really mattered was that Biggin Hill, Kenley and Manston and his Command were to be saved at the expense of London.

Meanwhile, the result of the Luftwaffe having chosen London as its target meant that Fighter Command was not that day in place to fend off the attack. Nevertheless, some interceptions were made. The most outstanding of these was when 303 Polish Squadron came onto a big group of Dornier 17 bombers flying some 4000 ft beneath them. The squadron dived, line abreast, each pilot selecting his target. They destroyed and damaged ten enemy aircraft. That day saw the first outing of Leigh-Mallory's big wing under Bader's leadership. The wing scored a number of victories. The RAF lost twenty-eight aircraft with nineteen pilots killed but shot down forty-one enemy aircraft.

Back in Germany, the Luftwaffe's achievements were already being hailed as a great success. Goering exulted that they had driven a sword into the heart of the enemy. Many German air crew had that day avoided the RAF. The conclusion was that the RAF was on its last legs.

In the early evening, there was a major attack on the London docks, and Battersea Power Station which sustained considerable damage. That night the Germans continued their attack with well over 200 bombers dropping their bombs on the burning targets. Not until five the next morning was the attack over. They left 400 civilians dead and several hundreds more injured. Next morning many Londoners had difficulty getting to work. Several mainline railway stations were closed.

73 Squadron Unofficial War Diary - 7 September

South of the Thames a terrific AA barrage was seen and a general rush in that direction resulted. The sky was absolutely stiff with aircraft. Bombers in stepped down formation of fives, with Me110s above, and He113s above them. The 113s were the 'crack' outfit with the yellow snouts. Red Section went head on for the bombers, and Yellow went for the 110s and Blue went for anything that was going. Dog fights broke out everywhere and Huns were falling all over the place.

The scores were as follows, PO Langham-Hobart, one Me110 definite, one very probable, Flt Lt Beytagh, one Me110 definite, Sgt Garton, one He111k probable, Sgt Marshall, one 111 probable, Sqdn Ldr Robinson, one definite. Flt Lt Lovett and Sgt McNay are missing, and Sgt Marshall landed at Burnham on Crouch, no details are as yet available. A second raid was seen coming in over Deal and Sgts Plenderleith and Brimble had a slap at them, but no definite results were observed. PO Marchand's 109 of yesterday has been confirmed. PO Hoole, the 'brains' of the Squadron, is in his element dashing from one to the other counting 'the bag'. Everyone is elated at our success but hope for good news of Flt Lt Lovett and Sgt McNay. A present of apples and plums in large quantity have been received from Miss Emsden. A letter of appreciation signed by each pilot has been sent to this lady. The evening has been spent filling in Form 'F' – the combat form. Everyone is mighty fed up with this task!

The CO saw the other day what he thought was a camouflaged aerodrome with a river nearby, he landed on this aerodrome, which wasn't, and finished up in the river which was!

249 Squadron Operational Record Book – 7 September

Two patrols were carried out in the morning, Flt Lt Barton, now leading the Squadron, owing to the Squadron Commander's absence in Maidstone Hospital. No contact made during these patrols. 11:30 hours third patrol at Rochester, 15,000 feet. Immediately on reaching patrol line, Squadron ordered to Maidstone in time to intercept a raid of thirty He111s with the usual escort of fighters above and at the sides. A quick flank attack was made on the bomber formation, but there was no time to observe the effect of the fire before breaking away. The Squadron was then attacked by Me109s and a dog fight followed. Six serviceable aircraft returned to base and were ordered off again within quarter of an hour. As these six took off, a large enemy force passed over the aerodrome but did not bomb until they reached NE London at 15,000 feet. The six aircraft of the Squadron then attacked an enemy force of approximately 100 aircraft, as a result of which 1 Do17 was destroyed and several damaged.

By far the heaviest day's fighting the Squadron has yet had. Enemy casualties: 4 ½ destroyed, 1 probable, 3 damaged. It is worthy of note that during this, the enemy's longest full-scale attack on the London docks, POs Meaker and Loweth had motored to Maidstone to collect the CO from the hospital there. On their return they arrived at Surrey docks about five mins before these attacks took place and spent a very undignified forty minutes lying on the pavement at the entrance to the Blackwall Tunnel.

PO D.H. Wissler Diary – 7 September

We had one short scrap with Me109s but I only had one short burst with no effect. These raids created a lot of damage in London, the provisional casualty list says 400 dead, 1500 seriously injured. What complete swines these Jerries are.

(Reproduced by kind permission of the Imperial War Museum and Copyright holder)

266 Squadron Operational Record Book – 7 September

Very warm – visibility excellent. Six aircraft operating from Coltishall. Two raid investigations from Coltishall during which one enemy aircraft (a Do 215) was shot down off Island of Walscheren near Flushing. Five Spitfire I aircraft delivered to no. 616 Squadron.

Reported Casualties (RAF Campaign Diary):

* Enemy: 74 confirmed, 34 probable, 33 damaged
* Own: 27 aircraft with 14 pilots killed or missing.

The Airfields
RAF Duxford

RAF Duxford began life at the end of World War One – initially as a training airfield for No 2 Flying Training School. Later 19 Squadron was formed there, and the Cambridge University Air Squadron flew from Duxford in the 1920s and 30s. In 1935, 19 Squadron provided the Silver Jubilee review at RAF Duxford in front of King George V and Queen Mary.

In 1938, 19 Squadron became the first to be equipped with the new Spitfires. Following Hitler's attack on Norway in April 1940, Duxford was rapidly expanded in readiness for the defence of Britain, as the Luftwaffe now had bases within striking distance of East Anglia and the East coast. RAF Duxford was the key defensive airfield to face attacks from across the North Sea.

The first new squadron to be based here was 310 Squadron, which was formed in July 1940 from Czech pilots who had escaped from France, equipped with Hurricanes. In August 1940, twelve Hurricanes of 242 Squadron arrived. Nearby RAF Fowlmere was designated as a satellite station for Duxford to handle all the additional aircraft and ground crew. The concentration of a number of squadrons into what became known as the 'Duxford Wing' was in preparation for a new though controversial tactic favoured by 12 Group's commanding officer Air Vice-Marshal Trafford Leigh-Mallory and his subordinate Squadron Leader Douglas Bader. In contrast to Keith Park's 11 Group's tactics of sending individual squadrons up to meet the incoming attacks – which allowed for speed and flexibility but led to large rates of attrition – the Big Wing involved sending up three to five squadrons together, to overwhelm the enemy.

The Wing's first outing was on September 9, when Duxford's three squadrons, acting in concert, attempted to intercept a large force of German bombers. However, the squadrons arrived late, though eleven enemy aircraft were claimed shot down. Subsequently two more squadrons were added to the Duxford Wing – 302 Squadron with Hurricanes and Polish pilots, and Spitfires from No.611 Auxiliary Squadron.

On 15 September 1940 this combined force of 60 Hurricanes and Spitfires intercepted a large German attack and prevented many of them from reaching London. The victories that day – across Southern England

– turned the tide of the Battle of Britain, and 15 September became the official Battle of Britain day to commemorate the Battle. However, the Big Wing tactics practised from Duxford were a source of bitter controversy between 11 and 12 Groups, and often led to 11 Group's airfields to the south being left undefended, since the time taken to put together such a large formation delayed arrival over the airfields.

RAF Fighter Command Squadrons which operated from RAF Duxford during the course of the war included : 19, 56, 66, 133, 181, 195, 222, 242, 264, 266, 310, 312, 601, 609, 611, and the Air Fighting Development Unit, which evaluated captured German aircraft as well as other new aircraft types.

In 1943 RAF Duxford passed to the USAAF and the Eighth Air Force fighter command.

Day 61 – 8 September 1940

Weather: fine.

Fighter Command Serviceable Aircraft as at 09:00 hours:

- Blenheim – 50
- Spitfire – 197
- Hurricane – 381
- Defiant – 23
- Gladiator – 8
- **Total – 697**

There was little activity this day. During the day Detling and West Malling were hit and in London an air raid shelter at Colombia Market was hit.

In Germany, Goering took over personal command of the air battle against Britain. As for the RAF, the system of rotating squadrons after they had been in action was being accelerated. Dowding had started a new system by which squadrons were being divided into three categories, those seriously fit for operations, those that needed careful handling and those that required to be taken out of combat altogether. The latter group was being stripped of its successful pilots who were transferred to the first group.

The RAF flew 305 sorties and shot down seven enemy aircraft, at a cost of four aircraft lost.

That night London was attacked again, in particular the docks. This time by over 200 bombers. The casualties this second night were 400 dead.
73 Squadron Unofficial War Diary – 8 September

A large 'flap' has developed! 'No. 1 Alert' is declared. After much seeking after knowledge we found that the aforesaid means that the great invasion is probably imminent. Everyone is confined to camp and armed to the teeth.

Reported Casualties (RAF Campaign Diary):

* Enemy: 7 confirmed, 3 probable, 8 damaged

Comments

Martin James: This was not the first time (or the last) that West Malling was bombed, but it was not actually operational as a Fighter Command airfield during the Battle of Britain. While in the geographical area of Group 11, the Battle of Britain was over when 29 Squadron, then flying Bristol Beaufighters, was posted there on 28 April 1941. I know this because I have a booklet belonging to my late father that was published by Tonbridge and Malling Borough Council in 1989 to commemorate the 50th Anniversary (1939-89) of RAF West Malling.

I quote from the booklet: 'no call was made upon West Malling, despite the present day myth that it was a BoB airfield' and '...between these dates (10 July-31 October 1940) no Hurricanes or Spitfires flew from the field, although some used it as an emergency landing field'.

May I also add that my Father joined 29 Squadron at Digby on 20 October 1940 as observer/navigator in the Bristol Blenheim night fighters that 29 was then flying. He is therefore one of the relatively few non pilots to be awarded the Battle of Britain Medal. And while the description of the Blenheim in a later 'post', and the accompanying comments, are not terribly complimentary about this aircraft, I understand from my father that it did perform a valuable service in being one of the first aircraft to be equipped with radar. I do feel that the well deserved adulation of the Battle of Britain fighter pilots tends to overshadow the just as valuable parts played by other aircrew.

May I further add, just for interest as a proud son, that when Flt Lt Guy Gibson joined 29 Squadron he chose my father as his navigator, and he retained that position when 29 Squadron moved to West Malling in 1941, by which time he had been promoted to Sergeant. Guy Gibson left 29 Squadron at the end of 1941.

Captains and Commanders
Adolf Hitler

When Hitler had finished with France in the summer of 1940, the only country he was left with still opposing him was Britain. His preference was not to have to fight Britain, but to receive her acquiescence in his triumph. He was prepared to settle for an arrangement which gave him complete control over Continental Europe in return for which he would acquiesce in Britain's overseas interests, her Empire guaranteed by her Navy. This is what he put, in not too graceful a way in his speech on 19 July. His phrase was that it was 'a last appeal to reason'.

When this was rebuffed by Halifax, who made it quite clear that Britain planned to continue the war, and had no interest in discussing terms or indeed anything else with Hitler, the dye was cast. On August 1, Hitler duly issued his Directive 17 to the effect that steps must now be taken to put the Royal Air Force out of action as a prelude to the launching of the seaborne invasion of Britain code named Sealion. Britain was to be put to the sword.

Having issued his new directive, he subsequently took relatively little part in the Battle, not bothering to oversee the next steps to be taken against Britain. The reason was that the Luftwaffe was in the personal hands and under the direct control of his trusted Nazi number two, Herman Goering. The fact was, the Luftwaffe was distinct from the other armed services in Germany at the time. The head of the Navy was Admiral Raeder, the Head of the Army was General Brauschitz. The Luftwaffe by contrast was under the personal control of Herman Goering who was given the newly created title of Reichsmarschall.

The fact that the German air force was professionally in the hands of a top Nazi, who admittedly had been a fighter pilot in the First World War, meant that Hitler had none of the latent mistrust which existed between him and the professional heads of the other services. It was almost as though he could rely on the Luftwaffe being within the overall Nazi element of the State. It meant also that it could do no wrong although it was to fail to carry out his Directive 17. It was never taken to task for this. It was, after all, the responsibility of his trusted Lieutenant, Herman Goering.

The further reason why Hitler never interfered or even bothered to comment on the clear failure of the Luftwaffe to execute his orders may have been the fact that Hitler never seemed to have his heart in the project to subjugate Britain that summer. If Goering had brought it off, all well and good. But the fact that he was not going to bring it off didn't seem to bother the Führer. An analysis of the German plans for Sealion show that it never got to a stage where it was a realistic prospect. He would come back to the subject of what to do about Britain when and after he had disposed of Soviet Russia.

Day 62 – 9 September 1940

Weather: showery.

Fighter Command Serviceable Aircraft as at 09:00 hours:

- Blenheim – 55
- Spitfire – 220
- Hurricane – 392
- Defiant – 22
- Gladiator – 8
- **Total – 697**

As well as the continuing attack on London, the enemy also launched a good number of attacks by pockets of bombers accompanied by the usual fighters on airfields of 11 Group. In combat that day the RAF lost twenty-one and managed to shoot down twenty-eight of the enemy aircraft.

The day's fighting was followed by a night attack on London by bombers resulting in over 350 people being killed. Birmingham, Liverpool, Nottingham and Derby were also bombed that night.

242 Squadron Operational Record Book – 9 September

Sqdn Ldr Bader leading wing consisting of 242, 310 and 19 Squadrons patrolling over London encountered large formation of e/a. bombers and fighters. 242 Squadron led the attack and shot down ten aircraft. No. 310 (Czech) Squadron shot down seven, and no. 19 Squadron two. One pilot of 242 killed (PO Sclanders). One pilot (Sgt Lonsdale) baled out and returned to Squadron next day unhurt. Congratulations received from Air Officer Command and Chief of the Air Staff.

Reported Casualties (RAF Campaign Diary):

* Enemy: 52 confirmed, 11 probable, 13 damaged
* Own: 20 aircraft with 5 pilots killed or missing.

The People in Support
Civilian Repair Unit

One of the advantages the RAF enjoyed during the Battle was that aircraft shot down could be recovered and recycled. This became the responsibility of the Civilian Repair Unit. Its job was to pick up RAF planes which had crashed or crash landed and take them back to the centre which was equipped to handle them. Many aircraft were repaired. Others which were too far gone, in terms of damage, were canabalised and the parts used to rebuild the other aircraft which were salvageable. By mid-July, 160 aircraft per week were being repaired and returned to operation.

This service had the benefit of a fleet of specially designed motor transport vehicles, some 30 ft long. A team would, when recovering a crashed aircraft, detach the wings and lift the fuselage onto the body of the vehicle fitting the wings alongside it. This form of transport vehicle was called a 'Queen Mary'. This method of handling crashed aircraft contributed a substantial source of almost mint aircraft being supplied to the Squadrons throughout the Battle.

Day 63 – 10 September 1940

Weather; cloudy with some rain.

Fighter Command Serviceable Aircraft as at 09:00 hours:

- Blenheim – 47
- Spitfire – 225
- Hurricane – 375
- Defiant – 21
- Gladiator – 8
- **Total – 676**

The day featured scattered attacks often by single aircraft, usually Me109s, carrying a single bomb. These attacks by Luftflotte 3 on airfields such as Tangmere and West Malling occurred in the late afternoon. Single aircraft attackers also came over from Luftflotte 2 hitting airfields in Kent.

The RAF shot down two enemy aircraft and lost none of its own.

That night St. Katherine's Dock was attacked resulting in a devastating fire. In all over a thousand incendiary bombs were dropped during the night raid on London.

Cyril Shoesmith, 14 years old, Bexhill-on-Sea, Diary – Tuesday 10 September

Had an air raid from 12:25pm-1:25. At 5:10pm-6:40 there was a second raid. Planes were heard. At 6 a big plane came over. There was machine gun fire. The plane was a bomber. We heard a queer humming sound. Then the plane was seen approaching from the town. It had been turned back by the Lewis guns. We heard about two loud explosions and machine guns. The plane came over our houses and I saw that it had two engines. I heard a whistling noise and then a very loud explosion. 8:25pm-4:45am – air raid.

(Reproduced by kind permission of the Imperial War Museum and Copyright holder)

73 Squadron Operational Record Book – 10 September – Castle Camps

Debden sent up a band at 19:00 hours which played good dance tunes outside the Mess and highly delighted an enthusiastic audience with 'request' numbers. The CO and Flt Lt Beytagh to Debden for supper and a discussion on tactics with OC 17 Squadron. Majority of those pilots left at F1 [Freddie 1 – satellite camp to Debden] repaired to an hostelry in the neighbourhood which was unanimously voted the best of its kind yet found locally. The stopping of the clock in the bar added to the enjoyment as the landlord did not notice the sabotage until 22:55 hours.

Reported Casualties (RAF Campaign Diary):

* Enemy: 2 confirmed, 1 probable, 0 damaged
* Own: 1 Spitfire, pilot safe.

Week 9 Summary: Operation Sealion

Statistical summary, Week 9:

- **Total Fighter Command Establishment:** *1558 planes*
- **Strength:** *1381 planes*
- **Balance:** *understrength 177 planes*
- **Losses:** *74 Hurricanes (+ 34 damaged), 52 Spitfires (+31 damaged), 4 Blenheims*
- **Aircraft Production:** *5 Beaufighters, 11 Defiants, 54 Hurricanes, 36 Spitfires*

Throughout that summer of 1940, the threat of German invasion was always present in British minds. Ostensibly, the air battle against the RAF was the prelude to that invasion. For Germany, the air battle was necessary to remove the danger of the RAF carrying out air attacks on

German forces as they crossed the Channel and, particularly, as they landed on the British coast. While the intention of invasion was real enough what could not be predicted was whether the RAF would meet final defeat that autumn and whether the weather would permit the launch of the invasion, particularly if this had to be in late September.

The answer to the conundrum was, had the conditions been met, they might indeed have come.

Had Goering not switched the Luftwaffe attack from the airfields of 11 Group to London itself, they might indeed have come. What then? For instance, had 11 Group been forced to withdraw from its airfields south of London and had the RAF been unable to contest control of the air over Sussex and Kent, the Fuhrer would surely have been tempted to land a force of Ju52 troop carrying aircraft. on airfields such as Manston. The point is that, had Fighter Command been overwhelmed, the Luftwaffe would have had all kinds of options open to them. They could, for instance, have adopted the policy which had proved so successful against Poland and Holland, namely the destruction of Warsaw and Rotterdam. Alternatively, they could have begun by wiping out large towns such as Guildford and Ashford. There was nothing the Navy or the Army could have done to stop them. It was only the continued existence of Fighter Command that prevented this kind of terror bombing. Without the RAF to protect it, holding Britain against the power of an unopposed Luftwaffe would have become impossible. Had Britain been subjugated Sealion would have become a formality. The Royal Navy in all its power would not have prevailed against the Luftwaffe. We were to see this in the Battle of Crete the following spring.

Day 64 – 11 September 1940

Weather: fine; some cloud on the south coast.

Fighter Command Serviceable Aircraft as at 09:00 hours:

- Blenheim – 61
- Spitfire – 214
- Hurricane – 387
- Defiant – 21
- Gladiator – 8
- **Total – 691**

From mid-afternoon onwards Luftflotte 3 delivered a raid on Southampton. This was followed by several raids on London by Luftflotte 2. As well as hitting London, aircraft attacked Biggin Hill, Kenley and Brooklands. Later that day raids also came in from the Cherbourg peninsula which once again ended up bombing Southampton and Portsmouth. There were also raids by Me109s which attacked Kenley, Detling and a convoy heading its way round the Kent coast. That day the RAF flew 678 sorties and lost twenty-nine aircraft with seventeen pilots killed. The Germans lost twenty-five aircraft.

Meanwhile there was intense speculation concerning the imminence of invasion. All this, however, was conditional on air superiority being achieved. At the same time it was noted by German aircrews that despite the losses inflicted on the RAF, the latter still appeared to have undiminished strength. Victory was still eluding the Luftwaffe.

That night Bomber Command hit French ports and damaged German invasion craft whilst the Luftwaffe continued to target London hitting Crystal Palace station and once again setting the Docks alight.

249 Squadron Operational Record Book – 11 September

Brought to readiness at 16:10 hours and ordered to patrol London Docks and Thames Estuary. Large formations of He111s with fighter escorts intercepted east of London. For the first time, it was possible to carry out a head-on attack, this resulted in two He111s being destroyed and one probable. Sgt Davis was wounded during this battle and had to bale out at Beneden owing to fire in his aircraft. Squadron patrolled Dover at 18:15 hours, and although a number of enemy fighters were seen high above, it was not possible to make contact. A stick of bombs was seen to fall slap outside the entrance to Dover harbour in the sea but no-one could see the enemy aircraft from which they were dropped.

Enemy casualties: 2 destroyed, 1 probable, 1 damaged

Reported Casualties (RAF Campaign Diary):

* Enemy: 89 confirmed, 34 probable, 52 damaged
* Own: 28 aircraft with 17 pilots killed or missing

Top Gun Gallery
Eric Lock

Eric Lock joined the RAF volunteer reserve just before the war. On the outbreak of hostilities he was duly called up to complete his flying training. He joined 41 Squadron, based at Catterick in Yorkshire, flying Spitfires. His squadron was redeployed to the south of England to RAF Hornchurch. Here he was soon in the thick of the battle in which he shot down an extraordinary figure of fifteen enemy aircraft, all in the space of nineteen days. He was awarded the DFC when half way through this total and a Bar when he had completed the total of fifteen victories. He was the highest scoring British fighter ace during the Battle of Britain. He went on to score a further clutch of kills reaching the total of twenty-six during the course of his involvement in the war. In one encounter, in November 1940, he was quite severely wounded, which kept him out of action for the next few months. However, he left his sick bed to attend an investiture at which he received the DSO.

He finally returned to operational flying in mid-summer 1941. On a fighter sweep across northern France on 3 August 1941, he went missing near Calais. Neither his aircraft nor his body has since been recovered.

Like Bob Doe, he was a quiet, unassuming and modest individual. He was known to his fellow pilots as 'Sawn Off Lockie', reflecting his very short stature.

Day 65 – 12 September 1940

Weather: unsettled with some rain.

Fighter Command Serviceable Aircraft as at 09:00 hours:

- Blenheim – 50
- Spitfire – 208
- Hurricane – 392
- Defiant – 21
- Gladiator – 8
- **Total – 679**

Once again, the main activity on the part of the enemy reconnaissance flights along with attacks by Me109s flying solo and small numbers of Ju88s. The weather held back the RAF in their pursuit of these marauders. In the early evening, Hornchurch was attacked by a single plane. That day there had also been bombs on Harrogate and Hastings.

That day a large delayed action bomb fell next door to the north wall of St. Paul's Cathedral in London which took several days to extract. The bomb disposal experts who extracted the bomb were awarded the George Cross. The RAF flew 247 sorties but lost no planes while the Germans suffered four aircraft destroyed.

That night Liverpool, London and Blackpool were bombed. Bomber Command carried out further attacks on the German barges.

266 Squadron Operational Record Book: 12 September

Cold, drizzle during the afternoon. Visibility poor. Six aircraft operating from Duxford. Owing to adverse weather only local flying was performed. Sqdn Ldr H.W. Mermagen, AFC, temporarily assumes Command of the Squadron.

Reported Casualties (RAF Campaign Diary):

* Enemy: 3 confirmed, 0 probable, 4 damaged
* Own: Nil.

Aircraft of the Battle
Bristol Blenheim

This aircraft could be said to have been the comparable aircraft with the Ju88. However, this was not a particularly effective aircraft though it got used in several types of activity by the RAF. It had been developed with funding from Lord Rothermere, the owner of the Daily Mail and entered squadron service in March 1937. When the prototype flew in 1935 it was the fastest light bomber, but was obsolete by 1939 and was consequently forced into service as a night fighter in 1940. The fact was that German anti aircraft fire was both intense and relatively accurate so that when used on daylight operations, the Blenheim became extremely vulnerable and suffered severe losses. Many Blenheims were lost in northern France.

Comments

Jim Kilduff: The Blenheim was totally out of its class when the Battle started, and it is unfortunate that it could not be replaced at that time. It was known amongst many aircrew as the Flying Coffin, for obvious reasons and a very well justified title. It was of a similar class s the Boulton Paul Defiant, an equally useless piece of equipment for the job in hand.

Day 66 – 13 September 1940

Weather: intermittent rain.

Fighter Command Serviceable Aircraft as at 09:00 hours:

- Blenheim – 51
- Spitfire – 208
- Hurricane – 393
- Defiant – 18
- Gladiator – 8
- **Total – 678**

In the morning several aircraft attacked single buildings in London. The targets included Downing St, Whitehall and Buckingham Palace. Some aircraft reached further inland and were able to attack parts of Oxfordshire and Berkshire. In the afternoon single seater fighters were despatched by Luftflotte 2. They aimed for Biggin Hill but were turned back by Fighter Command. The RAF lost One aircraft and the Luftwaffe lost four.

London was targeted that night. Clapham Junction and a school in West Ham, which was being used as a reception centre, were just two of the areas hit.

73 Squadron Unofficial War Diary – 13 September

Mrs Robinson, the CO's better half, has got us adopted by a knitting circle…Mrs R also collected all our 'smalls' and took them off to launder them.

PO D.H. Wissler Diary – 13 September

Bed at 10:30 thinking very hard of Mummy and Pop as I could see a hell of a barrage over town. God Damn and blast Hitler.

Reported Casualties (RAF Campaign Diary):

* Enemy: 3 confirmed, 0 probable, 3 damaged
* Own: 1 Hurricane of which the pilot is safe.

The Squadrons
73 Squadron
Tutor et ultor – Protector and Avenger

73 squadron was formed in July 1917 at Upavon. In 1918 the squadron saw service in France as bomber escorts for missions over the Western Front. The squadron was disbanded in July 1919.

In March 1937 the squadron was reformed at Mildenhall. It received Hurricanes in 1938 and following the outbreak of the Second World War was sent to France as an attachment to the Advanced Air Striking Force. The squadron returned to Britain in June 1940. During the Battle of Britain the squadron was initially based at Church Fenton and was later moved south to Debden. After the Battle the squadron served in the Middle East and Yugoslavia.

Following the end of the war the squadron was based in Cyprus for a number of years. It was eventually disbanded in March 1969.

Comments

Jim Kilduff: It is disturbing to see and hear so much about the Spitfire having 'won' the Battle of Britain. In fact there were at least double the numbers of Hurricanes engaged in the Battle as Spitfires, and although the Hurricane was marginally slower, (not 'much' slower as is said by many modern commentators – only c. 30 – 40 mph) it could take much more punishment than the 'Spit', and in fact more enemy aircraft pro rata were shot down by Hurricanes than by Spitfires. The Hurricane did not perform at the higher altitudes as well as the Spitfire, but the task of the Hurricane pilots was to attack the German bombers flying at lower altitudes, which were a greater threat to the civilian population than the single-seat fighters, and they carried out this duty extremely well. The Spitfire had several flaws which caused some dismay amongst aircrews – such as the tendency to flip over when taxi-ing, due to the very long blades of the airscrew, and its lack of stability as a gun platform.

Day 67 – 14 September 1940

Weather: showery.

Fighter Command Serviceable Aircraft as at 09:00 hours:

- Blenheim – 52
- Spitfire – 215
- Hurricane – 403
- Defiant – 16
- Gladiator – 7
- **Total – 693**

Activity this day was once more concentrated on attacks by single aircraft. The targets were south of London and on London itself. Attacks took place on radar stations and on Eastbourne and Brighton where a cinema was hit killing thirty-five people.

In Berlin, Hitler blamed the difficulties being experienced in the battle against the RAF on the weather. The point is that the Germans had missed the fine weather earlier in the month. It was then that they had failed to dominate the RAF. Now it was getting too late to launch an invasion. Yet the Germans managed to get the impression that once again the RAF was showing signs of being near defeat. The RAF lost fourteen and the Luftwaffe lost seven.

73 Squadron Operational Record Book – 14 September

This turned out to be our blackest day. Twelve machines took off, seven returned in disorder. FO Smith, supported by two others, reports that Spitfires attacked the formation and broke up the rear section. Smithy followed one Spitfire right down almost to the ground, hence the forcefulness of his statement that they attacked our formations. Of the seven that returned, PO Marchand was battered about a bit, having a bullet through his port tank, one through the port aileron passing through the main spar and emerging from the landing light, and one clean through the top of the W/T mast just above his head.

Flt Lt Beytagh got a bullet in his radiator and force landed at West Malling. Sgt Marshall was shot down by a Me109 near Dover, Sergt Leng was also shot down by one of the same tribe, near Gravesend. The CO was reported missing, also Sgt Brimble. Sgt Griffin was shot in both legs and baled out. A pall of gloom spread over the whole unit.

Reported Casualties (RAF Campaign Diary):

* Enemy: 16 confirmed, 3 probable, 12 damaged
* Own: 12 aircraft with 4 pilots killed or missing.

The Airfields
RAF Middle Wallop

RAF Middle Wallop was originally opened as a training school, home of the 15th Service Flying Training School flying Oxfords and Masters, which arrived in June 1940. The airfield and base had taken 18 months to build.

With the fall of France and the outbreak of the Battle of Britain, however, the airfield was soon in demand for operational purposes, and it became a sector operations HQ (Y Sector) for 10 Group. Both fighters and light bombers were based here.

'Y' sector had responsibility for defending the naval base of Portland, as well as the Supermarine aircraft factory on Southampton and the Isle of Wight. After the beginning of the Blitz in September 1940 its duties extended to defending the cities on the South Coast.

Squadrons stationed here included 236 Squadron (flying Blenheim light bombers), 238 Squadron (Hurricanes) and 401 (RCAF – Hurricanes) from June 1940, 501 Squadron (Hurricanes), 609 Squadron (Spitfires) and 604 Squadron (Blenheims) in July, 222 Squadron (Spitfires) in August, and 238 Squadron (Hurricanes) and 23 Squadron (Blenheims) in September. 604 squadron was later equipped with Beaufighter nightfighters flown by Sqdn Ldr John Cunningham.

609 Squadron was perhaps the most famous squadron to be based at RAF Middle Wallop during the Battle, being the first to down 100 enemy aircraft. On August 13, the squadron intercepted a raid over Portland. They claimed at least 13 enemy aircraft downed and several more 'probables'. On the next day the Luftwaffe visited their revenge – a single German bomber dropped five bombs on the airfield, damaging hangars four and five. Three airmen died as they were trying to close the vast doors to protect the aircraft inside.

RAF Middle Wallop was also used by the United States Army Air Forces Ninth Air Force as IX Fighter Command Headquarters beginning in November 1943. Today the airfield is the home of the Army Air Corps.

Comments

Stan Hurrell: Middle Wallop was also the home of FEE (Fighter Experimental Establishment) formed from 93 Squadron and later renamed TFU (Telecommunications Flying Unit) which in 1941 experimented with the laying of aerial minefields using Wellingtons and even Handley Page Harrows. The mines consisted of 4lb bombs suspended from long lengths of piano wire and, vectored by Ground Control, laid in quantities across the front of the incoming enemy bomber force. The EA was then supposed to fly into it and a steadying parachute at the upper end of the wire pulled the bomb up until it impacted with the underside of the wing and exploded. Surprisingly we got several successes with this Heath Robinson scheme which was the brain child of a Cmdr. Dove of the Royal Navy. The BBC reported these sucesses as due to 'other devices'.

Day 68 – 15 September 1940

Battle of Britain Day

Weather: fine.

Fighter Command Serviceable Aircraft as at 09:00 hours:

- Blenheim – 47
- Spitfire – 192
- Hurricane – 389
- Defiant – 24
- Gladiator – 8
- **Total – 660**

Weather wise this was finally the opportunity the Luftwaffe had been waiting for. Accordingly, in mid-morning the radar along the south coast picked up evidence of mass raids which duly appeared over southern England heading for London. All three groups, 10, 11 and 12 in southern England now played their part in intercepting the incoming armada. There were no less than thirty squadrons engaged in intercepting and contesting the progress of this vast fleet of German bombers. Furthermore, the latter was accompanied by a very strong force of Me109s. Naturally, despite the aerial battles which developed, substantial damage was done to London. This was partly due to the manner in which the German bombers jettisoned their bombs when under attack.

Bombs fell again on Buckingham Palace. One sergeant pilot who shot down a Do17, from which the German crew managed to parachute to safety, was himself shot down and managed to bale out ending up in a dustbin in Chelsea. Proceedings that day demonstrated beyond doubt that Fighter Command, far from being on the verge of collapse, was on vigorous form. Despite the RAF claiming that it had shot down no less than 183 aircraft, when the actual figure was fifty-six, for a loss of twenty-six aircraft, the result was almost three to one in the RAF's favour. For the Germans it was the sheer experience of having to fight their way to London and back when they had been assured that the opposition was almost at an end, that so riled them.

Meanwhile, in the early evening there had been an attack on the Supermarine Spitfire factory near Southampton but this had been driven off by intense anti-aircraft fire.

The significance of this day was, that in terms of publicity, the British had got a wonderful boost to their morale. Everybody in the land had listened to the nine o'clock news on the BBC that night. Although the day had been fine, the weather was in fact breaking up. It was going to be too late to mount an invasion. The Germans had missed the boat. Yet despite the events of these couple of days, Goering was not giving up. Indeed a new plan was announced. It would be a renewed attack on Fighter Command airfields carried out mainly by hoards of Me109s. The RAF, he confidently asserted, would be finished within four days. That was what everyone had heard at the beginning of Adler Tag. The weather would last another six weeks but the decisive day, which has gone down in history as Battle of Britain day, was on this date the 15 September. Britain had survived the onslaught.

249 Squadron Operational Record Book – 15 September

Squadron patrolled with no. 46 Squadron at 12:00 hours and intercepted twenty Do215s South of London, and carried out a beam attack. Enemy casualties: one destroyed, one probable and one damaged. Our casualties: nil. At 13:40 hours, Squadron again ordered to patrol and intercepted fifteen Do215s over South London. A beam attack cracked this formation wide open, the result being that 5 ½ bombers were destroyed and 8 ½ probables and three damaged. One reason for this success was that the German fighters failed to do their stuff, probably due to their attention already being diverted by being attacked from above by

Spitfires. Further patrol with 46 Squadron carried out over Shellhaven during the evening; nothing seen. This was by far the most successful day in the Squadron's history. Total to date 185 enemy aircraft destroyed.

Enemy casualties: 8 ½ destroyed, 9 ½ probable, 4 damaged.

73 Squadron Unofficial War Diary – 15 September

At 14:45hrs our five serviceable machines took off to investigate an 'X' raid near Maidstone. Over 100 EA nearly all bombers, were contacted and the boys waded in. PO Langham-Hobart set about a Me110 and saw one engine on fire. Sgt Ellis tackled a He111k and damaged it, both of these were highly probable, Sgt Garton damaged a Do17.

News came through later that PO Roy Marchand had crashed at Sittingbourne, Kent, and was unfortunately killed. No details are available...The task of breaking the news to Mrs Marchand. Roy's wife, fell to Flt Lt Beytagh and PO Hoole. The whole Squadron mourns the loss of this popular, cheery, happy-go-lucky, but gallant pilot.

Cyril Shoesmith, 14 years old, Bexhill-on-Sea, Diary – Sunday 15 September

The first air raid today was from 11:40am-1:10pm. Saw a Hurricane about 12:30, and just before the 'all clear' went we saw a squadron of 'Hurricanes' and a squadron of 'Spitfires'. At 2:45pm the 'take cover' was sounded. We saw a German bomber being attacked by three Spitfires. Also about thirty German planes in one formation heading towards the sea. A big number of English planes headed towards Eastbourne. The raid lasted one hour.

(Reproduced by kind permission of the Imperial War Museum and Copyright holder)

Reported Casualties (RAF Campaign Diary):

* Enemy: 186 confirmed, 42 probable, 72 damaged
* Own: 25 aircraft with 13 pilots killed or missing.

Comments

Peter Stapleton: I wrote this some years ago, and seems only fitting to have it on the web today, 15 September, the 70th anniversary. It's my tribute to those for whom tomorrow never came, but without who's sacrifice we would simply not be here.

"This day is never done"

I can't believe it's over
Is this day really done?
And have the Germans gone to bed
Just like the setting sun?

I can't believe it's over
The wingco said 'Stand Down',
Lads, the evenings yours
Why not go into town?

I can't believe it's over
But beer I cannot face
Whilst the spirits of those who died today
Are still about this place

And so I'll sit and muse awhile
And remember them all
Their laughs and smiles
And so I'll sit and cry

For tomorrow when the klaxon comes
We'll be in the skies and with our guns
Goering's planes we'll kill and maim
With steady hand and steady aim
And so I'll sit and wait.

I don't believe it's over
Our day is NEVER done
And perhaps tomorrow, Monday
The reaper to me may come.

So off to bed and off to sleep
But before I go, in the diary I keep –

Sunday, 15th September
God, what a day to remember!
'Bandits blasted from the skies by the score'
But tomorrow they'll be back for more.

I won't believe it's over
I won't believe this day is done
Until the bastards stay away
Until they never come.

Could there be a chance, just a chance,
That tomorrow they won't? .

John Morris Bush: I well remember this day when it was announced that 185 enemy planes had been shot down for the loss of twenty-six RAF with a number of our boys safe. We went out into the street and cheered and cheered and cheered. The news vendors placards gave the scores each day as if it was a cricket match, 185 for 26. I cannot remember ever being told we lost more than the Germans, and it wasn't for a long long time afterwards that the 185 was amended, but it didn't matter then as the invasion had been averted. You can have no idea how that figure of 185 bucked us all up.

becky burdick: Even though I knew what would happen, it's oddly a great relief to read this post! Here in America, I'm ever grateful for the outcome of this day.

Glorious and heartbreaking. So much, much more to come....
Have always been in awe of the raw courage of those times – can't imagine what it was like to endure that war, day after day, night after night, not knowing what tomorrow would bring, and still keep going.

Captains and Commanders
Winston Churchill

It was Neville Chamberlain who declared war on Germany on September 3 1939, but it was left to his successor, Winston Churchill, actually to make war when he succeeded to the premiership on May 10 1940. Chamberlain who, though he had declared war, had no appetite for actually making war. He loathed the idea of war. He knew it was inevitable but he wasn't really the man for it. When on May 10 he was forced out, it undoubtedly hurt his parliamentary pride. But the way that he moved into his new position, as a key member of Churchill's five man inner war cabinet and the way he gave Churchill absolute loyalty, seemed to suggest that he was ready and almost relieved to pass over responsibility for the conduct of hostilities to his successor, Churchill.

Churchill inherited Fighter Command under Dowding, as the instrument of war which was both to save Britain and, indeed, make his political career. Dowding's letter to the Under Secretary of State for Air, dated 16 May, showed that that there was no lack of will on the part of the RAF. All Churchill had to do was to back Dowding and this is what he did.

During the Battle he made several visits, first to Dowding and then to Keith Park. He did so to experience the drama of the Battle.

Comments

Roy Watts: It is unfortunate that Churchill's backing for Dowding evaporated the moment the Battle was over. If the Battle did indeed make Churchill's political career, it was, to say the least, an act of spectacular ingratitude on his part to summarily remove not only Dowding but AVM Park and the AOC 10 Group from their posts. One suspects that, like all politicians, Churchill had a low tolerance of being crossed. Thus he did not take kindly to Dowding's refusual to send further hurricane squadrons to the Continent towards the end of the battle for France despite the rash promises Churchill had made to the French government. His irritation will have been made worse by the fact that Dowding was proved right, irrespective of the fact that Dowding's stand on this issue was probably a key factor in winning the battle. Churchill had marked Dowding's card and he and his two key lieutenants in the Battle were dispensed with at the earliest opportunity.

Andrew: I don't think that Churchill was behind Dowding's sacking but he should have stepped in to sort out the bad guys in the RAF and Air Ministry. The RAF had the wrong leaders at the top for the next few years with some exceptions, notably in the Mediterranean.

The Battle of Britain was truly the RAF's defining moment then it slipped into mediocrity and the lessons on how not to run a bombing campaign were forgotten. Park, Saul and Brand should have been given more prominent roles at the top of the RAF after the Battle of Britain.

Churchill should also have made sure that Dowding was appointed Marshal of the RAF particularly when the King suggested it.

Despite all the research in to the Battle of Britain and the RAF in World War Two it is still a great mystery as to why Dowding was humiliated instead of rewarded and honoured. Park, Brand and Saul were badly needed at the top but were sidelined due to their association with Dowding and Battle of Britain success.

Who was behind this fiasco that robbed the RAF of some of its best leadership? Why didn't Churchill (and Beaverbrook) step in, what was Sinclair's role at the Air Ministry, Newall or Portal could have taken more definitive action or were they occupied passing on the baton and under the influence of retired Marshals of the RAF, Trenchard and Salmond? Dowding himself, why didn't he sack Leigh Mallory when it was plainly clear he wasn't doing his job and then reprimand Bader and send him to 11 Group to keep him occupied doing something useful? Newall could have stepped at that stage in too and backed Dowding in that necessary duty.

Tony Rudd: The questions you ask are absolutely relevant. The answer has to be complicated. Dowding had tremendous qualities, but being able to deal with personalities wasn't one of them. He picked the most important man in the battle, namely Keith Park. After all he promoted him over Trafford Leigh Mallory who was his senior. He, of course, was very much not one of the group in the Air Ministry itself. As for Churchill, Beaverbrook and co., the only person that could have done more for Dowding was, I think, Churchill himself. The reason for his reluctance to get involved was, I suggest that the inner workings of the RAF at the top was a subject he knew very little about. So in a way it's difficult to blame him. As for the rest of it, we just have to accept the way the chips fell. It was very unfortunate but there it is.

Day 69 – 16 September 1940

Weather: cloud and rain.

Fighter Command Serviceable Aircraft as at 09:00 hours:

- Blenheim – 60
- Spitfire – 216
- Hurricane – 356
- Defiant – 19
- Gladiator – 8
- **Total – 659**

That day Goering held a conference with his commanders in France at which he announced a return to a policy of hitting Fighter Command and its airfields. At the same time, he said that bomber formations were to be reduced and the covering fighters increased. The key was to draw up RAF fighters and destroy them. He envisaged that in four to five days the job would be done and the RAF fighter strength eliminated.

At Uxbridge, Park was trying to tighten up the battle procedures of 11 Group. Despite the achievements of the previous day, in his opinion there was still more that could be done. For instance, to intercept the second and third waves of the German attacks, he wanted to ensure that squadrons should be in pairs, or if there was time, to be formed into wings of three squadrons. In Germany in the meanwhile, it was announced that that day the Reichsmarschall had flown over London in a Ju88. To accommodate his rather large girth this would have a massive modification to the air frame. There was some doubt in England anyway as to whether this had actually happened.

Due to the bad weather there were only a number of small incursions mainly over Kent. Nine German aircraft were destroyed at the cost of one RAF fighter.

That night some 170 bombers launched an attack on London. Liverpool and some other provincial cities, including Coventry, also came under attack.

266 Squadron Operational Record Book – 16 September

Average temperature, drizzle afternoon and evening. Visibility poor. Practices included formation flying – Fighter Command attacks. PO A.H. Humphrey, PO H.A.R. Prowse and Pilot Sgts L.C. Allton, R.A. Boswell, R.A. Breeze, J.T. Dunmore and A.N. MacGregor reported for flying duties from no. 7 Operational Training Unit.

Reported Casualties (RAF Campaign Diary):

* Enemy: 2 confirmed, 0 probable, 1 damaged
* Own: One Spitfire of which the pilot is safe.

The People in Support
Airfield Repair Services

As the German attack intensified, particularly on the airfields of Fighter Command, the business of repairing damage, so that the airfields could remain operational, gave rise to problems. As a result of some attacks, the area of the airfield, used as the runway, was often pitted with literally dozens of craters. They were for the time being unusable. Churchill seeing such an airfield, after a raid, decided that what was needed were several hundred strong groups armed with proper equipment and able to be deployed immediately after a raid. These groups did sterling service and were responsible for many an airfield being made usable again in a matter of hours or certainly by the next morning enabling the airfield once more to be operational.

Day 70 – 17 September 1940

Weather: rain and cloud.

Fighter Command Serviceable Aircraft as at 09:00 hours:

- Blenheim – 49
- Spitfire – 222
- Hurricane – 362
- Defiant – 23
- Gladiator – 8
- **Total – 659**

Faced with the prospect of further bad weather, Hitler yet again postponed Sealion.

Despite the conditions, Luftflotte 2 sent over small pockets of fighter bombers together with a mass of Me109s to harass the defences. The idea was that the bombers would attract RAF fighters who would then run into the Me109s who would slaughter them. The RAF flew 540 sorties, lost five of their number but shot down eight of the enemy.

By night, there was a heavy attack on London by over 260 bombers. The West End took the brunt of this night's raids. There was a great deal of damage and in particular John Lewis in Oxford Street went up in flames. There was direct hit on the telephone exchange at Greenwich and Marble Arch tube station was also hit. Merseyside and Glasgow were further targets that night.

RAF Bomber Command continued its night raids on the concentrations of barges in the French ports along the Channel.

73 Squadron Unofficial War Diary - 17 September

At 15:50 hrs the Squadron was ordered to 'scramble' to Hendon, angels fifteen, and join up with 257 Squadron. A glorious shambles was the result. The Squadron arrived over Hendon to find the sky absolutely stiff with aircraft, which on closer inspection proved to be British. If the number of aircraft shot down by the Hun is as great as he claims then after this afternoons display we are quite ready to believe that our production of aircraft and fighter pilots must have reached astronomical figures.

501 Squadron Operational Record Book - 17 September

One patrol (two aircraft) took off on patrol at 13:50hours. Twelve aircraft took off at 15:03 hours in company with 253 Squadron over Ashford. They were attacked by twenty Me109s. Sqdn Ldr Hogan attacked one Me109 and hit it in the radiator. This aircraft was seem to turn inland. Damage to this aircraft was not seen. Sgts Lacey and Egan were reported missing in this engagement but information was received that Lacey was uninjured but had baled out.

Reported Casualties (RAF Campaign Diary):

* Enemy: 10 confirmed, 4 probable, 2 damaged
* Own: Five aircraft of which four pilots are safe.

Comments:

Keith at Tregenna: Also on this day: U-boat U-48 torpedoed and caused the sinking of the SS City of Benares, killing 77 British children and 248 crew en-route to Canada. The ship, part of convoy OB-213, had departed from Liverpool, England, for Montreal and Quebec City, Canada, on 13 September carrying 199 passengers, 90 of whom were children. The children were being transported to Canada as part of a government programme. A few hours after the Royal Navy escort had withdrawn, the ship was torpedoed at 56.48N, 21.15W. The torpedo hit the ship on the port side and she sank after a short time. Only 57 passengers, including thirteen children, were rescued. Immediately after the sinking, the British government ceased the transportation of children to Canada and South Africa.

Week 10 Summary: The Poles become Operational

Statistical summary, Week 10:

- *Total Fighter Command Establishment: 1662 planes*
- *Strength: 1492 planes*
- *Balance: understrength 170 planes*
- *Losses: 59 Hurricanes (+ 20 damaged), 28 Spitfires (+15 damaged)*
- *Aircraft Production: 6 Beaufighters, 10 Defiants, 56 Hurricanes, 38 Spitfires*

It could be said that in the Battle of Britain the Poles played the part which Blucher had done for Wellington at Waterloo. Some might argue that this is an exaggeration but, the fact is, that when the Poles came into the Battle, Fighter Command's effectiveness was being worn down by the loss of really experienced pilots. What the Poles represented was an infusion of exactly what was lacking, namely really experienced pilots. Not only were they fully trained, they also had a tremendously personal urge to get to grips with the enemy. The British pilots had the incentive of preventing the enemy winning because this would have delivered their country into Hitler's hands. They could imagine what this might mean. But the Poles actually knew what this meant. They had experienced the Nazi takeover of their country. They wanted revenge.

What the Poles also had was an élan peculiar to them. They were proud to be Polish. In fact, they loved being Polish and they didn't mind showing it. Moreover, they fitted into the RAF perfectly. There were no problems converting them to Spitfires and Hurricanes. They took to these new planes like a ballerina to her shoes. It was as if these two aircraft had been waiting for them to fly them. There was only one problem. The language. The Poles liked expressing themselves. In battle there was no holding them. The radio transmitters, the RT became crowded with what an RAF pilot called 'Polish chatter'. Furthermore, they had to learn RAF procedure. But finally they got it. At the beginning of September pressure on Fighter Command was such that Dowding when pressed on the subject again quietly gave in: 'Yes make them operational'.

303 Squadron became operational at Northolt just to the west of London. It is where the Polish air force memorial stands, commemorating their participation in the Battle. 303 achieved an exceptional record in the Battle of Britain. It won the greatest success in the number of kills of any squadron in the whole Command. The number of kills was only exceeded by the number of hearts broken in the West End by those good looking guys.

But having praised the Poles, we must mention the Czechs. While the Poles fielded some 140 pilots in the RAF during the war, the Czechs put some 30 pilots at the RAF's disposal. They too had a record similar to that of the Poles. They also were extremely successful and for fundamentally the same reasons. They were very professional and very well trained and had the experience.
After them came the French and Belgians. Small in number but eager in spirit.

It was an honour to have them all and we shall not forget them.

Comments:

Mike: Yes, the Polish pilots were so pivotal to our efforts in the Battle, but oh how shamefully we treated them after the war!

Tony Rudd: Yes, we totally agree with you. I was a navigator flying on Mosquitoes on 305 (Polish) squadron based at Epinoy in Northern France when the news came through that the British Government had transfered recognition from the London Poles to the Polish Communist Poles. It was indeed a sad day, but even then, they carried on flying until the very end. It was a sad day indeed.

Day 71 – 18 September 1940

Weather: variable.

Fighter Command Serviceable Aircraft as at 09:00 hours:

- Blenheim – 51
- Spitfire – 212
- Hurricane – 362
- Defiant – 25
- Gladiator – 5
- **Total – 655**

This was to be a busy day. Several large attacks were mounted by the Luftwaffe. Only fighters were involved. Over Kent, they were intercepted with major battles following. In the afternoon further attacks were mounted and duly intercepted not only by 11 Group squadrons but also by the Duxford wing. The wing, led by Squadron Leader Bader achieved considerable success though not as great as that claimed. The score that day was fifteen enemy destroyed at a cost of twelve RAF fighters. The RAF had flown 1165 sorties that day.

That night London was again the main target of the Luftwaffe bombing effort. County Hall, Westminster was hit. Bomber Command launched several attacks on French ports aiming at the barges.

73 Squadron Unofficial Diary – 18 September

At 4pm the 'Scramble' and patrol Colchester, angels fifteen given. Led by PO Scott the Squadron began a game of hunt the slipper. 'Patrolling J for Johnny' reported Scotty, 'Orbit'replied Ops, then 'Patrol Chelmsford'; 'Patrolling Chelmsford' reported Scotty a few minutes later. 'Orbit' said Ops. So we orbited and peace reigned for a few minutes, then 'Vector 180° for two minutes, four bandits closing coast'. So off we went, and sure enough there was something about 10,000 feet above us. 'Can you see the bandits?', Sgt Garton replied, 'yes I can see them, but God knows how we're going to get up to the b******s'. This seemed to shake Ops for a bit, for we were told to patrol Colchester again. Arriving there we received the order to 'Pancake'. So off we started for home and tea, when suddenly 'Patrol K for King below cloud base'. This was done, and then we were ordered back to Colchester, angels ten. After an hour and forty minutes, the Ops graciously allowed us to return and refuel. Sgt Perkin went a drift, but landed at North Weald, and came on here later.

303 Squadron Operational Record Book – 18 September

Visit from General Sikorski.

Reported Casualties (RAF Campaign Diary):

* Enemy: 33 confirmed, 16 probable, 19 damaged
* Own: Twelve aircraft of which nine pilots are safe

Top Gun Gallery
Stanislaw Skalski

Of the many Poles who served with the RAF, Stanislaw Skalski was probably the most distinguished.He started his career in Poland, joining the Polish Air Force in 1936, where he trained as a pilot. He flew against the Germans during the invasion of his country and was credited with some seven victories. Escaping via Rumania at the end of the Polish campaign, he made his way to France. From there he came to England in time to fly in the Battle of Britain. He joined 302 squadron in August 1940, however, 302 was not then operational and he was quickly moved to 501 squadron. He scored a total of twenty-two victories during the war. On 5 September he was shot down and suffered severe burns, despite his injuries he was anxious to return to operations and rejoined his squadron after only six weeks.

After the Battle, he continued a very successful career as a fighter pilot, not only flying from Britain, but going on to operations in North Africa and Italy. Finally, he ended up in England commanding a wing with the rank of Wing Commander. During the war, he was awarded the DFC and Bar and DSO.

On returning to Poland, in 1947, he rejoined the Polish Air Force, but, in 1948, he was arrested by the Communist regime, accused of spying. First being condemned to death and, then, when this sentence was commuted, continued in prison. He was finally released in 1956, when he resumed his air force career, mainly on staff duties. He was a wonderfully brave and resolute man.

Day 72 – 19 September 1940

Weather: mild with showers.

Fighter Command Serviceable Aircraft as at 09:00 hours:

- Spitfire – 211
- Hurricane – 364
- Defiant – 21
- Gladiator – 7
- **Total – 654**

That morning London was clearing up after further considerable damage to the West End. The day was marked by sporadic raids either by single aircraft or small groups. These tried to reach the capital but were intercepted and turned back. During the afternoon Walthamstow and Hackney were machine gunned. In the evening, the Luftwaffe launched bombing raids against London. Losses this day were eight Luftwaffe aircraft with no losses reported by the RAF.

In Germany Hitler gave the order to disperse the barges which had been waiting in the French ports to take part in the invasion. Keeping them there was only providing RAF Bomber Command with attractive targets. This was a signal that Sealion had been cancelled, at least for the winter.

266 Squadron Operational Record Book – 19 September

Average temperature – visibility very good. Practices included battle climb to 30,000 feet, flight formation – formation attacks and cloud flying.

Reported Casualties (RAF Campaign Diary):

* Enemy: 6 confirmed, 1 probable, 0 damaged
* Own: Nil.

Aircraft of the Battle
Gloster Gladiator

This aircraft represented the tail end of the bi-plane fighter which had been standard in Fighter Command before the arrival of the single seater fighter. Several squadrons of Gladiators had been lost in the Norwegian campaign in April and they had also served in France with the BEF. Fortunately they never saw serious operational service in the Battle of Britain with only one RAF squadron equipped with them. Had they done so, they would have been very vulnerable in the company of Me109s.

Day 73 – 20 September 1940

Weather: mainly fair, intermittent showers.

Fighter Command Serviceable Aircraft as at 09:00 hours:

- Blenheim – 55
- Spitfire – 237
- Hurricane – 391
- Defiant – 21
- Gladiator – 7
- **Total – 711**

There were several major incursions by mixed groups of bombers surrounded by large concentrations of fighters which ranged over Kent with some aircraft penetrating to London. However, four squadrons of the RAF managed to intercept. In Brighton, eleven people were killed during a morning raid. In the air fighting that day, eight German aircraft were destroyed for a loss of seven RAF fighters.

That night the London Docks were once again targets and Lambeth Palace was damaged.

266 Squadron Operational Record Book – 20 September

Average temperature – visibility very good. Practices included battle climb, squadron formation flying – fighter command attacks and dog fighting.

Reported Casualties (RAF Campaign Diary):

* Enemy: 6 confirmed, 1 probable, 2 damaged
* Own: 7 aircraft with 4 pilots killed or missing.

The Squadrons

85 Squadron

Noctu diuque vanamur – We hunt by day and night

85 squadron was formed in August 1917 at Upavon. In May 1918 the squadron was sent to France where it undertook patrols over the Western Front. It was disbanded in July 1919.

The squadron was reformed on 1 June 1938 at Debden and was equipped with Gladiators. In September 1938 these were changed for Hurricanes. In September 1939 the squadron was sent to France with the BEF where it remained until its bases were overrun during the invasion in 1940. On returning to Britain the squadron took part in the first part of the Battle of Britain before being moved north in September 1940 when it changed to flying night patrols. Later in the war the squadron flew bomber support missions.

The squadron was disbanded on 31 October 1958.

Day 74 – 21 September 1940

Weather: fine.

Fighter Command Serviceable Aircraft as at 09:00 hours:

- Spitfire – 215
- Hurricane – 394
- Defiant – 27
- Gladiator – 8
- **Total – 700**

Relatively little enemy activity in the morning. Brooklands was attacked by a single Ju88 in a low level operation at fifty feet. Middle Wallop was also targeted but suffered no damage. There were also minor attacks on Biggin Hill and Kenley. Fighter Command flew 560 sorties, destroyed nine enemy aircraft at no loss to the RAF.

There was widespread bombing that night over London, Liverpool and Nottingham.

266 Squadron Operational Record Book – 21 September

Warm – visibility excellent. Practices included formation flying – Fighter Command attacks and affiliation exercise with Blenheim aircraft of no. 218 Squadron, escorted by six Hurricane aircraft from no. 7 Squadron. Pilot Sgt W.T. Ellis posted to no. 92 Squadron for flying duties.

Reported Casualties (RAF Campaign Diary):

* Enemy: 2 confirmed, 1 probable, 6 damaged
* Own: Nil.

The Airfields
RAF Hendon

RAF Hendon, just eight miles north west from central London, was established during World War One on the site of one of the world's first commercial airfields. Ballooning had been popular on a reservoir near here in the late 19th century, and at the beginning of the 20th early aircraft production was taking place at neighboring Colindale. The aviation pioneer Claude Grahame-White bought the airfield and established his aircraft factory here in 1911, and that year the world's first official airmail flight flew between Hendon and Windsor. In 1912 Grahame-White organised the world's first air show here.

In the first world war the airfield was taken over by the Admiralty and early machines of the Royal Naval Air Service fly air defence of London from Hendon. In 1916 the civilian training school was taken over by the Royal Flying Corps (to become the RAF in 1918) to train its pilots. After the First War, Military Air shows became a regular event in the 20s and 30s, becoming known as Empire Air Day. The auxiliary 604 squadron was formed and flew from Hendon in the 1930s.

The airfield was little used for operational flying in the Battle of Britain, but mainly for transport and communications activities. Today it is the home of the RAF Museum.

Day 75 – 22 September 1940

Weather: dull and cloudy.

Fighter Command Serviceable Aircraft as at 09:00 hours:

- Blenheim – 58
- Spitfire – 237
- Hurricane – 384
- Defiant – 20
- Gladiator – 8
- **Total – 707**

A relatively quiet Sunday. Fighter Command flew 158 sorties. Enemy losses amounted to five aircraft while the RAF again lost none. If the day had been quiet, the night was far from being so. Direct hits took place on air raid shelters in Poplar and Lambeth. In Ilford, a mine exploded destroying 100 houses.

73 Squadron Unofficial War Diary – 22 September

Another day of Pilot's weather. After 257 [Squadron] had joined us the mess was crowded and we 'local inhabitants' couldn't get near the stove for the 257 lads. Cards and darts were the order of the day, but these diversions palled after a while and a deep depression settled over us. We had some good news however. 'The Powers That Be' have decided that no Night Operations shall take place by single seat fighters. Deep sighs of relief from us. As someone remarked 'only bats and owls fly by night – and even they pack up when it gets really dark'.

Most of us adjourned to the 'Fox and Hounds' in Steeple Bumpstead and imbibed quantities of ale.

Reported Casualties (RAF Campaign Diary):

* Enemy: 1 confirmed, 0 probable, 1 damaged
* Own: Nil.

Captains and Commanders
Herman Goering

Goering took personal charge of the Luftwaffe in the Battle of Britain. He issued the orders. It was his instructions which the officers commanding the air fleets took. Goering ran the Battle through a series of personal conferences carried out by his air fleet commanders. These conferences took place at various locations. The first devoted to discussing tactics, was held in The Hague. Subsequently, the meetings usually took place at Karinhall, his huge hunting lodge south of Berlin. But, because Goering enjoyed maintaining personal contact with the pilots who were doing the fighting, he used a magnificently appointed special train which moved about the French railway network in northern France during the Battle. Goering was in a sense 'one of the boys', amongst the pilots, at least he liked to think that he was.

As the Battle progressed it was Goering who laid down the tactics which were to be followed. He became irritated and frustrated at the failure of 'his' Luftwaffe to deliver the goods. The problem was that for all his enthusiasm he didn't really understand the tactics of modern air warfare. He couldn't grasp how Fighter Command operated. He underestimated the significance of radar. The result was a growing lack of trust between the Higher Command and the pilots who were doing the fighting. Matters came to a head when Goering himself accused his aircrews, not just of a lack of dash, but of cowardice. This reached a dangerous point during a personal confrontation when, in answer to Goering's question of what did the pilots want in order to improve their performance, Adolf Galland answered, a squadron of Spitfires.

Day 76 – 23 September 1940

Weather: fine.

Fighter Command Serviceable Aircraft as at 09:00 hours:

- Blenheim – 60
- Spitfire – 237
- Hurricane – 401
- Defiant – 18
- Gladiator – 7
- **Total – 723**

This day the Luftwaffe launched a series of wide fighter sweeps over south east England. Hornchurch and Northolt were attacked but suffered no damage. Fighter Command launched twenty-four squadrons to intercept them. In the day's fighting, which was intense, eleven RAF planes were lost while the Germans suffered sixteen aircraft destroyed.

That night Bomber Command mounted a raid of over 100 aircraft on Berlin in retaliation for the bombing of London. The Luftwaffe's night attack on London was the largest so far consisting of over 250 aircraft. The capital was turned into an inferno.

73 Squadron Unofficial War Diary – 23 September

In spite of the bright sunny morning our spirits sagged – and our stomachs revolted – when we had our breakfast placed before us. It purported to be mince, but it gave us all many unpleasant thoughts and even the most hardened stomachs decided to go breakfastless.

If our breakfast was bad, worse and infinitely more tragic hours awaited us. At 09:20 hours twelve of our machines, leading 257 took off, and were to be covered by 17 Squadron from Debden. 17 Squadron failed badly in their necessary task, and aided by what can only be described as class stupidity of the part of Ops. The Squadrons were broken up by Me109s. While patrolling at 20,000 feet the Squadron was ordered to 10,000 feet. Smithy, who was leading, promptly and wisely questioned this, but the order was confirmed, so being left no option he began to go down. Disaster then came among us. At 12,000 feet when 17 Squadron had left the tail completely uncovered, Me109s and He113s hurtled down from the sun and the formations went over like nine pins.

The first news the ground staff had of the debacle — for debacle it was — was the arrival of Sgt Webster, seething with rage, and with his machine well bullet marked. One bullet had struck and ammo tank in the port gun bay and exploded a belt of rounds, and weakened the wing struts. From him we were prepared for the further bad news that followed. Of the twelve machines which had taken off only eight returned. PO Hobart's section, of which Sgt Webster was no.3, had suffered worst. PO Hobart and PO Kinder were both reported missing, Sgt Leng was known to have baled out near Detling, and Sgt Perkin also baled out near Harty Ferry. He landed on a sandbank in the Estuary and was rescued by two men in a boat.

303 Squadron Operational Record Book – 23 September

09:30 hours

Combat Thames Estuary to Calais. Vectored south of Biggin Hill and then towards estuary. Saw about twenty streamers approaching from South. Squadron at 22,000 ft then saw about twenty Me109s at 30,000 to 25,000 ft circling the estuary. Wing circled slowly and enemy aircraft made no attempt to attack. Then about twelve Me109s came behind from some other formation, apparently trying to break up the wing. Red Section attacked and e/a fled southwards. Flt Lt Kent caught up one Me109 diving for France and shot it down in the sea fifteen miles from French coast. The pilot baled out at 4,000 ft. On returning Flt Lt Kent saw probably a Potex flying low towards England. Enemy aircraft turned and Flt Lt Kent saw De Wilde hitting e/a, but his own began labouring, and he returned to base. Sgt Szaposznikow also over took one Me109 and shot it down in flames near French coast. Enemy fighters made no attempt to fight Hurricanes and showed no aptitude for evasion. Potex, painted mottled dark grey with black crosses. No return fire noticed. Evasive tactics slow turns over sea.

Reported Casualties (RAF Campaign Diary):

* Enemy: 11 confirmed, 7 probable, 6 damaged
* Own: 11 aircraft with 3 pilots missing.

The People in Support
The GPO

In those days, the telephone system in the country was provided by the GPO, the General Post Office. The Defence Control System of Fighter Command relied entirely on land lines for its communications. Thousands of miles of new landlines were laid, linking the radar installations on the coast to Fighter Command Headquarters at Bentley Priory, and from this control centre to Group Headquarters, to the Sector Stations and to the Squadrons on the airfields. As the Luftwaffe raids intensified on airfields, it was these vital communications which were, just as much, the target as the aircraft themselves.

Teams of GPO engineers were kept frantically busy by bombs destroying telephone lines and telephone exchanges. It was a matter of the highest priority to restore damaged facilities to working order. GPO engineers were immediately on the scene following a raid and were straight away at work, putting the system together again. Nobody who saw the work they did at the time ever complained about the GPO in later life.

Day 77 – 24 September 1940

Weather: hazy and cloudy.

Fighter Command Serviceable Aircraft as at 09:00 hours:

- Blenheim – 58
- Spitfire – 233
- Hurricane – 380
- Defiant – 19
- Gladiator – 8
- **Total – 698**

Potentially the most dangerous raid this day was on the Spitfire works near Southampton. Nearly 100 Supermarine workers were killed when their shelter was hit. Eleven German aircraft were shot down at the loss of four RAF aircraft.

That night The Times offices and Blackfriars Station were hit.

73 Squadron Operational Record Book – 24 September

In the evening a dance organised for the Squadron took place in the village hall of Steeple Bumpstead at 20:00 hours. All the officers and pilot sergeants attended as did most of the other non commissioned officers. About 120 men also attended. For our enjoyment approximately 50 WAAFs from Debden were invited together with a number of local ladies and the WAAF officers from Debden. A bar was run and so popular was it that everything except beer had been sold long before 23:00 hours the time at which the dance finished. It was voted a great success but was spoilt a little by the crowded state of the room. It has been decided to hold any subsequent dance in a hut on the camp.

17 Squadron Operational Record Book – 24 September

The Squadron took off at 08:30 hours and joined 73 Squadron over base. Thirty bombers were sighted over the Thames Estuary approaching London with masses of fighters above them. 17 Squadron acting as rear guard were attacked by the fighters and in the dog fight which followed FO Bird-Wilson was shot down and baled out. FO Czernin, PO Stevens and Sgt Griffiths circled over him until they saw him picked up safely by a boat off Chatham. Later it was reported that FO Bird-Wilson had been taken to the Royal Naval Hospital, Chatham, suffering from burns about the legs and face, but he is not on the danger list. PO Wissler's a/c was hit by cannon shell and he was slightly wounded in the arm. His a/c crashed on landing at Debden. He is not seriously hurt. Ten aircraft landed safely at Debden at 09:30 hours, FO Czernin having probably destroyed one Me109 over the sea off Foreness and PO Pittman having damaged another.

PO DH Wissler Diary – 24 September

We were attacked by Me109s and having made one attack on a 109, I was making a second at four who were well above when I realised that I should stall so I levelled off. Suddenly there was a blinding flash on my port wing and I felt a hell of a blow on my left arm, and then blood running down. I went into a hell of a dive and came back to Debden. A cannon shell had hit my wing and a bit of it hit me just above the elbow and behind. The shell had blown away most of the port flap so I tried to land without flaps. I could not stop and crashed into a pile of stones just off the field, hitting my face and cutting it in two places. I was taken to Saffron Walden General Hospital. They operated but had to leave small pieces as it had penetrated the muscle.

(Reproduced by kind permission of the Imperial War Museum and Copyright holder)

Reported Casualties (RAF Campaign Diary):

* Enemy: 7 confirmed, 8 probable, 13 damaged
* Own: Five aircraft with two pilots killed or missing.

Week 11 Summary: The Empire Group

Statistical summary, Week 11:

* **Total Fighter Command Establishment:** *1662 planes*
* **Strength:** *1509 planes*
* **Balance:** *understrength 153 planes*
* **Losses:** *12 Hurricanes, 7 Spitfires (+9 damaged), 7 unidentified to date*
* **Aircraft Production:** *4 Beaufighters, 6 Defiants, 57 Hurricanes, 40 Spitfires*

Having sung the praises of our continental allies of 1940, let us turn now to the many who came from the Dominions, in what was, in those days long past called the Empire. What the RAF had done before the war was send out a recruiting team to offer the young men of the day the chance to fly for the RAF, on short service commissions. It was a brilliant idea. The RAF managed to recruit over 200 volunteers this way, who became pilots. The RAF certainly got some star performers by casting its net so far and wide.

For instance, from New Zealand, its recruits included Alan Deere who managed more than half a dozen extraordinary hairy incidents and in the process became an outstanding ace. Then there was 'Sailor' Malan from South Africa who got an amazing reputation as the best shot in Fighter Command. Both of these men were real leaders. 'Sailor' Malan became an early CO of 54 Squadron.

It wasn't just the capacity of these recruits from New Zealand, South Africa, Australia and Canada to fly and fight, they had real powers of leadership. They instilled confidence in other members of their squadrons. They didn't want to add only to their number of kills, they minded about their compatriots and the reputation of their squadrons.

What complemented the eagerness of these young men from the Dominions, was what the RAF offered. It gave them the opportunity of flying. The Hurricane and the Spitfire were both British models of the front line fighter of the day. It was the single seater monoplane fighter, capable of 300 miles per hour plus, which became every schoolboy's dream to fly. Coming of age, no wonder they wanted to grasp that opportunity. Furthermore, war was coming. They had all known that. They had heard from their parents what it had been like last time. Not for them a heroic death on the Somme. Not for them, all that stuff about King and Country. They were opting for a cleaner way to fight. One in which they could pit skill against skill. If you had to go, it was better to go this way than suffer all that mud and blood in the trenches. This is what attracted them.

Comments:

Charles Davenport: Again, I learn something I never knew. I did not know RAF recruited some of its pilots. Was that also the case with the few Americans who came over?

Tony Rudd: No, I very much doubt it. They were from a neutral country and although they volunteered their services, I don't think we would have been allowed actively to recruit them. It was a different matter in, for instance, New Zealand because they were a Commonwealth country at war with Germany being both an ally of ours as a member of the Commonwealth.

Day 78 – 25 September 1940

Weather: fine, some haze in the south.

Fighter Command Serviceable Aircraft as at 09:00 hours:

- Blenheim – 48
- Spitfire – 218
- Hurricane – 376
- Defiant – 19
- Gladiator – 8
- **Total – 669**

The attacks this day launched by Luftflotte 3 consisted of a major incursion aimed at Bristol. Serious damage was done to the Bristol Aeroplane Company works at Filton, just outside Bristol where over 250 people were killed or injured. In all that day Fighter Command had flown 668 sorties, had shot down thirteen enemy aircraft and lost four RAF fighters.

The railways in London were the main targets that night.

266 Squadron Operational Record Book – 25 September

Average temperature – visibility very good. Practices included formation flying – flight cloud penetration – dog fighting – interception exercise. Pilot Sgt D.E. Kingaby posted to no. 92 Squadron for flying duties.

Reported Casualties (RAF Campaign Diary):

* Enemy: 26 confirmed, 8 probable, 12 damaged
* Own: Four aircraft with two pilots killed or missing.

Top Gun Gallery
Josef Frantisek

Joseph Frantisek was a young Czech pilot who joined 303 Polish Squadron. The Poles were happy to have him. He was an amazingly successful pilot, but with a certain defect, namely a lack of discipline in flying with his colleagues. He invariably broke off to go on his own, earning him the nickname 'the lone wolf'. After some outstanding difficulties in this regard, the squadron accepted his indiscipline and just allowed him to operate independently.

He was an experienced pilot having joined the Czechoslovak Air Force in 1934. When the Germans invaded Czechoslovakia in March 1939, Frantisek fled to Poland and joined the Polish Air Force, where he fought against the Luftwaffe during the Blitzkrieg on Poland. He escaped Poland via Romania and finally reached Britain on 21 June 1940.

Frantisek duly racked up a remarkable score in individual combats with the enemy. He succeeded in achieving sixteen kills. However, once again, on an individual foray on 8 October 1940, he crashed near Ewell in Surrey. His body was buried at the Polish Air Force cemetary in Northolt. His career may have been sadly short, but it was a remarkable one.

Day 79 – 26 September 1940

Weather: cloudy, with some bright intervals.

Fighter Command Serviceable Aircraft as at 09:00 hours:

*   Blenheim – 56
*   Spitfire – 203
*   Hurricane – 392
*   Defiant – 15
*   Gladiator – 7
*   **Total – 673**

Once again the Luftwaffe launched an attack on the Spitfire works at Woolston near Southampton. It was carried out by over 70 aircraft from Luftflotte 3. In a five minute attack the installation was hit by over 70 tons of bombs. One bomb hit a shelter killing thirty of the workers. Production was halted. However only one or two aircraft were wrecked. A number were damaged but were repaired within a couple of days to be delivered to squadrons. The German aircraft which had attacked were intercepted by 10 Group Squadrons. Both the RAF and the Luftwaffe lost nine aircraft each.

That night, in London a bomb exploded on the corner of Denbigh Street and Belgrave Road trapping people in an underground shelter. Liverpool docks were also hit and the Standard Motor company in Coventry suffered £100,000 worth of damage.

266 Squadron Operational Record Book – 26 September

Cold – visibility moderate. Practices included formation flying – cloud penetration and dog fighting. Fourteen pilots proceeded to Sutton Bridge and carried out Air to Air firing programme. One Spitfire II aircraft piloted by PO R.J.B. Roach sent to Hendon for demonstration of factory observers. Wg Cdr J. Barwell from Headquarters, no. 12 Group, visited

Squadron respecting training of new pilots. Pilot Sgts K.C. Pattison, W. Sadler and J.A. Scott posted to no. 611 Squadron for flying duties.

Reported Casualties (RAF Campaign Diary):

* Enemy: 33 confirmed, 11 probable, 13 damaged
* Own: 10 aircraft with 3 pilots killed or missing.

Comments:

Mark: You wrote …'Wg Cdr J. Barwell from Headquarters, no. 12 Group, visited Squadron respecting training of new pilots'. This was Wg Cdr Philip Reginald Barwell, the older brother of PO Eric Gorden Barwell. He was educated at Perse School, Cambridge; their archives show him as one of many pupils who joined the RAF but the only one who flew in the Battle of Britain with 242 Squadron. My interest is that he was in command of 46 Squadron at RAF Digby when my brother, Sgt Stanley Andrew, was posted there in September 1939 and he is shown in the photographs taken when the King visited the Squadron.

He led a flight of 6 Hurricanes on October 21 1939 to intercept German planes approaching a Convoy and he shot down a He 115 and shared another. He was awarded a DFC on November 28 for his involvement in one of the first engagements of the war. He was posted away to Command Sutton Bridge that month. Barwell was lost on July 1 1942 after being attacked by a inexperienced Spitfire over the Channel, he is buried in the Calais Canadian War Cemetery.

We hope Perse School will accept a Battle of Britain Historical Society Memorial Plaque and that the 46 Squadron Association will send a representative.

Aircraft of the Battle

The Westland Lysander

In July 1940, the AOC of 11 Group, Air Vice Marshal Park secured twelve Lysanders which were pressed into service as part of a make shift air sea rescue service. They were a high wing light plane with a single engine and a fixed under carriage. They had been designed for army cooperation and had operated in France where they suffered heavy losses. They were not particularly effective in the air sea rescue business. They only came into their own when used for ferrying Special Operations Executive agents, often at night, into occupied France. This made better use of their capacity to land in very restricted space.

Day 80 – 27 September 1940

Weather: fair with some rain.

Fighter Command Serviceable Aircraft as at 09:00 hours:

- Blenheim – 53
- Spitfire – 214
- Hurricane – 391
- Defiant – 19
- Gladiator – 7
- **Total – 684**

The first main attack this day was by Me110s, acting as bombers accompanied by a large number of Me109s. The plan was for the Me109s, having escorted their charges, to remain over the capital and provide cover for a second wave of bombers Do17s and Ju88s. The plan misfired. The bombers came on alone. The Me109s with their fuel running low made for home. The bombers were intercepted by the RAF fighters. The same combination of plane attacked aircraft works at Filton and Yeovil.

Later that day, 80 German aircraft flew towards Bristol but were intercepted and forced to drop their bombs on the suburbs. Around midday nearly 300 aircraft made for London but most got no further than mid Kent having been intercepted by a number of 11 Group squadrons.

Eventually, some twenty aircraft made it to the centre of London. The day had been full of action. The RAF had shot down fifty-four German aircraft and had lost twenty-eight themselves.

303 Squadron Operational Record Book – 27 September

09:00 hours

Eleven Hurricanes left Northolt at 09:00hours. Squadron working with No. 1 Canadian Squadron were sent out and encountered the enemy in the Horsham area at 15,000 feet. The enemy consisted of thirty He111 protected by 50 to 60 Me109s. Bombers in vics of three line astern stepped up behind. It was noticed that the majority of the He111s had a vertical white stripe on the tail fin and from a distance they gave the impression of friendly aircraft. The squadron attacked the bombers from astern and were themselves engaged by enemy fighters which fled in disorder. In the meantime the bombers had wheeled and were heading south and the squadron went in to attack from astern. Vics of bombers maintained formation throughout, closing up when one or more were shot down. Other Hurricanes came in to attack the bombers and immediately afterwards the squadron noticed about 40 Do17s approaching head on in single line astern formation supported by Me109s above. Upon going in to attack the bombers formed a defensive circle and the enemy fighters formed a similar circle above. Only one pilot attacked Hes and Dos and succeeded in shooting one down on land. Two other squadrons of Hurricanes came in and attacked the Dos and as far as is known broke them up and inflicted heavy casualties. Our fighters did not follow down the individual e/a claimed as destroyed but it is believed that almost all were shot down on land.

Enemy casualties: 4 Me109, 4 He111, 1 Do17, 1 Me 110 – destroyed

1 Me109 – probable, 1 He111 damaged.

Our casualties: FO Paszkiewicz crashed at Borough Green, pilot killed in the air. Sgt. Andruszkow crashed at Cowden, pilot killed in air. FO Zak baled out near Leatherhead and taken to Leatherhead Hospital suffering from burns to face and hands. One Hurricane cat. 3.

As on 26 September, just before going in to attack the Squadron received orders on the R/T 'apany leader pancake'. This was not given by controllers at this station but was given in good English and in an authoritative manner.

249 Squadron Operational Record Book – 27 September

Three very successful sorties carried out with 46 Squadron. Our casualties were POs Burton and Meaker killed. Although two of our most gallant comrades were lost, to-day was a glorious day in the history of the Squadron. From reports later received it appears that PO Meaker attacked a close formation of five Ju88s on his own and his aircraft was completely shot up by the heavy cross fire from the cannons now fitted in the rear of these aircraft. From reports from the Hailsham district Observer Corps, it appears that PO Burton has been attacking an Me110 for some time and was seen to climb above it and dive down on to it, he rammed it and cut it's tail off and both aircraft crashed. PO A G Lewis, DFC on this day destroyed 6 aircraft himself and was subsequently ordered a bar to his DFC.

Enemy casualties: 21 destroyed, 6 probable, 3 damaged.

266 Squadron Operational Record Book – 27 September

Squadron ordered to patrol in Duxford Wing and investigate activity North Weald-Biggin Hill area as near cloud base as possible (17,000 feet). No enemy aircraft or AA fire seen. Another wing of Hurricane and Spitfire aircraft seen over Sheppey area. Wing was then ordered to return and land at Duxford.

Cyril Shoesmith, 14 years old, Bexhill-on-Sea, Diary – Friday 27 September

The next raid came at 3pm. We heard heavy machine-gun fire and four bombers came over the trees. As they came closer we could see six fighters on their tail. One of the German bombers had been set alight by our fighters for there was black smoke pouring out of its tail. We watched them until they were out of sight heading towards Galley Hill. Three of the Germans were shot down in the sea. Many fighters circled round and a formation of twenty-four went over. There was more machine gun fire and the 'raiders passed' came at 4:10. At 11:30 there was a raid which ended at 6:15am.

(Reproduced by kind permission of the Imperial War Museum and Copyright holder)

Reported Casualties (RAF Campaign Diary):

* Enemy: 133 confirmed, 55 probable, 52 damaged
* Own: 27 aircraft with 18 pilots killed or missing.

The Squadrons
601 Squadron

601 squadron was formed in October 1925 at Northolt as part of the Auxiliary Air Force. Initially it was a light bomber force, but in January 1939 it received Blenheims which were replaced with Hurricanes in March 1940. The squadron spent a week in France before returning to Britain to take part in the emerging Battle of Britain.

Following service in the Middle East and North Africa, the squadron was disbanded on 14 August 1945. In June 1946 it was reformed as part of the Auxiliary Air Force. The Auxiliary Air Force was eventually disbanded in 1957 and the squadron was also disbanded.

Day 81 – 28 September 1940

Weather: fine, some patchy cloud.

Fighter Command Serviceable Aircraft as at 09:00 hours:

- Spitfire – 214
- Hurricane – 390
- Defiant – 12
- Gladiator – 8
- **Total – 681**

Churchill, deeply impressed by results of the previous day caused a congratulatory message to be sent to Fighter Command. A force of some thirty Ju88s accompanied by no less than 200 Me109s crossed over the Channel and targetted London and Portsmouth.

Pilots were becoming exhausted. It was the same for the Luftwaffe, which lost no less than seven aircraft in accidents. The Luftwaffe was having its problems too. The Command had in fact decided that day their use of twin engined bombers in the battle was becoming too expensive. As an interim measure, the ratio of fighters to bombers was once again to be increased in favour of fighters.

The RAF lost sixteen aircraft against four German planes destroyed.

That night 200 bombs were dropped at the Vickers Armstrong factory and several London hospitals were also hit.

Reported Casualties (RAF Campaign Diary):

* Enemy: 6 confirmed, 4 probable, 1 damaged
* Own: 16 aircraft with 9 pilots killed or missing.

The Airfields
RAF Northolt

RAF Northolt opened in May 1915 as a base for the new Royal Flying Corps, with its aircraft flying defensive patrols against the German Zeppelins. In the 1930s, RAF Northolt was the first station to operate the Hurricane.

During the Battle of Britain it was the site of a Sector Operations Room and Staff, and the following Squadrons were based here during the Battle:
* No 609 Squadron from 19 May 1940
* No 257 Squadron from 4 July 1940
* No 303 Squadron from 22 July 1940
* No 43 Squadron from 23 July 1940 to 1 August 1940
* No 1 Squadron RCAF from 1 August 1940
* No 401 Squadron RCAF from Mid-August 1940
* No 615 Squadron from 10 October 1940
* No 302 Squadron from 11 October 1940

264 Squadron was also stationed here for a while, flying the doomed Boulton Paul Defiants. 303 (Polish) Squadron clocked up the highest allied scores during the Battle, with Czech Sergeant Josef Frantisek, becoming the highest scorer of the Battle. He is buried at Northolt. He shot down seventeen enemy fighters in a thirty day period before crashing through tiredness and dying at the age of twenty-four.

Day 82 – 29 September 1940

Weather: fine but turning cloudy.

Fighter Command Serviceable Aircraft as at 09:00 hours:

- Spitfire – 227
- Hurricane – 387
- Defiant – 16
- Gladiator – 8
- **Total – 697**

Several groups of high flying aircraft penetrated Southern England. As a result of RAF interceptions the Germans lost ten aircraft as against five British fighters destroyed.

Reported Casualties (RAF Campaign Diary):

* Enemy: 6 confirmed, 3 probable, 2 damaged
* Own: 5 aircraft with 3 pilots killed or missing.

Captains and Commanders
Sir Archibald Sinclair

The man Dowding was immediately responsible to was the Secretary of State for Air, Sir Archibald Sinclair. He, in turn, reported to the War Cabinet which ultimately meant to Churchill. Sinclair presented a somewhat old fashioned personality, even in those days. He always wore a stiff high starched wing collar which gave him a somewhat antique appearance. He had been brought in by Churchill in early May, although Chamberlain had invited him to take office in September 1939 but Sinclair had declined. He was and had been in his career a Liberal politician, but, before that, he had served in the Army. During the First World War he formed a close friendship with Churchill. And in 1916, when Churchill had temporarily fallen out of the War Cabinet and put on a khaki uniform to take command of a battalion in the trenches, Sinclair had, for a few months, become his number two.

He had a strained relationship with Dowding who blamed him for allowing fighter squadrons to be sent to France in the spring of 1940. The relationship declined further still following the Battle of Britain when Dowding was retired in November 1940.

Sinclair remained in office until 1945.

Day 83 – 30 September 1940

Weather:fine with some cloud.

Fighter Command Serviceable Aircraft as at 09:00 hours:

- Spitfire – 218
- Hurricane – 403
- Defiant – 13
- Gladiator – 8
- **Total – 687**

Two attacks by between 200 and 300 aircraft were set in train by Luftflotte 2. However, both raids were intercepted by large numbers of RAF fighters and both were turned back before they could reach London. At midday, heavy fighting took place over Kent. That afternoon, following some sporadic individual raids, a major onslaught occurred across Kent aiming for London. Some thirty aircraft penetrated to the capital. At the same time, a force of some 180 aircraft approached the capital from near Slough. Finally, a force of some 50 aircraft from Luftflotte 3 headed towards Yeovil. The target being the Westland works nearby. However, when the Luftwaffe aircraft got there, the target was obscured by cloud so they had to bomb blind. Most of the bombs fell on the surrounding area.

So ended the last big daylight raid of the battle. So also ended the use by the Luftwaffe of massed formations of twin engined bombers attacking Britain by daylight. Like the Ju87 Stukas, these aircraft too were to be withdrawn from their daylight role. Henceforward, they would operate at night in what the British were to dub the 'Blitz'.

The Luftwaffe lost forty-seven aircraft and the RAF lost twenty.

303 Squadron Operational Record Book – 30 September

16:40 hours

Combat at Brooklands at 16:50 hours. Ten Hurricanes left Northolt at 16:40 hours...Squadron was ordered to patrol base and then to join number 1 Canadian Squadron at 229 Squadron who had taken off fifteen minutes earlier. Climbed at full boost and Flights became separated but neither could join the wing. A Flight was broken up by Me109s of which FO Urbanowicz destroyed one. In this area were 150 to 200 Me109s and 110s and odds were too great. Cloud cover alone saved heavy casualties. B Flight made towards bombers going SE near Croydon. Sgt Belc broke away to protect Hurricane, pilot baled out and being attacked by Mes and after seeing him safe never rejoined Flight. Remaining four were dived upon by Me109s when four to five miles from bombers. Sgt Frantisek broke off upwards in order to cover flight from enemy attack. He caught one Me on the turn and destroyed it and in subsequent fight with six probably destroyed another. He escaped with great difficulty in cloud. Rest of Flight tried to continue toward bombers but were broken up by Me109s.

Enemy casualties: 2 Me109s destroyed, 1 Me109 probable

Our casualties: nil

Reported Casualties (RAF Campaign Diary):

* Enemy: 46 confirmed, 32 probable, 29 damaged
* Own:20 aircraft with 8 pilots killed or missing.

The People in Support
The ARP

When the Luftwaffe switched its attack from Fighter Command airfields to London itself on September 7, the preparations which had been made, in 1937, to handle this kind of eventuality, swung into operation. A body had been formed, under the name of Air Raid Precaution, commonly known as the ARP, which was to be responsible for handling the problems and the damage created by air raids.

The system involved the creation of a network of ARP wardens who were situated in ARP posts dotted around urban areas. They were equipped with first aid items and were linked by telephone to the Police and the Fire Brigade.

Once the air raid siren, warning of an incoming raid was sounded, they took charge. They saw to it that people were guided to the appropriate shelter. Then, as a raid progressed and as the bombs fell, they located buildings which were damaged and had suffered casualties. They directed ambulances and the Fire Brigade to where they were needed. It was they who tried to exert a measure of control over chaotic events. They did a wonderful job.

Ground crew and armourers refill ammunitions belts

Receiver hut at Ventnor Chain Home

Underground operations room

Observer Corps

Sector G operations room at Duxford, Cambs

An armourer re-arms a Spitfire at RAF Fowlmere

Auxiliary air force pilots

Observer Corps post

WAAF plotters in the operations room

*An example of a Chain
Home Low station*

WAAF radar operator plotting aircraft movements

The End of the Battle
October 1 – October 31 1940

The End of the Battle
October 1 – October 31 1940

Day 84 -1 October

Weather: fair with some cloud.

Fighter Command Serviceable Aircraft as at 09:00 hours:

- Blenheim – 37
- Spitfire – 225
- Hurricane – 368
- Defiant – 17
- Gladiator – 8
- **Total – 655**

Mid-morning, a concentration of about 100 aircraft from Normandy attempted to bomb Southampton and Portsmouth. The force was made up entirely of Me109s and Me110s. A third of the Me109s had been converted to carry a single bomb. The Me110s were all carrying bombs. Fighter protection was provided by the two thirds of the Me109s which were unconverted. The enemy flew at a very considerable height, nearly 30000 feet. This was the new pattern of attack. It caused the RAF considerable difficulty. The formation was nevertheless intercepted. One Me109 was shot down at the cost of two Spitfires shot down. That morning there had also been an attack on Aberdeen and other targets in Scotland.

Mid afternoon, three slightly smaller groups of Me109s and Me110s came across the Channel from behind Calais. These were met by four RAF squadrons which were involved in some serious combat. A dive bomb attack on Uxbridge that afternoon killed thirteen people and damaged 400 houses.

Later in the day, at 16:10, a force of some 125 enemy aircraft flew across the Channel from Calais and reached Maidstone and Biggin Hill. There, part of the force flew off to the south west while the remainder pressed on to London. Meanwhile, a third section of some 75 aircraft headed for London and Kenley, but was intercepted before flying across the coast.

An attempt that day had been made by the RAF to deploy a new weapon, a Heath Robinson device consisting of a cable on a parachute with a bomb on the other end, some 200 ft below. The idea was the enemy would run into the cable and explode the bomb and themselves. The weapon was not successful.

As the evening wore on, the night attack on London and other provincial cities developed. The RAF that day had flown 723 sorties. It lost four aircraft against the enemy loss of six aircraft.

266 Squadron Operational Record Book - 1 October

Average temperature – visibility moderate. Practices included Squadron formation flying, Fighter Command attacks. Six aircraft available – Sgt Breeze, R.A. and Sgt Dunmore, J.T., posted to 222 Squadron for flying duties.

Reported Casualties (RAF Campaign Diary):

* Enemy: 4 confirmed, 1 probable, 5 damaged
* Own: 5 aircraft with 4 pilots killed or missing.

Weekly Comment: The Pilot Shortage

Statistical summary: Week 12:

- *Total Fighter Command Establishment: 1662 planes*
- *Strength: 1581 planes*
- *Balance: understrength 81 planes*
- *Losses: 46 Hurricanes (23 damaged), 32 Spitfires (24 damaged)*
- *Weekly Aircraft Production: 0 Beaufighters, 10 Defiants, 58 Hurricanes, 34 Spitfires*

The most difficult part of the Battle for Dowding and Park was the problem posed by the growing shortage of pilots. Although, on the British side the RAF had the advantage of pilots who were shot down, often surviving to fight another day, there just weren't enough trained, let alone experienced, pilots available to fill the gaps in the squadrons.

So the inevitable result was that the trainee pilots had their training cut short. Courses were shortened and drastically. The time the young pilot got on single seater fighter flying was, in particular, cut short. Training went from months to weeks. A young pilot would get posted to a squadron when he only had five to ten hours flying experience on a Spitfire or Hurricane. A few, of course, were naturals who took to flying a fighter like duck to water. It was they who had a very strong survival instinct but most were still nervous if not downright frightened at this first experience of flying such a demanding airplane. The result was that when they got on the squadrons, what was asked of them far exceeded what they were capable of. They just weren't up to the challenge however hard they might have tried.

The difficulty was that there was little the squadron itself could do about it. The experienced pilots were too much in demand to fill their operational time in the squadron for them to have the time, let alone the patience, to nurse the newcomers into coping with the day-to-day exposure involved in fighting the Luftwaffe. They might try but seldom did they succeed in prolonging the life of the novice.

Perhaps more should have been done to expose the trainees at the operational training units, the OTUs of Fighter Command, to pass on the experience of pilots from the squadrons to give a taste of what it was like to do the real fighting. Perhaps some system should have been organised whereby the experienced pilots on the squadrons should have been given a couple of days off in return for an hour or two with the trainee pilots for the purpose.

Keith Park, when he left 11 Group after the Battle was over and was posted to Commander of a group in Training Command, found in many respects the OTUs were out of touch with reality. It shocked him. He did his best to cope with the problem which, indeed, persisted well into the war.

Day 85 – 2 October

Weather: fine.

Fighter Command Serviceable Aircraft as at 09:00 hours:

- Blenheim – 41
- Spitfire – 224
- Hurricane – 383
- Defiant – 19
- Gladiator – 7
- **Total – 674**

In the morning the Luftwaffe laid on a large heavy raid which attacked Biggin Hill, Kenley and other airfields south of London. Smaller groups of enemy aircraft attacked in the afternoon, again they headed towards Biggin Hill and Kenley. There were many engagements. A total of seventeen German aircraft were shot down with the loss of only one RAF fighter.

This daylight success was however followed by substantial night attacks involving over 100 enemy bombers. Individual aircraft from this mass attacked various targets in the suburbs of London and in central London, spreading destruction far and wide.

17 Squadron Operational Record Book - 2 October

The Squadron took off from Debden at 08:40 hours, joining 73 Squadron over base, and patrolled Hornchurch. While returning after 90 minutes patrol the Squadron was vectored to intercept a Do17. Four a/c returned to base short of fuel and the remainder chased and attacked the Do17. Yellow Section after making an attack landed at Martlesham to re-arm and re-fuel, later returning to Debden. Flt Lt Bayne attacked, but had to return to base owing to lack of fuel. FO Blatchford and PO Fajtl (Czech) continued the attack, and force-landed in fields near Pulham Aerodrome, returning by transport later. PO Ross force landed in a field after seeing the Do crash nearby. He inspected the crash and saw the crew taken prisoner, after which he managed to take off and return to Debden having been refuelled from Martlesham.

Reported Casualties (RAF Campaign Diary):

* Enemy: 10 confirmed, 1 probable, 2 damaged
* Own: One Spitfire of which the pilot is safe.

Top Gun Gallery
Brian Kingcome

Kingcome was a regular in the RAF, which he had joined in 1936. After training at Cranwell and getting his wings, he joined 65 Squadron flying Gladiators from Hornchurch. He converted to Spitfires and was appointed a Flight Commander in 92 Squadron in May 1940. He was active on operations before the official start date of the Battle and, in particular, shot down two He 111s and damaged a third on June 2.

He had a particular tactic in the Battle, in his words 'to leap into the middle of them and run amok, firing at everything in sight and hitting as many as you could as often as possible.' By the end of the war, he was officially credited with eleven kills, though his real score was said to have been nearer twenty. He was awarded a DFC in 1940, a Bar in 1941, and a DSO the following year, which reflected his very active career during the war. This included leading a wing of five squadrons in North Africa, Sicily and finally in Italy. At the end of the war he was a Group Captain, aged only twenty-five.

He retired from the RAF in 1954. He died at the age of 76.

Day 86 – 3 October

Weather: rain in the Channel; visibility poor over the mainland.

Fighter Command Serviceable Aircraft as at 09:00 hours:

- Blenheim – 31
- Spitfire – 226
- Hurricane – 403
- Defiant – 12
- Gladiator – 8
- **Total – 680**

The poor weather led to sporadic attacks by single aircraft or by small groups of enemy planes. Many coming over the coast of East Anglia from bases in Holland and Belgium. Some bombs were dropped in and around North Weald. Interception by RAF fighters was virtually impossible as a result of poor visibility. The RAF flew 173 sorties and lost no aircraft, but the Luftwaffe suffered nine aircraft destroyed.

Around 60 bombers attacked the south that night.

73 Squadron Operational Record Book - 3 October

Rained nearly all day and it early became apparent that flying would be almost impossible for this Squadron. At about mid-day the Squadron was released for the rest of the day. Despite the poor weather the pilots could hardly believe that the order had been given. Some went to London – some to Cambridge and some to Debden and Saffron Walden. There were very few inmates of the mess by 18:00 hours.

Reported Casualties (RAF Campaign Diary):

* Enemy: 1 confirmed, 0 probable, 0 damaged
* Own: Nil.

Comments:

Mark: 'Rained nearly all day'. Repeated 70 years later.

Aircraft of the Battle
Fw 200 Condor

Originally designed as an airliner in 1936 the Fw 200 was used in 1940 as a maritime patrol and reconnaissance aircraft. Equipped with anti-shipping mines it carried out a number of attacks on British shipping during the early part of the Battle of Britain. These attacks intensified as the Battle went on and the Fw 200 is credited with sinking 90,000 tons of British shipping between August and October 1940. It was also used for occasional night raids over Britain.

Day 87 – 4 October

Weather: rain; visibility poor.

Fighter Command Serviceable Aircraft as at 09:00 hours:

- Blenheim – 49
- Spitfire – 230
- Hurricane – 400
- Defiant – 20
- Gladiator – 8
- **Total – 707**

Interceptions continued to be difficult. However, in the afternoon some were achieved, particularly when single enemy aircraft were caught over Central London. Park recognised the difficulties being encountered by controllers. They were trying to get squadrons positioned in time to intercept individual raiders. This was difficult when trying to manoeuvre a wing of three squadrons into a promising position. He reiterated, however, the main priority which was to intercept the raiders before they could drop their bombs.

Three RAF fighters were lost but twelve enemy aircraft were shot down. At night heavy raids on London, Kent, Surrey and Suffolk. Liverpool and Newcastle were visited but not bombed.

85 Squadron Operational Record Book - 4 October – Church Fenton

Bad weather. No flying. Aircraft given a spring clean. Relaxation at night came in form of a dance at Sergeants' Mess.

Reported Casualties (RAF Campaign Diary):

* Enemy: 2 confirmed, 3 probable, 4 damaged
* Own: 3 aircraft with one pilot missing.

Comments:

Mark: The weather that day appeared to cause the forced landing of Sgt J H ' Ginger' Lacey of 501 Squadron in Hurricane V7498 at Ockley Manor Farm, Keymer.?He was born in Wetherby Yorkshire and is remembered on the Battle of Britain Historical Society School Memorial Plaque at King James School, Knaresborough and in Bridlington Priory.

The Squadrons
253 Squadron

Come one, come all

253 Squadron was formed in June 1918 at Bembridge on the Isle of Wight. Equipped with seaplanes if flew anti-submarine patrols during the last months of the First World War. It was disbanded at the end of May 1919.

The squadron reformed in October 1939 at Manston and was equipped with Hurricanes in February 1940. In May 1940 the squadron spent four days in France, with flights at Vitry and Lille. The squadron was involved in the Battle of Britain from the end of August when it moved from Prestwick to Kenley. During the rest of the war, the squadron saw service in North Africa and Italy. It was disbanded in May 1947.

253 squadron had a brief post-war existence when it was re-formed as a night fighter squadron in 1955. It was eventually disbanded in 1957.

Day 88 - 5 October

Weather: bright intervals.

Fighter Command Serviceable Aircraft as at 09:00 hours:

- Blenheim – 59
- Spitfire – 232
- Hurricane – 419
- Defiant – 16
- Gladiator – 8
- **Total – 734**

Three raids developed that morning all heading for Kent and to airfield targets south of London. West Malling was bombed. The first was by thirty aircraft whilst the next was larger and consisted of several groups making just under 100 in all. The final group consisted of a fighter sweep of twenty-five Me109s.

The switch by the Luftwaffe to fighter and fighter-bomber preponderance as against the old formula of twin-engine bombers escorted by fighters, meant that the days were now seeing much more in the way of dog fighting between fighters which were often persistent and bitter. It was, of course. a great spectacle for those, particularly in London and the south east, who were able to watch the aircraft high in the sky leaving their telltale contrails of white vapour visible against the bright blue sky. There were great patterns as the planes manoeuvred desperately weaving in and out as they fought to gain advantage.

The final air battles that day were between aircraft from Luftflotte 3 which had flown over Kent and a second group which had attacked Southampton. The score that day was eleven RAF aircraft lost and twelve Luftwaffe planes lost.

That night 200 bombers attacked London and some of the usual provincial targets. Portland Dockyard was bombed that night and the West India Docks were hit which caused a large fire.

303 Squadron Operational Record Book - 5 October

11:05 hours

Combat over Rochester, Channel 11:40 hours. Twelve Hurricanes left Northolt 11:10 hours to rendezvous with no. 1 Canadian Squadron leading. The wing flying southward met enemy fighters flying northward to east of them over Rochester. When the squadron was at 18,000 feet and alto cirrus layer of cloud at 5/10 to 3,000 feet and alto cirrus 10/10 at 25,000 to 30,000 feet. Me 109s descended from upper cloud in fives and threes. One group of Me 109s turned 180 degrees and attacked No. 1 Canadian Squadron and dived away southwards. About sixty e/a and forty friendly fighters were locked in running individual and section dog fights, rolling southwards, to the channel. Over Lympne were about fifteen Me110s at about 20,000 feet, which formed a defensive circle, and there were great numbers of Me109s above them in the high clouds. Our aircraft attacked the circle singly from head on and below, and broke it up, inflicting heavy casualties in spite of attacks by Me109s. Over the Channel, the Squadron was ordered home. Sqdn Ldr Kellett damaged one Me 109, seeing pieces fly off the engine and wing, and the enemy aircraft disappeared in a steep dive. PO Ferie destroyed one Me110 which crashed near the coast on land. FO Henneberg destroyed one Me110 but the position of the crash not visible. FO Pisarek destroyed one Me109 which exploded, Sgt Palak destroyed one Me109 near Lympne and damaged one Me110. Sgt Belc destroyed one Me110 near Lympne, one man baling out. Sgt Suidak destroyed two Me109s, one near Ashford and one in the sea off Littlestone. He attacked a Me110 to starboard, with a Spitfire attacking to port, and the e/a was destroyed. Sgt Suidak landed at an unidentified aerodrome near Rochester and was ordered to proceed to Gravesend when after refuelling and rearming he returned to Northolt.

Enemy casualties: 4 Me110, 4 Me109 – destroyed, 2 Me110, 1 Me109 – damaged

Our casualties: 1 Hurricane missing, FO Januszewick crashed in flames at Hawkinge and was killed.

Reported Casualties (RAF Campaign Diary):

* Enemy: 22 confirmed, 5 probable, 16 damaged
* Own: 9 aircraft with 2 pilots missing.

The Airfields
RAF Croydon

Croydon originally comprised two airfields, Beddington and Waddon. During the First World War the sites were used by the Royal Flyng Corps to defend London against Zeppelins, being just to the south of Central London, as well as for training new pilots. Immediately after World War One, Croydon Aerodrome was created out of the two original airfields and became London's first international airport, and the home base for the newly formed Imperial Airways, which began life here in 1924. The famous terminal building and Aerodrome hotel were built during this period in the Art Deco style, and formed the centrepiece of the newly named Croydon Airport which opened in 1928. Many famous aviators of the period flew in and out of Croydon, including Charles Lindbergh, Amy Johnson and Winston Churchill, who took flying lessons here with near disastrous consequences.

At the outbreak of war in 1939, Croydon once again became a military base, this time under Fighter Command. Squadrons based here at one time or another during the Battle of Britain included 111 Squadron, 501 Squadron, 401 Squadron RCAF, 85 Squadron, 72 Squadron, and 605 Squadron. The airfield was targeted by the Luftwaffe several times during the Battle.

In 1944, Croydon became the base of RAF Transport Command, and the airfield returned to civilian use in 1946. However, by then the new jetliners needed longer runways, and the new London airport was sited at Heathrow.

Day 89 – 6 October

Weather: persistent rain.

Fighter Command Serviceable Aircraft as at 09:00 hours:

- Blenheim – 48
- Spitfire – 229
- Hurricane – 411
- Defiant – 18
- Gladiator – 8
- **Total – 714**

This day began with a single bomb carrying aircraft attacking Biggin Hill which, though alone, did considerable damage. Later in the day a more substantial group of aircraft formed up behind Calais and came across the Channel to attack Middle Wallop, Northolt and Uxbridge. The RAF, despite difficult conditions, did well, losing one aircraft to an enemy toll of six.

That night German aircraft attacked the De Havilland works which were lucky to escape without much damage. The Hawker factory at Slough was also attacked, as well as the Royal Arsenal at Woolwich, but little damage was done. That night only seven bombers attacked central London, leaving the populace with a relatively quiet sleep.

303 Squadron Operational Record Book - 6 October

10:30 hours

Enemy attack on the aerodrome by one aircraft. Sgt Suidak was killed by a bomb which fell between the hangars. Aircraft totally destroyed. FS Kanis rejoined the Squadron from no. 6 OTU.

Reported Casualties (RAF Campaign Diary):

* Enemy: 1 confirmed, 0 probable, 1 damaged
* Own: One Spitfire with the pilot missing.

Captains and Commanders
Hans-Jürgen Stumpff

In charge of Luftflotte 5, situated mainly in Norway with its headquarters in Stavanger, was Generaloberst Hans-Jürgen Stumpff. Stumpff had started his military career in 1907 when he joined the army. He rose through the ranks, and by 1918 had been promoted to the rank of Captain. In 1933, following Hitler's rise to Chancellor, Stumpff was made head of personnel in the Luftwaffe. Between 1937 and 1939, Stumpff served as Chief of Staff of the Luftwaffe.

In the context of the Battle of Britain, his command was doomed not to play much of a role. Geography was against him. The North Sea, at the Latitude of Norway, was just too wide to enable aircraft from his Luftflotte to constitute a major threat to Britain. As it was, German intelligence had deduced that the continuous pressure from Luftflotte 2 under Kesselring would inevitably mean that Dowding would have to transfer all his fighter strength down to 11 Group to fight the battle there. This would mean that in the north, there would be no fighter cover. None that would be available to oppose an incursion from Lufftflotte 5 in Norway.

But when Stumpff's forces tried to attack Britain in the north, it was a sheer disaster. Dowding hadn't, after all, transferred his fighter strength down from 13 Group in the north down to the south. Stumpff's forces were met by a serious number of Spitfires and Hurricanes. They shot down many of Stumpff's bombers without any loss to themselves. That was the end of any action in the Battle from Stumpff's forces. Eventually, he was required to send his Me109s down to Luftflotte 2 to help participate in the battle there.

He continued to command Luftflotte 5 until the end of 1943. Stumpff was the official Luftwaffe representative at the signing of the surrender in May 1945. He died in 1968.

Day 90 – 7 October

Weather: cloudy with some showers.

Fighter Command Serviceable Aircraft as at 09:00 hours:

- Blenheim – 33
- Spitfire – 226
- Hurricane – 416
- Defiant – 9
- Gladiator – 8
- **Total – 692**

This was to be a busy day. It started with an attack of just over 120 aircraft searching for targets in Kent. They were met by some sixteen RAF squadrons. There was widespread combat.

A second attack developed that morning, again involving over 100 Me109s which broke up into single intruders or small groups. They too were intercepted by, not only 11 Group, but also 12 Group aircraft.
A third attack occurred in the afternoon consisting of some 50 Me109s which headed for London and Biggin Hill.

At 15:30, a further attack, this time by a mixed force of fighters Me110s and Ju88s, went for the Westland works at Yeovil. A shelter was hit in Yeovil town causing many casualties. Following this, a number of individual aircraft or small groups attacked various targets along the south coast.

That day Goering put the final touches to yet another plan to encompass the final defeat of the RAF in a conveniently short time, namely four days. This was, in essence, a plan to bomb London to bits. Fighter Command flew 829 sorties that day for the loss of seventeen aircraft against the Luftwaffe's loss of ten planes destroyed.

That night, Hendon airfield was bombed and some serious damage was done with a complete flight destroyed and offices and hangars hit. During the night raids hit Tottenham and destroyed the gas works there. Flying in the opposite direction that evening were some 150 twin-engined RAF bombers heading for Berlin.

501 Squadron Operational Record Book - 7 October

The Squadron was ordered away at 12:50 hours. They joined up with 605 Squadron. They intercepted two Me109s north west of Ashford, five Me109s came behind the Squadron. Dog fights ensued and two Me109s were destroyed and one probably destroyed. PO Mackenzie attacked the rear guard of another formation of Me109s. He damaged the glycol tank and forced it into the sea by ramming its tail with his wing tip. He was then attacked by two e/a. He evaded them (having used all his ammunition) and force landed his badly shot up aircraft one mile north of Folkestone. The Squadron did not take off again during this day.

Reported Casualties (RAF Campaign Diary):

* Enemy: 27 confirmed, 5 probable, 14 damaged
* Own:16 aircraft with 6 pilots missing.

The People in Support
Fire Services

Before the war there was no national fire service, instead there were locally organised fire brigades who were often poorly equipped. These brigades were put into the front line of the war once the bombing began. As well as high explosive bombs, the Luftwaffe attacked with incendiary bombs. They were relatively small and made of manganese. Thousands would be dropped in the average raid. What the enemy was aiming for was to set light to swathes of houses and buildings, turning them into a raging inferno.

London was a prize target for this kind of attack. From 7 September onwards, large areas of the docks and streets of small terrace houses became the target of these attacks. Big warehouses, often full of food, became targets of choice for the Luftwaffe.

Meanwhile, the peace time fire brigades had already been enlarged by the establishment of the Auxiliary Fire Service, the AFS, which played an important part in the recruitment of volunteers to become auxiliary firemen. It was the equivalent of doing national service in the armed services.

The firefighters created a wonderful record for themselves in the work that they did trying to contain the fires created by the German attacks. By the autumn of 1941 the system of local fire brigades had been reorganised to create a national fire service.

Day 91 – 8 October

Weather: cloudy in the south east, fair elsewhere.

Fighter Command Serviceable Aircraft as at 09:00 hours:

- Blenheim – 50
- Spitfire – 228
- Hurricane – 423
- Defiant – 14
- Gladiator – 8
- **Total – 723**

In the morning raids of 150 aircraft from Luftflotte 2 crossed the coast and headed towards London. Bombs were in fact scattered over a number of targets, including central London. Several raids developed in the afternoon involving substantial numbers of aircraft. The RAF flew 639 sorties. RAF losses were four aircraft against fourteen Luftwaffe planes shot down. However, the Czech pilot, Josef Frantisek crashed and was killed.

During the following night there were serious raids on London.

303 Squadron Operational Record Book - 8 October

09:00 hours

Twelve Hurricanes left Northolt 09:00 hours. Landed 09:55 hours. No contact made. Sgt Frantiszek crashed at Ewell, near Sutton and was killed.

Reported Casualties (RAF Campaign Diary):

* Enemy: 6 confirmed, 2 probable, 3 damaged
* Own: 4 aircraft with 4 pilots missing.

Weekly Comment: Trouble in the Command

Dowding was a hugely successful commander except in one respect. He allowed a disagreement between two key subordinates, Keith Park and Trafford Leigh Mallory, to erupt into a row which in the end cost him his command and Park his job in 11 Group.

Dowding was a quiet, reserved man, not an extrovert at all but he was so professional, so clearly devoted to the young pilots who flew in his command that he had their loyalty. The trouble in his command started when Keith Park got the job a year or two before the war began as head, that is Air Officer Commanding, of 11 Group. Park had a history as a fighter pilot. He had been decorated for his flying in the last part of the First World War. That was his trade, a tough New Zealander fighter pilot. Trafford Leigh Mallory was quite a different proposition. He had a brother who had died on Everest, reaching the top but dying on his way down. He was a very English man, part of the establishment and a very clubbable man. He had never been a fighter pilot, yet he was very much part of the RAF establishment. He was also ambitious. When Park was made AOC of 11 Group, Leigh Mallory felt put out. He would have liked the post himself. Yet he got 12 Group where he became AOC. He also didn't really like Dowding who wasn't his kind of man. Unfortunately, he let Park know. Park didn't like that. He was a very loyal man.

The trouble began as the Battle progressed. Park's growing problem was having to expose his airfields to attack by sending off their squadrons to intercept the enemy in the south of England. He asked 12 Group, which was situated north of 11 Group and slightly to the north of London, to cover some of his airfields to prevent them being attacked. But it didn't always happen. For instance, there was an incident when he had asked Leigh Mallory to cover Debden, whose squadrons had been sent south, to intercept the enemy. The help never arrived. Debden was left undefended against a very devastating raid by the Luftwaffe. Park was furious.

What next happened in this turn of events was the rise of Bader, the legless pilot who was CO of 242 Squadron. He conceived the idea of forming a wing of three squadrons, with him at the helm, leading them all. His idea was to hit the enemy in strength. In its way it was a great notion. RAF squadrons were always being outnumbered and this would cure that. The only trouble was that 11 Group seldom had the time to assemble squadrons into a wing. They had to intercept the enemy with little time to spare. That was if they wanted to hit the enemy before it had dropped its bombs. When Park did have time to assemble a wing, he did so.

The fact was that with 12 Group being situated north of London, it usually had much more time to form up a wing. What was possible for it just wasn't on for 11 Group. Bader was fortunate to have had Leigh Mallory as his AOC. Mallory backed Bader and his tactics. The two formed a close partnership, in which each understood the other. Bader never really appreciated the 'Dowding System' of defence which had grown out of the work of such men as Tizard and Watson Watt. Bader took the view that the only man who could take decisions in the air was the person up there flying and in charge. He didn't like the idea of having to obey a controller on the ground telling him what to do. His heroes were the pilots of the First World War like Ball and McCudden. Added to all this was the fact that Bader was a tremendous leader and an immensely strong character who was used to having his own way. He was the product of an appalling accident which had led him to lose his legs in 1933 but had also seen him recover.

The next step in the saga was the chance that the adjutant of his squadron, Flight Lieutenant Peter McDonald also happened to be a sitting MP at the time. He picked up the story of Bader's frustrations about not getting his own way at all times particularly on the subject of the big wing formation. On one of his visits to Parliament, he told the story to the Under Secretary State for Air, Balfour. Balfour passed it on to the Minister who in turn passed it on to Churchill. The fat was in the fire. Very soon the story was common knowledge in the higher reaches of the Air Ministry. The fuse was lit.

Comments:

Andrew: While 12 Group did have more time to form a big wing they still didn't turn up at the right place at the right time, the bombing of Debden being a typical example. So the big wing (for 12 Group) was definitley very badly used (further evidenced by Mallory and Bader's lack of thought to its implementation) and even if it had been properly planned it may have been the wrong tactic most of the time.?The big wing controversy is also portrayed as a row between Park and Mallory. I would call it poor behaviour by one commander rather than a row between two, Park was rightly furious at Mallory's lack of ability and deliberate undermining of Fighter Command stategy. He was also not impressed by a junior and inexperienced officer (Bader) being allowed to influence strategy in such a way, Park had hundreds of fighter pilots under his command better qualified to comment on strategy but it was not necessary to involve them in high level meetings.

Tony Rudd: I think you have hit the nail on the head. It was the culmination of the emerging disagreement at that Air Ministry meeting when Leigh Mallory took Bader and Sholto Douglas was clearly biased in their favour which was really disgraceful. Such an unhappy note in which to end this amazing and wonderful performance.

Day 92 – 9 October

Weather: cloudy with rain.

Fighter Command Serviceable Aircraft as at 09:00 hours:

- Blenheim – 38
- Spitfire – 229
- Hurricane – 394
- Defiant – 17
- Gladiator – 8
- **Total – 686**

In the morning a large force of Me109s attacked airfields south of London, particularly those which had suffered so much damage in the summer. This was a repetition of those earlier heavy raids. A second raid developed in the mid-afternoon, this time with even greater numbers. Nearly 200 enemy aircraft attacked East London and the East Ham Memorial Hospital was hit. The RAF flew over 400 sorties and lost one aircraft but destroyed nine of the enemy.

That night St. Paul's Cathedral was hit with the choir stalls and altar being damaged.

85 Squadron Operational Record Book - 9 October, Church Fenton

15 hours 25 minutes non-operational flying consisting of bad weather flying attacks, camera gun and low flying attacks for aerodrome defences. PO J.J. Robinson posted from 6 OTU and Fg Off I.D. Watson (RCAF) attached from 151 Squadron.

Reported Casualties (RAF Campaign Diary):

* Enemy: 4 confirmed, 4 probable, 5 damaged
* Own: One aircraft with pilot safe.

Top Gun Gallery
Geoffrey Wellum

Geoffrey Wellum was a young fighter pilot who joined his Squadron, no. 92, flying Spitfires in May 1940. The squadron was initially based at Northolt, but moved to Biggin Hill during the Battle. The remarkable thing about Wellum was his youth. His nickname was 'Boy' because of it. He had joined the RAF at the end of July1939, only weeks before the war began. He had timed his entry to coincide with the end of the cricket season in the last summer of peace.

He was credited with several kills and received the DFC in 1941. Interspersed with several rest periods, he spent three years flying Spitfires after the Battle. First, these involved flying in fighter sweeps over northern France, then a period at Malta flying there. He, subsequently, became a test pilot helping with the development of the Typhoon.

He wrote a memoir, *First Light*, of his experiences in the RAF, from which he retired in 1961. The book was published by Penguin and became a great success. It contains the most illuminating description of the RAF in 1939 and 1940, from training as a pilot to service on a squadron. It is a 'must' read.

Day 93 – 10 October

Weather: showery.

Fighter Command Serviceable Aircraft as at 09:00 hours:

- Blenheim – 53
- Spitfire – 226
- Hurricane – 387
- Defiant – 14
- Gladiator – 8
- **Total – 688**

The Luftwaffe was now adopting the tactic of sending in streams of single or very small groups of aircraft instead of the massive attacks which they had favoured up until now. This new system presented the RAF with some problems.

At lunchtime, over 100 enemy aircraft came over Lulworth Cove. In the late afternoon two waves of enemy aircraft came over Kent, this was followed in the early evening by an attack on the General Aircraft Company works. This day the RAF lost five aircraft to an enemy loss of only four aircraft.

At night London, Liverpool and Manchester were attacked along with a number of airfields.

85 Squadron Operational Record Book - 10 October

10 hours 20 minutes non-operational flying consisting of attacks, camera gun, formation, aerobatics.

Reported Casualties (RAF Campaign Diary):

* Enemy: 5 confirmed,   0 probable, 5 damaged
* Own: 5 aircraft with 3 pilots killed.

Aircraft of the Battle
He 59 Floatplane

The Germans provided a remarkably efficient and widespread air sea rescue service for its pilots. Particularly, during the first part of the Battle: the Kanalkampf. The aircraft carried civilian markings and a large Red Cross painted on the fuselage. Unhappily, the aircraft also carried a rear gunner firing a heavy machine gun. This armament compromised their role as Red Cross aircraft. The RAF also suspected them of being used for reconnaissance purposes, and on 14 July 1940 the British government stated that any He59s not overtly undertaking rescue missions were legitimate targets. Nevertheless, these German seaplanes were an undoubted advantage to the Luftwaffe and during the fighting managed to pick up a number of downed German pilots, saving them from drowning.

Day 94 – 11 October

Weather: fair with some coastal showers.

Fighter Command Serviceable Aircraft as at 09:00 hours:

- Blenheim – 40
- Spitfire – 240
- Hurricane – 384
- Defiant – 18
- Gladiator – 8
- **Total – 690**

For most of the day RAF fighters were kept busy seeing off a series of attacks by Me109s. Mid-morning, a group of Me109s went inland to attack Biggin Hill. In the afternoon sweeps of 100 Me109s attacked Southend, and later, Maidstone. The RAF flew 949 sorties, destroyed seven enemy aircraft but lost nine aircraft.

At night German bombers ranged far and wide visiting Southampton, Portsmouth, Dorset, Berkshire, Surrey, Kent, Norfolk and parts of Scotland. The Lever factory at Port Sunlight was also hit.

85 Squadron Operational Record Book - 11 October

19 hours 55 minutes non-op flying consisting of camera gun and formation. Sgts Gray, Muchowski and Paleniczer carried out dusk landings.

Reported Casualties (RAF Campaign Diary):

* Enemy: 8 confirmed, 4 probable, 1 damaged
* Own: 9 aircraft with 3 pilots lost.

The Squadrons
501 Squadron
Nil Time

501 squadron was formed in 1929 as a Special Reserve unit with day bomber duties. In 1936 the squadron was transferred to the Auxiliary Air Force and was converted to a fighter unit two years later. The squadron was equipped with Hurricanes in March 1939 and in May 1940 flew fighter cover for the Advanced Air Striking Force in France. The squadron was based in the south throughout the Battle of Britain, flying variously from Croydon, Middle Wallop, Gravesend and Kenley.

The squadron was disbanded in the 1950s. Some fifty years later it was reformed, in 2001, at RAF Brize Norton, as a Force Protection unit and part of the Royal Auxiliary Air Force.

Day 95 – 12 October

Weather: widespread mist.

Fighter Command Serviceable Aircraft as at 09:00 hours:

- Blenheim – 46
- Spitfire – 217
- Hurricane – 368
- Defiant – 16
- Gladiator – 8
- **Total – 655**

An active day. In the morning, there were attacks on Biggin Hill, London and Kent. In the afternoon over 100 enemy aircraft reached South London. In the late afternoon there were raids of over 100 enemy aircraft over south east Kent and there was a small raid on Biggin Hill. Fighter Command flew 797 sorties. They lost ten aircraft but shot down eleven enemy aircraft.

That night the Luftwaffe visited and bombed Hastings, Coventry and Trafalgar Square.

85 Squadron Operational Record Book -12 October

12 hours 35 minutes non-op flying consisting of formation and cloud flying. Practice squadron formation, pilots were Sqdn Ldr Townsend, Flt Lt Marshall, FO Hemingway, Sgt Goodman, Sgt Webster, Sgt Berkeley, Sgt Gray, Flt Lt Allard, PO Thompson.

Reported Casualties (RAF Campaign Diary):

* Enemy: 11 confirmed, 11 probable, 7 damaged
* Own: 10 aircraft with 4 pilots lost.

The Airfields
RAF North Weald

RAF North Weald in Essex began life as a RFC base in 1916. In the interwar years the airfield and facilities were expanded by the RAF, and by May 1940 it housed a squadron of Hurricanes, which saw action over Dunkirk. Bristol Blenheim night fighters were also stationed here. In 1941 one of the newly formed Eagle squadrons (manned by American volunteers) arrived at North Weald, and in the following year a Norwegian squadron was based here.

RAF North Weald was home to the North Weald Sector Operations Room in 11 Group.

One of the most famous – or rather notorious – actions in World War Two to involve North Weald was the 'Battle of Barking Creek' on only the third day of the war, when the Spitfire claimed its first 'kill' and the battle claimed first RAF airman to be killed in the war. The downed pilot came from North Weald, and the plane the Spitfire shot down was, unhappily, his Hurricane – a bad case of mistaken identity.

North Weald was targeted on numerous occasions by the Luftwaffe during the Battle. The first major raid took place on 24 August, when more than 200 bombs fell on the airfield, many were killed, and the Officers Mess and married quarters were damaged.

The airfield was in the thick of the Battle. The two squadrons to be based here in the first phase of the battle, 56 and 151, took a terrible battering. 56 Squadron lost 11 aircraft in just five days and 151 was reduced to just ten Hurricanes. By the end of August both squadrons had to be withdrawn as non-operational due to the loss of pilots and machines. They were replaced on 1st September by 249, 46 and 25 squadrons. On 3 September, just as the planes were taking off, the Luftwaffe again bombed North Weald. Aircraft and hangars were destroyed and five people killed. However, throughout the Battle the airfield was never put out of action.

Although attacks abated as the Luftwaffe turned their attention to London, the airfield was hit again on 29 October, when six were killed.

Day 96 – 13 October

Weather: fine, cloud in the afternoon.

Fighter Command Serviceable Aircraft as at 09:00 hours:

- Blenheim – 38
- Spitfire – 221
- Hurricane – 359
- Defiant – 13
- Gladiator – 8
- **Total – 639**

The first enemy attack was on a convoy off the coast of East Anglia. At lunch time, however, several attacks developed on London. The first of these was by a force of fifty Me109s. This was followed by a slightly larger group. A third attack in the afternoon came in from twenty-five Me109s. This last penetrated to the centre of London where it attracted continuous harassment from RAF fighters. The RAF that day flew 590 sorties. The British lost two aircraft but succeeded in shooting down five of the enemy.

That night bombs hit a shelter of a block of flats in Stoke Newington and killed 154 people.

17 Squadron Operational Record Book - 13 October

While on patrol, Sgt Sewell and PO Ross were weaving behind the Squadron in the Chatham area, when anti-aircraft fire opened up just behind them. Soon afterwards PO Ross was missed. The rest of the Squadron landed at Martlesham at 14:55 hours. Later PO Ross was reported in Gravesend RAF Hospital with slight shrapnel wounds in the left leg, side and neck. His aircraft was hit by cannon-shell (which it is thought may have been from A/A guns) and PO Ross baled out.

Reported Casualties (RAF Campaign Diary):

* Enemy: 2 confirmed, 5 probable, 0 damaged
* Own: 2 aircraft which the pilots are safe.

Captains and Commanders

Lord Beaverbrook

Lord Beaverbrook, the Canadian press baron was the third member of Churchill's tight inner circle, formed when the latter took office on May 10. For those who were still suspicious of Churchill, Beaverbrook's appointment confirmed the criticism of Churchill that he surrounded himself by questionable figures.But Churchill knew what he was doing. In the Battle, when we would be fighting for our lives, the supply of new fighters from the factories was going to be crucial. First, Churchill needed to separate aircraft production from the Air Ministry. So a new ministry of Aircraft Production was duly set up. Secondly, he had to appoint somebody to run it. For this, he selected his old friend Beaverbrook.

Like it or hate him, nobody could say that Beaverbrook lacked dynamic energy. If anybody could be relied upon to cut through red tape, to energise established figures and to generate real action, it was Beaverbrook. That said, he was a notorious bully and his harsh tactics weren't without consequences. Beaverbrook fired the general manager of Supermarine, who had been successfully dealing with the problem of Spitfire production; shortly afterwards, the general manager shot himself.

Beaverbrook's first action was to deal with the difficulties which had arisen at the 'shadow' factory at Castle Bromwich, just outside Birmingham. What he did was to wrest the factory away from Lord Nuffield's control and transfer it to the engineering giant, Vickers. That caused an explosion. Nuffield went straight to Churchill and demanded Beaverbrook's dismissal. He got nowhere. Instead, Beaverbrook went from strength to strength. He galvanised the industry. He would ring up managers at all hours of the day and night. He expected them to work a seven day week. Churchill gave Beaverbrook the recognition for the enormous growth in aircraft production during the summer of 1940, yet this ignores the fact that much of the machinery for production was already in place. The real heroes of aircraft production were the hundreds of workers who worked 13 or 14-hour shifts, seven days a week.

Beaverbrook was a talented marketing man, and his 'Saucepans for Spitfires' scheme captured the public's imagination. He called for donations of aluminum, and housewives readily donated their pots and pans, happy in the knowledge that their sacrifice could help to win the war.

His reign remains controversial. But Churchill himself was controversial. This was how we were going to fight the war.

Comments:

Rod Sanders: Lord Beaverbrook took most of the credit that should have gone to Sir Wilfrid Freeman. Freeman was behind the Spitfire, Mustang,Lancaster and the Mosquito, also known as 'Freeman's Folly'. Much of the work to do with establishing shadow factories and the civilian repair organisation is down to him. Ignored as was Dowding & Park.

Day 97 – 14 October

Weather: autumnal; rain.

Fighter Command Serviceable Aircraft as at 09:00 hours:

- Blenheim – 41
- Spitfire – 222
- Hurricane – 391
- Defiant – 19
- Gladiator – 8
- **Total – 681**

This proved not to be a day for interception. Bombs were, however, dropped on London. During the day attacks took place on Portsmouth by thirty enemy aircraft. Duxford and Hawkinge were bombed in the early afternoon.

That night heavy attacks took place on Coventry and London. A direct hit on the Carlton Club, London, spared the members, none of whom were seriously hurt. 'The devil looks after his own' was the verdict of a labour MP. Unhappily, there were no less than 500 casualties inflicted that day and night on the civilian population. Worse was to come.

17 Squadron Operational Record Book - 14 October

FO Czernin and PO Pittman took off from Martlesham at 14:40 hours and intercepted a Do17 with British markings on the tail-fin, upper wing surfaces and fuselage. As the e/a turned away, black crosses were seen on the underside of the wings and FO Czernin attacked leaving the port engine on fire. The e/a fired two rockets, which were however incorrect colours. Later PO Pittman attacked, but the Do17 escaped by flying through Harwich balloon barrage. The two a/c landed at 16:00 hours and claimed a Do17 damaged.

PO Dennis Wissler Diary - 14 October

We did no flying today at all. 'A' Flight had a crack at a Do17 which was sporting British markings but did not shoot it down for certain.
(Reproduced by kind permission of the Imperial War Museum and Copyright holder)

Reported Casualties (RAF Campaign Diary):

* Enemy: 0 confirmed, 0 probable, 3 damaged
* Own: Nil.

The People in Support
McIndoe's Guinea Pigs

The casualties of the Battle included a regrettably large number of pilots, who, when shot down, suffered terrible burns in the process. The cockpits of fighter aircraft often filled with petrol vapours. There was also a potential danger from the sighting of the fighters' fuel tank just in front of the cockpit. The result was that all too often enemy fire not only damaged the aircraft but also led to the cockpit filling with flames and turning it into the equivalent of a blow torch. This meant that the pilot had to escape very rapidly if he was to avoid being burnt. In many cases the cockpit canopy was difficult to unlock. The result was that many a pilot suffered appalling burns to his face and hands.

To deal with this situation, a special unit was set up under a brilliant plastic surgeon, Sir Archibald McIndoe, who created a burns unit at the Queen Victoria Hospital in East Grinstead, where victims could be treated.

Often the treatment required literally dozens of operations on the single patient. It was all a matter of affecting a series of skin grafts. Each one had to 'take' before the next could be started. It was a terrible and very painful process. Where McIndoe was brilliant was, not only in his surgery which was ground breaking, but in his recognition that morale had to be kept up in very trying circumstances. He insisted that all the nurses at East Grinstead were of exemplary beauty. He was equally as committed to rehabilitating his patients into civilian life, even, in some cases, lending them money. He was knighted in 1947 in recognition of his work. McIndoes' patients became known as McIndoe's Guinea Pigs. They were disfigured for life, but they wore their disfigurement with great honour.

Day 98 – 15 October

Weather: fair but some cloud.

Fighter Command Serviceable Aircraft as at 09:00 hours:

- Blenheim – 53
- Spitfire – 208
- Hurricane – 405
- Defiant – 18
- Gladiator – 8
- **Total – 692**

The day opened with new instructions from the AOC of 11 Group. It was in response to the new tactics being employed by the Luftwaffe in which twin-engined bombers had been more or less eliminated from their battle order. They were being replaced by strong forces of Me109s and 110s. Secondly they were flying at much higher altitude than before. Sometimes as high as 30,000 feet. All this meant that German aircraft were arriving over London between seventeen and twenty minutes after the radar stations had given the first warning. As they might be flying as high as 30,000 feet, RAF fighters were often unable to intercept, as it took them at least fifteen minutes to achieve the requisite altitude. The answer was to have squadrons patrolling at 20,000 feet or thereabouts, enabling them to intercept the enemy. The result was that, throughout October, the number of enemy aircraft shot down by the RAF fell in relation to the losses suffered by Fighter Command. It had become a battle of fighter versus fighter.

In the morning, some thirty Me109s hit London, including Waterloo Station. The station was subjected to further attacks that night, wrecking a train and two platforms. A second force of enemy aircraft attacked the capital in the middle of the morning while further enemy aircraft hit the suburbs. There were also raids on Kent, Biggin Hill, Kenley and

Southampton. The RAF flew 743 sorties, lost fifteen aircraft and shot down fourteen enemy planes.

That night London was heavily bombed by 410 aircraft, which dropped 538 tons of bombs. Over 400 people were killed. BBC Broadcasting House was hit whilst Bruce Belfrage read the 9 o'clock news. Despite being covered in plaster and debris, Belfrage continued with his broadcast.

85 Squadron Operational Record Book - 15 October

22 hours 5 minutes non-op flying comprising formation air drill, air fighting and camera gun. Night flying carried out by PO Arbon, Sgts Gray, Berkeley and Hutton. PO W.H. Hodgson awarded DFC and Sgt H.N. Howes, DFM.

Reported Casualties (RAF Campaign Diary):

* Enemy: 19 confirmed, 5 probable, 10 damaged
* Own: 15 Aircraft of which 9 pilots are safe.

Weekly Comment: The Denouement

Dowding had been teetering on the edge of enforced retirement for more than a year. He was now 58 years old. He had never been popular in the upper reaches of the Service. Ever since his appointment as AOC in C of Fighter Command, on that Command's creation in the summer of 1936, he had fought tooth and nail to get what he thought he needed for his command. He tended to ignore the fact that other commands in the RAF also had needs which required attention. He had been in line for the ultimate post for Chief of the Air Staff, that is Head of the Air Force, but he was passed over. He took that reasonably well. He was, after all, totally committed to the task of preparing Fighter Command for battle.

He was told he was going to have to retire shortly before the war began but when it did begin and there being no candidate to replace him being immediately available, he was asked to stay. The date of his retirement was moved forwards. It happened twice more until the date of his retirement was fixed for November 1940.

Coincidentally, the tactics followed during the Battle and, in particular, the question of the Big Wing, became the subject of a major meeting at the Air Ministry which was called for 17th October. The conference was to be chaired by the Chief of the Air Staff. Dowding and Park were duly called. When they got to the Air Ministry, the meeting turned out to be taken by Air Vice Marshal Sir Sholto Douglas, the Deputy to the Chief of the Air Staff who was unavoidably away. Also attending was Air Vice Marshal Leigh Mallory. He turned up with Douglas Bader in tow. It was Bader who was to steal the show.

Dowding had been given no indication of what the meeting was to be about. In particular, he had not been warned that Bader would be there. Otherwise he might have brought one of at least a dozen fighter pilots from 11 Group.

When the meeting got under way, Leigh Mallory soon introduced Bader. He was the only person in the room who had been flying in the Battle. He spoke with enormous energy and enthusiasm about the question of tactics and in particular his take on them. It was clear that the Big Wing thesis was to win the day. And it did.

When Dowding and Park left, Park wanted to ensure that the other side of the argument was incorporated into the minute which would undoubtedly be written. So he went straight back to Uxbridge to write it. When he sent his draft into the Air Ministry, the notion of incorporating it into the minute of the meeting was duly rejected.

The upshot was that Dowding was retired. Park was removed from his post and sent to command a Group in Training Command. The Air Ministry produced a slim pamphlet giving an account of the Battle which failed to mention Dowding or, indeed, Park. Churchill remarked that it was like an account of Trafalgar without any mention of Nelson.

Air Vice Marshal Sholto Douglas then took over the command of Fighter Command. Trafford Leigh Mallory took over from Park at 11 Group. Bader was to get further promotion to Wing Commander and took over command of a wing at Tangmere.

Thus ended the drama of the Battle of Britain. It was not a particularly happy ending. The majority view in the command amongst the pilots was that Dowding and Park had been shuffled out of their positions, mainly as a result of politics. There is no doubt about the fact that the Battle had been the most important in British history since Trafalgar and Waterloo. Dowding's reputation has survived his dislodgement from office and his standing now compares with that of Admiral Nelson. He was one of those very few Englishmen to win a military contest on which the future of the country depended, decisively. Park is now emerging as Dowding's main instrument in the victory achieved that year.

Comments:

James Mackie: I have enjoyed reading all the posts regarding the Battle Of Britain. Hugh Dowding was born in the southern Scottish town of Moffat in 1882 and received his early education at St. Ninian's Boys' Preparatory School in Moffat, which his father, Arthur Dowding, had been instrumental in founding.

Day 99 – 16 October

Weather: widespread fog.

Fighter Command Serviceable Aircraft as at 09:00 hours:

*   Blenheim – 46
*   Spitfire – 225
*   Hurricane – 421
*   Defiant – 17
*   Gladiator – 8
*   **Total – 717**

The day saw a number of individual attacks by lone Me109s. RAF Ternhill was bombed, destroying a hangar and damaging others. The RAF managed to fly 275 sorties, destroyed seven enemy aircraft, losing one RAF fighter.

That night 300 bombers attacked Britain.

85 Squadron Operational Record Book - 16 October

Order for one section to scramble. Flt Lt Marshall, Sgt Webster and Sgt Goodman took off 07:15 and landed 07:35. Conditions difficult owing to mist and low cloud at 300ft. 11 hours 40 mins non-op flying, consisting of a battle climb to 25,000 feet, fighter attacks, camera gun and aerobatics. POs A. Velebnovsky and E. Foit (Czechs) posted from 6 OTU.

Sqdn Ldr Townsend accompanied by FO T.J. Molony, motored to Speke to sit on court of enquiry. Sgt Johnson posted to 145 Squadron, Tangmere.

Reported Casualties (RAF Campaign Diary):

* Enemy: 2 confirmed, 0 probable, 1 damaged
* Own: 1 Hurricane of which the pilot is safe.

Top Gun Gallery
Adolf Galland

In the Battle of Britain, the RAF were up against an extremely able and professional group of experienced German fighter pilots flying a very formidable plane, the Me109.

Galland was born in 1912, a member of what was originally a Huguenot family. From an early age, he was deeply interested in everything aeronautical. Having received early experience on gliders, he undertook his pilot's training in 1932 as part of Germany's secret military training programme. In 1933 he joined the Luftwaffe.. He was twice injured in early flying accidents, but emerged in 1937 as an extremely competent fighter pilot, flying as part of the Condor Legion in Spain, of course on Franco's side.

When war started, he took part in the Polish campaign. In the Battle of Britain he flew numerous successful missions against Fighter Command. Like all fighter pilots who survived, he had a number of narrow escapes. But from all of them, he emerged to live on and continue the fight. When Goering decided to promote certain operational pilots to senior commands, he was a beneficiary, and late in August he was promoted Reichsmarschall and took over a senior command.

He was both a hugely successful operational pilot and a very independent minded critic of higher command. He was a hero to his pilots and a thorn in the side of the Nazi dominated command structure. In the Battle, he shot down in the region of forty British aircraft.

He was a great character and after the war, formed several notable friendships with air aces Stanford Tuck, Bader and Johnnie Johnson. He was an inveterate cigar smoker.

Day 100 – 17 October

Weather: some bright intervals but flying conditions remained difficult.

Fighter Command Serviceable Aircraft as at 09:00 hours:

- Blenheim – 46
- Spitfire – 217
- Hurricane – 404
- Defiant – 17
- Gladiator – 8
- **Total – 692**

There was little combat this day. However, Kenley was attacked in the late afternoon. The RAF lost three aircraft and the Luftwaffe lost five.

That night bombs fell on London, Birmingham and Liverpool. The Vickers Armstrong factory was seriously damaged. Park issued another stream of instructions designed to improve the rate of interceptions particularly of high flying intruders.

74 Squadron – Combat Report - 17 October

Squadron was ordered on patrol and 11 aircraft took off from Biggin Hill at 15:10 hrs on 17 October 1940. Later the squadron was ordered to intercept enemy fighters approaching London from the south. Sqdn Ldr Malan attacked from the sun and picked out one Me109. He delivered a two second burst with a quarter deflection from 200 yds closing to 150yds when he delivered another two second burst. This he followed with a four second burst from 100 yds which appeared to damage the elevator control of the enemy aircraft, which was seen in a vertical dive, during which time a final four second burst was delivered and the enemy aircraft emitted black smoke. Sqdn Ldr Malan could not follow the enemy aircraft as he himself 'blacked out' for two seconds.

Reported Casualties (RAF Campaign Diary):

* Enemy: 4 confirmed, 6 probable, 5 damaged
* Own: 3 aircraft and 3 pilots killed or missing.

Aircraft of the Battle
Bristol Beaufighter

The Beaufighter came into Fighter Command service in September - just in time to take part in the Battle. It was a substantial addition to the RAF's attack potential. It was a twin-engined monoplane with pilot and navigator sitting almost side by side. It was powered by two Bristol radial engines which was a departure from the more normal use of "in-line" engines. They were, however, powerful and gave this fighter bomber a top speed of over 300 miles per hour. The armament was 6 Browning machine guns, 3 mounted in each wing. This was supplemented by four 20mm Hispano cannons.

The Beaufighter was a truly formidable aeroplane. It subsequently saw service abroad, particularly in the Middle East. It ended up a true fighter bomber, seeing much service in such operations as shipping strikes. It was later superseded by the twin-engined Havilland Mosquito which was lighter, faster but just as well armed.

Day 101 – 18 October

Weather: fair. A relatively calm day.

Fighter Command Serviceable Aircraft as at 09:00 hours:

- Blenheim – 43
- Spitfire – 218
- Hurricane – 408
- Defiant – 16
- Gladiator – 7
- **Total – 692**

Sporadic attacks on London, Kent and South East coast. However, Liverpool and Birmingham were bombed that night. Luftwaffe losses amounted to fifteen aircraft as against the RAF loss of four planes.

1 Squadron Operational Record Book - 18 October – Wittering

Three weather tests; searchlight co-operation, formation air test, air drill, camera gun and formation cloud flying.

Reported Casualties (RAF Campaign Diary):

* Enemy: 0 confirmed, 0 probable, 1 damaged
* Own: Nil.

The Squadrons
266 Squadron
Hlabezulu – the stabber of the sky

266 squadron was formed in September 1918 at Mudros. The squadron was equipped with seaplanes and flew anti-submarine patrols over the Aegean Sea. It was disbanded in September 1919.

The squadron was reformed in October 1939 at Sutton Bridge. Intended to be a Blenheim squadron it never received the aircraft, and was equipped with Spitfires in January 1940. In June 1940 the squadron flew patrols over the evacuation from Dunkirk. During the Battle of Britain, the squadron was based at Wittering, Tangmere, Eastchurch and Hornchurch. In 1942 the squadron was re-equipped with Typhoons and in 1944 became part of Second TAF in France. The squadron was disbanded in July 1945.

Re-formed in 1946, the squadron had a number of post-war incarnations before finally being disbanded in 1964.

Day 102 – 19 October

Weather: cloudy with some mist.

Fighter Command Serviceable Aircraft as at 09:00 hours:

- Blenheim – 47
- Spitfire – 233
- Hurricane – 412
- Defiant – 22
- Gladiator – 7
- **Total – 721**

A few individual sorties were reported in the morning, mainly heading for London. In the afternoon a group of about 60 Me109s flew over Kent. They were intercepted by RAF fighters and fierce dog-fights took place in which the RAF lost five aircraft shooting down two of the enemy.

That night heavy raids took place on London and Coventry. Mile End Hospital was partly destroyed.

1 Squadron Operational Record Book - 19 October

Flying consisted of weather test by A/C. Formation, air drill, cine camera. During a scramble by Flt Lt M.H. Brown, PO Chetham and PO A.V. Clowes DFM, a Hun was sighted on top of a cloud, but he got away through the clouds before attacked.

Reported Casualties (RAF Campaign Diary):

* Enemy: 2 confirmed, 0 probable, 1 damaged
* Own: Two aircraft. One pilot missing.

The Airfields
RAF Martlesham Heath

RAF Martlesham Heath in Suffolk was the most northerly of the 11 Group airfields during the Battle of Britain, used as a satellite station for North Weald and Debden. It had begun life as an experimental airfield in 1917, when the RFC and then the RAF tested new aircraft.

As World War Two broke out Blenheims from 604 squadron were based here, to be joined by Hurricanes towards the end of 1939. Boulton Paul Defiants of 264 squadron were also based here.

The airfield was attacked on 10 July and 15 August 1940, causing little damage as most of the aircraft were airborne. Initially the runway was grass covered, and at one time during the Battle Robert Stanford Tuck and Douglas Bader were based there, as was Peter Townsend and 85 Squadron for a short time. In 1943 it was handed over to the United States Air Force. Squadrons based here during the Battle included 25, 17, 85 and 257.

Day 103 – 20 October

Weather: cloudy with some haze.

Fighter Command Serviceable Aircraft as at 09:00 hours:

- Blenheim – 44
- Spitfire – 226
- Hurricane – 411
- Defiant – 20
- Gladiator – 7
- **Total – 708**

This day, there were raids at 9;35, 11:00, 13:15, 14:20 and 15:00 on London and the south east but a number of interceptions were made by the RAF. The RAF flew 745 sorties and lost four aircraft but succeeded in shooting down fourteen enemy aircraft.

The coming night, London was given a hard time by a force of no less than 300 bombers which pounded the city. Coventry was also heavily bombed and many fires were started.

1 Squadron Operational Record Book - 20 October

Practice flying: fighter attacks, vector by R/T, high flying tactics. Blue section (B Flight) scrambled base, 20,000 ft, but no e/a sighted. Sgt A. Zavoral landed at Cottesmore. Sgt. H.E. Pettit posted to no. 605 Squadron, Kenley.

Reported Casualties (RAF Campaign Diary):

* Enemy: 9 confirmed, 7 probable, 6 damaged
* Own: Three aircraft. Pilots safe.

Captains and Commanders

Erhard Milch

On the German side, a great deal of the professional staff work which sustained the Luftwaffe with its thousands of aircraft and aircrew was done by a large staff at the Air Ministry, housed in a huge building in Berlin on the Unter den Linden. The key personality here was Erhard Milch. He was second only in rank to Goering. Milch was an extremely able but very ambitious man. During the Twenties, he had been in civilian aviation, as director of Lufthansa, biding his time until Germany could form its new air force which it did in 1935, in contravention with the Versailles Treaty.

Milch did a great deal of the work that reduced the massive tactical air force which went to war so successfully in Poland and then in France.

It was Milch whose idea it was to attack Britain early in June before it had had time to recover from the loss by the British Expeditionary Force of all its arms which had been left on the beaches of Dunkirk. Milch had his plan turned down by Goering who had thought, at the time, the plan was superfluous. Milch, who might be said to have been the brains of the Luftwaffe, went on throughout the war at the Air Ministry working on his plan to usurp Goering's position at the head of the service. He was one of those who, in 1944, pleaded with Hitler to remove Goering from the command of the Luftwaffe. In the event, this attempt to get rid of Goering came to nothing. Hitler remained loyal to his old colleague and to their Nazi past.

Day 104 – 21 October

Weather: cloudy with fog and rain.

Fighter Command Serviceable Aircraft as at 09:00 hours:

- Blenheim – 32
- Spitfire – 227
- Hurricane – 410
- Defiant – 13
- Gladiator – 7
- **Total – 689**

There were sporadic raids by single or small groups of Me109s over much of the southern counties and the Midlands, with some reaching as far north as Lancashire and Liverpool. Interception was difficult on account of the weather. The RAF flew 275 sorties but lost no aircraft, yet shooting down six enemy planes. One of these was a Ju88 which had tried to disguise itself as a Blenheim. The ruse did not work and the enemy aircraft was shot down on its way back to the coast.

At night Coventry suffered heavy raids, considerable damage being done to the Armstrong-Siddeley works. There were also raids over London, Birmingham and Liverpool.

245 Squadron Operational Record Book - 21 October

One operational flight called for at 14:20 by 1 section. Dog fighting. Formation and attack exercises carried on throughout the day. 1 section took off at 12:05 for Sydenham to meet and escort the aircraft conveying HRH the Duke of Kent, who visited Aldegrove station in the course of his Ulster tour of inspection. After lunch and an inspection of the station, a section of Hurricanes escorted HRH back to Sydenham. Hurricane P3657 piloted by Sgt E G Greenwood did not return from battle climb. News later received from the police at Toombridge that the a/c was observed to dive into Lough Neagh at high speed, exploding on impact.

73 Squadron Operational Record Book - 21 October

There was too much mist and the weather altogether too bad for the Squadron to operate as a unit, but twice during the day a pair of Hurricanes were despatched to intercept single raiders. Sqdn Ldr Murray and Flt Lt Smith patrolled over the SE coast in the morning and Flt Lt Smith and Sgt Price were ordered in the afternoon to patrol base at 9000 feet. No e/a was seen but a Wellington which did not appear to have the proper markings was challenged but it soon proved itself as friendly. 'Stefan' has arrived this afternoon and been accorded the Honorary Rank of Group Captain. 'Stefan' is a Borzie presented to the Squadron as a mascot by friends in Cambridge.

Reported Casualties (RAF Campaign Diary):

* Enemy: 2 confirmed, 0 probable, 3 damaged
* Own: Nil.

The People in Support
Training the Aces

Derby winners are the product of trainers. So are successful fighter pilots. All pilots who fly in war or peace are the product of instructors who have taught them to fly. The RAF, at the time of the Battle of Britain and now, pays a great deal of attention to the training of their air crew. Pre-war training of pilots tended to take place at a somewhat leisurely pace. Directly the country went to war, there was a speeding up of the process. Anybody interested in finding out what it was like could do no better than to read Geoffrey Wellum's book, First Light, in which he describes his experience of joining the RAF just before war broke out in September 1939 and the conclusion of his training when he joined 92 squadron flying Spitfires in May 1940.

There were two parts in the process of training: flying training and the intellectual task of learning what flying was about. You had to pass both to qualify.

The flying took the form of three stages. The first was the gentle art of learning to fly a really simple training plane. In 1939 it was the De Havilland Tiger Moth, a very light two-seater bi-plane. This is the aircraft in which the trainee pilot first got his experience of going solo which usually occurred after doing some seven or eight hours of instruction.

The next stage was, in those days, when the pilot graduated onto the Harvard. This was an American built and designed two-seater trainer which was a monoplane with a good deal more powerful engine than that of the Moth. It had some of the characteristics of a fully fledged fighter aircraft. In it the trainee pilot was moved from the simple aerodynamics of the Tiger Moth to the more demanding performance resembling that of a Hurricane or Spitfire.

Then came the third and most demanding stage of the training when the trainee was subject to the real test, both of skill and nerve of flying a real fighter, which in those days meant the Spitfire. This last stage was when the trainee really had to learn his stuff.

It was at this stage that the relationship between the instructor and his pupil became really crucial Wellum's description of his instructor tells the story. When Wellum, the newly commissioned trainee, met his instructor for the first time, he addressed him as 'Sir'. The answer came back, 'You don't call me, "Sir", Sir. You call me Flight Sergeant or Flight'. What this hardened instructor, in his late twenties, with sharp bright blue eyes and thin lips wanted was perfection. He was a hard task master and kept Wellum at it until he was satisfied. But he was probably responsible for Wellum's survival when it came to the Battle that summer. The skills he had taught Wellum lasted him, not only through the Battle, but for two long years afterwards until Wellum came home from Malta at the end of his third tour. He owed his life to that instructor.

Throughout the Battle the RAF turned out pilots at an increasing rate to fill the gaps caused by operations, on the squadrons. The service never ran short of pilots, but there was undoubtedly a diminution in the performance of the newly qualified pilots as a result of the time pressure Training Command was under to get them onto the front line. It meant that the squadrons were having to rely on younger and less experienced pilots than they had started with. It was inevitable but regrettable.

Day 105 – 22 October

Weather: fog and widespread rain causing poor visibility.

Fighter Command Serviceable Aircraft as at 09:00 hours:

- Blenheim – 40
- Spitfire – 234
- Hurricane – 402
- Defiant – 19
- Gladiator – 7
- **Total – 702**

Fog grounded most of 12 Group and some of 11 Group. That afternoon, a convoy off Dover was attacked unsuccessfully. Later small groups of Me109s, targeting another convoy, were plotted off the south coast. On being intercepted, dog-fights developed. As a result eleven enemy aircraft were destroyed while six RAF planes were lost. Despite the weather, the Luftwaffe succeeded in attacking London.

At night, Coventry was once again a major target with 200 people being made homeless. Bombs were also dropped on Windsor Great Park.

74 Squadron – Combat Report - 22 October

Patrol Maidstone at 15,000 feet in company with 92 Squadron. Sqdn Ldr Malan attacked the leading enemy aircraft in a fast dive and fixed bursts from 200 to 50 yds range. The enemy aircraft smoked heavily after the second burst but carried on. Sqdn Ldr Malan continued to fire but had to break off momentarily to wipe ice off his windscreen. He then followed the enemy Me109 to the coast and saw the aircraft crash into the sea five miles out from the Hastings-Dungeness area.

73 Squadron Operational Record Book - 22 October

Thick fog until 12:00 hours. Nothing was done in the morning except to walk Hon. Group Captain 'Stefan' across the aerodrome in the hope of setting up a hare. In this FO Hoole and PO McFadden were successful, but Hon. Group Captain 'Stefan' having sighted the hare did not make any attempt to chase. In good time he will undoubtedly realise what his duties to the mess are. There was no flying throughout the day.

Reported Casualties (RAF Campaign Diary):

* Enemy: 3 confirmed, 1 probable, 1 damaged
* Own: 6 aircraft with 4 pilots killed or missing.

Weekly Comment: The end in sight

In effect, the issue over which the Battle had been fought had been decided back in September, during the battles over London on September 15 and September 27. As October began, the Germans withdrew their twin-engined bombers from daylight operations over Britain. The Do17, the He111 and the Ju87 Stuka dive bomber were no longer to be seen in the skies of this country. It was the same with the invasion fleet and the barges in the French ports which were already being withdrawn. The threat of the invasion, Sealion, was over. The fact was the RAF had thwarted the Luftwaffe in its effort to wipe out Fighter Command. The RAF had not ceded control over British airspace to the enemy. The German order had been quite clear. It had been to defeat Fighter Command so that the Spitfires and Hurricanes would no longer contest a German invasion. The German pilots understood quite clearly what they had failed to achieve. That ace pilot, Galland, had no doubt about what had happened. There had been a muddle and they had paid for it. Tactically, it was the switch from attacking Fighter Command's airfields to the whole force attacking London which was their big mistake. We shall never know, had they not made the switch, whether their persistent attacks on Fighter Command airfields might not have forced Dowding to withdraw his forces to airfields in the Midlands. As it was the Germans lost the chance to find out.

It had been a very close run thing. The RAF hadn't defeated the Luftwaffe and Britain was very far from knocking Germany out of the war. But what the RAF had done was to thwart German intentions. To that extent, it was a great victory.

Day 106 – 23 October

Weather: heavy cloud.

Fighter Command Serviceable Aircraft as at 09:00 hours:

- Blenheim – 47
- Spitfire – 225
- Hurricane – 412
- Defiant – 26
- Gladiator – 8
- **Total – 718**

The weather conditions hampered Fighter Command which only flew 90 sorties. Fighter Command lost six aircraft against a German figure for the day of four destroyed.

That night, substantial damage was done in the bombing of London. The National Gallery was hit. Scotland was also targeted, with £20,000 worth of damage being inflicted on a saw mill in Stirlingshire. Glasgow was also hit.

73 Squadron Operational Record Book - 23 October

There was operational flying during the day. The most important news to-day is that 73 Squadron is to become a night fighter Squadron immediately. There is no doubt that every pilot is disappointed and dislikes the prospect of night flying, but the CO has given each pilot the opportunity of being posted away.

Reported Casualties (RAF Campaign Diary):

* Enemy: 0 confirmed, 0 probable, 1 damaged
* Own: Nil.

Top Gun Gallery
Werner Mölders

Werner Mölders, a fighter pilot who scored a number of victories in the Battle of Britain, was the most significant and influential pilot in the Luftwaffe. He was only a year younger than Galland with whom he served in Spain in the Condor Legion. It was during the missions over Spain that he had developed the key German fighter tactics. This was a formation consisting of two pairs (each pair known as a Rotte) of aircraft in a formation called the Schwarm. When adopted by the RAF, it was rechristened the Finger Four. The point of this revolutionary change was that it gave the pilots clear visibility and flexibility in responding to enemy attack.

Mölders was a very strong character as well as being a natural pilot. He was a staunch Catholic and retained his faith despite the regime, until his death in a flying accident in late 1941. He left a record whose influence long outlasted his life. It is still felt to this day.

Day 107 – 24 October

Weather: improved.

Fighter Command Serviceable Aircraft as at 09:00 hours:

- Blenheim – 38
- Spitfire – 229
- Hurricane – 420
- Defiant – 12
- Gladiator – 8
- **Total – 707**

A few individual raiders and reconnaissance planes flew over Britain. This quieter day enabled Dowding to try and straighten out the difficult relations between Keith Park at 11 Group and Leigh Mallory at 12 Group. He told the former to make allowances for the latter's difficulties when trying to send reinforcements. However, subsequent events showed it was really too late to mend these fences. Things had gone too far. The RAF flew 476 sorties resulting in eight German aircraft being destroyed; several the result of accidents while Fighter Command lost none.

At night 50 aircraft attacked London. In the provinces, Birmingham was the main target while Basingstoke was also hit.

1 Squadron Operational Record Book - 24 October

Destruction of a Junkers 17. Red Section were ordered to intercept raid 10 at 12:04 hours. Personnel: Flt Lt M.H. Brown, PO A.V. Clowes, DFM, PO A. Kershaw. E/a sighted 3,000 ft above cloud. As a result of the ensuing engagement the e/a was brought down at St. Neot. During the engagement some fire was experienced from the e/a rear gunner, and our side used up 1911 rounds. All three pilots expressed the opinion that the e/a did not make very good use of cloud cover before the attack and the only evasive action taken was diving into the clouds. He appeared to be an inexperienced pilot. Searchlight co-operation. Blue Section (B Flight) scrambled base, nothing sighted.

Reported Casualties (RAF Campaign Diary):

* Enemy: 2 confirmed, 0 probable, 2 damaged
* Own: Nil.

Aircraft of the Battle
Ju52

This aircraft was the Luftwaffe's basic transport plane, originally designed as a civil transport aircraft it went on to be used in bomber training. It saw a great deal of service during the Spanish Civil War and the land battles in Europe during the Second World War. It was a sturdy aircraft with capacity for seventeen passengers. It was powered by three engines, one in the wing each side of the fuselage, with a third engine in the nose of the aircraft. This may have seemed unusual but it was very effective. Had Fighter Command not seen off the Luftwaffe in the Battle of Britain there is no doubt that we, in Britain, would have seen many more Ju52s than was actually the case in 1940.

Day 108 – 25 October

Weather: dry but overcast.

Fighter Command Serviceable Aircraft as at 09:00 hours:

- Blenheim – 38
- Spitfire – 232
- Hurricane – 413
- Defiant – 12
- Gladiator – 8
- **Total – 703**

Dornier 17s came back into battle this day. These twin-engined bombers were, however, heavily protected by a number of Me109s. In the early morning there were raids over Biggin Hill, Maidstone, Kenley, Hastings and London. This was followed later that morning with a raid from 100 aircraft over Maidstone. In the afternoon there were attacks on central London, Kenley and Tangmere. The RAF flew 809 sorties against the considerable number of enemy raids over Kent and London. Twenty enemy aircraft were destroyed at a cost of ten RAF fighters.

This was the day that the Italian Air Force finally joined the battle. It proved to be more of a political gesture than a serious act of war. Sixteen of these Italian aircraft took off that night to bomb Harwich. Milch complained that this Italian initiative caused more trouble than it was worth.

At night London and Birmingham were the main targets.

1 Squadron Operational Record Book - 25 October

Air firing at Sutton Bridge. Searchlight co-operation. Dusk landings. The night readiness section had to scramble base for 15 mins but no enemy aircraft was sighted.

Reported Casualties (RAF Campaign Diary):

* Enemy: 14 confirmed, 12 probable, 16 damaged
* Own: 10 aircraft with 3 pilots killed or missing.

The Squadrons

1 Squadron

Fugo non fugio – I put to flight, I do not flee

1 squadron can be traced back to 1878 when it was 1 Balloon Company of the Royal Engineers. In 1912 the unit was transferred to the RFC and became number 1 squadron. During the course of the First World War the squadron flew many missions over the Western Front. Following the end of the war, the squadron was disbanded in 1919 only to be re-formed the following day. During the inter-war years the squadron saw service in Iraq.

In 1938 the squadron, which was based at Tangmere, was equipped with Hurricanes. Following the outbreak of the Second World War, the squadron was sent to France as part of the Advanced Air Striking Force. Returning to Britain in May 1940 the squadron was once again based at Tangmere and Northolt, during the first part of the Battle of Britain. The squadron was moved to Wittering for rest in September 1940.

The squadron has seen service in the Suez Crisis, the Falklands, Iraq and continues to serve in Afghanistan.

Day 109 – 26 October

Weather: cloudy with some bright intervals.

Fighter Command Serviceable Aircraft as at 09:00 hours:

- Blenheim – 46
- Spitfire – 216
- Hurricane – 405
- Defiant – 10
- Gladiator – 8
- **Total – 685**

While the daylight fighter bomber attacks on London were maintained it was evident that the main effort of the Luftwaffe was taking the form of night bomber attacks on London and countrywide cities. Throughout the day, a number of intruder groups flew over Kent with some penetrating to London where the Royal Chelsea Hospital was hit. The RAF flew 732 sorties, ten German aircraft being destroyed while two British fighters were shot down.

Arrangements were now in hand whereby the Duxford wing informed 11 Group of its day's intentions so that operations of the two groups could be coordinated. Certain aircraft were nominated to act as the line of communications between the two groups, meaning that they were furnished with the correct crystals for the task.

Once more the night time raids hit London and Birmingham heavily. New Street station in Birmingham had to be closed due to an unexploded bomb.

85 Squadron Operational Record Book - 26 October

Pilots flew to Kirton Lindsey in morning for visit to the station of Secretary of State for Air (Sir Archibald Sinclair) and the AOC (Air Vice

Marshal T Leigh Mallory, CB, DSO) who spoke to them on the fine records of the squadron. Sqdn Ldr Townsend had a long talk with Sir Archibald at lunch on the subject of night fighting. Pilots returned to Caistor. Flt Lt Marshall carried out night patrol (19:00-20:00).

Reported Casualties (RAF Campaign Diary):

* Enemy: 5 confirmed, 4 probable, 8 damaged
* Own: 2 aircraft with both pilots missing.

The Airfields
RAF Coltishall

RAF Coltishall in Norfolk became operational in May 1940, and was active until 2006. Initially conceived as a bomber base, it was pressed into service as a fighter airfield in 12 Group as battles in the air increased in intensity in May 1940. The first squadron to operate from here was Sqdn Ldr Rupert Leigh's 66 Squadron flying Spitfires.

Squadrons based here during the Battle included 66 Squadron from 29 May 1940, 242 Squadron from 18 June 1940, 616 Squadron from 3 September 1940, 74 Squadron from 9 September 1940 and 72 Squadron from 13 October 1940. Douglas Bader was CO of 242 Squadron, which later in the Battle moved to Duxford. He joined his new squadron, mostly made up of Canadian pilots flying Hurricanes, at Coltishall.

Aircraft flying from Coltishall were part of the famous 'Big Wing' operating out of Duxford. Pilots who flew from here included Stanford Tuck, 'Sailor' Malan, 'Cats Eyes' Cunningham and Johnnie Johnson.
The airfield was attacked by the Luftwaffe on 18 August but little damage was caused.

Day 110 – 27 October

Weather: cloudy with a few bright intervals.

Fighter Command Serviceable Aircraft as at 09:00 hours:

- Blenheim – 46
- Spitfire – 215
- Hurricane – 393
- Defiant – 15
- Gladiator – 8
- **Total – 677**

In the morning formations of up to 50 aircraft attacked targets in Kent and in London itself. In the afternoon, an attack was launched by Luftflotte 3 on Southampton. Martlesham Heath was also hit. The RAF that day flew 1007 sorties with the RAF losing ten fighters as against fifteen German aircraft destroyed.

At night, Coventry was hit heavily. The Armstrong-Siddeley factory and the Royal Naval Ordnance Store were both heavily damaged. London, Liverpool and Bristol were also bombed.

85 Squadron Operational Record Book - 27 October

Day and night patrols. At 18:00 hours Heinkel III suddenly appeared over Caistor aerodrome flying very low and proceeded to machine gun it. Sqdn Ldr Townsend, PO I.E. La Bouchere and Flt Lt Marshall rushed to their machines and took off. Flt Lt Marshall chased e/a west. Orbiting Kirton Lindsey at 1,000 ft he sighted e/a to the South West some 2,000 ft above him flying West. He climbed to attack and fired two one second bursts at 300 yds from slightly below and to the starboard quarter. MG fire was opened at him from the Dorsal turret at 500-800yds but it was low and to the right.

E/a turned right and made for cloud cover to the East. Flt Lt Marshall put in a three second burst as he entered cloud and another of 3 seconds from slightly above and astern at 250yds as he emerged. E/a entered second cloud but the next cloud it entered was thin and Flt Lt Marshall was easily able to follow and finished his ammunition with a six second burst at 250 yds closing to 200 from astern and to the port quarter allowing ¼ deflection. This burst was particularly effective and he could see bullet holes being torn in e/a's fuselage. E/a dived for cloud heading east and Flt Lt Marshall being out of ammunition returned to Caistor at 18:20

The e/a was subsequently confirmed as being destroyed, a searchlight near Salt Fleet having reported an e/a down in the sea at approximately 18:10 hours. Before being engaged by Flt Lt Marshall the e/a dropped six sticks of bombs on and near Kirton Lindsey aerodrome. One stick fell on no. 7 hangar and demolished the Squadron Orderly room and Adjutant's Office. FO Molony and the orderly room clerks were not in the office at the time. A runner (AC2 Jordan) who was in the Orderly Room escaped with a shaking.

Reported Casualties (RAF Campaign Diary):

* Enemy: 10 confirmed, 7 probable, 9 damaged
* Own: 8 aircraft with 4 pilots killed or missing.

Captains and Commanders
Henry Tizard

No account of the RAF's success in the Battle of Britain should omit mention of Henry Tizard. He was the man who led the science base research in the Thirties which produced the winning formula of a radar based air defence system.

Tizard had long been a leader in scientific research particularly applied to the air. Like that other physicist who was to play an important part, Frederick Lindeman, he had begun as a researcher in physics. He had become acquainted with his colleague Lindeman, originally from Alsace, when they had met in Berlin in 1909. After the First World War, in which both men had served at Farnborough, their paths diverged. Lindeman became Professor of Physics at Oxford University, while Tizard went off to Imperial College in London. A few years later, in the Twenties, Lindeman met Churchill and began a long cooperation with the man who was to become Prime Minister in 1940. Tizard, meanwhile, became the most influential scientist at the Air Ministry during the Thirties. It was his committee which recruited Watson Watt to develop the radar. Cooperating with Dowding, Tizard's group was largely responsible for Fighter Command's ability to withstand the German onslaught in the Battle of Britain. Tizard's name should not be forgotten, and indeed he deserves his own statue for playing such an important, indeed, crucial role for preparing the RAF for the Battle.

Day 111 – 28 October

Weather: cloudy with large patches of fog.

Fighter Command Serviceable Aircraft as at 09:00 hours:

- Blenheim – 44
- Spitfire – 219
- Hurricane – 385
- Defiant – 18
- Gladiator – 8
- **Total – 674**

There were a number of incursions by groups of enemy aircraft with between 50 and 100 aircraft in each group. Their targets were the same as before. The main object being attacks on London and the South East. The RAF were up in strength this day intercepting these attacks. They flew 639 sorties, losing two aircraft in the process but destroying eleven German aircraft.

At night, Birmingham was once again attacked and the cathedral was hit. Incendiary bombs were showered on Biggin Hill without much damage being done while in London a public shelter in Southwark was hit causing many casualties.

242 Squadron Operational Record Book - 28 October

Visit to Squadron by AOC who congratulated pilots on efficiency of Squadron which he said was equal, if not superior, to any Squadron in RAF. Operational patrols carried out over London.

Reported Casualties (RAF Campaign Diary):

* Enemy: 5 confirmed, 7 probable, 8 damaged
* Own: Nil.

The People in Support
Bomber Command and its part in the Battle

The honours in the Battle of Britain have tended to go exclusively to Fighter Command. Yet other commands, particularly Bomber Command played an important part in the contest. Furthermore, Bomber Command suffered much higher casualties in 1940 than did Fighter Command. From July till the end of the year, Bomber Command suffered the loss of 1400 aircrew and lost 330 planes. This reflected the fact that the average bomber carried four to five aircrew so that each plane suffered much higher casualties than Fighter Command when the loss of a single fighter incurred the maximum of one pilot killed. But, of course, many RAF pilots shot down survived to fight another day.

The targets for Bomber Command in 1940 were, first, the canals in Western Europe down which the barges requisitioned for the cross Channel invasion were travelling. Secondly, once the barges had arrived in the Channel ports, they became a target as they lay berthed waiting to play their part in 'Sealion', Hitler's planned invasion of Britain.

The canals represented a vast target. There were thousands of miles of such waterways in Western Europe. Nevertheless, Bomber Command managed to block the Dortmund/Ems canal so effectively that virtually the whole waterway system of Western Europe was paralysed for a week. Unfortunately, it was only for a week as the impact of this amazingly accurate bit of bombing was cleared in a few days.

However, the barges, once they were located in the Channel ports, were much more vulnerable. As a target they were easy to find. Moreover, once hit they tended to burn. One RAF pilot observing the effect of Bomber Command's attack on the Channel Ports described the sight of the fires generated by the bombing as being reminiscent of pre-war Blackpool illuminations, so enormous were the fires. It was said that on some nights, the fires were visible from the south coast of Britain.

The Bomber Command success was all the more remarkable considering the aircraft the RAF were flying. They were all twin-engined aircraft, originally designed for use by day. They were the Wellington, Hampden and Whitley bombers. These attacks represented the Command's first taste of real war. Nonetheless, they were all approaching obsolescence. When it came to mounting a serious onslaught on Germany, it wasn't until the advent of the four engined bomber fleets that really serious damage was done. Nevertheless, in the summer of 1940, the Command completed a remarkably successful role.

Its final achievement was to bomb Berlin in response to what turned out to be an error by the Luftwaffe when London was bombed in July. When Hitler heard about it, he was furious. Nevertheless Churchill seized the opportunity to use the occasion to bomb Berlin. This really upset the Fuehrer. He, in response, ordered the bombing of London. This resulted in a switch in tactics. It gave up bombing 11 Group airfields south of London and on September 7 launched its whole strength against London. The Luftwaffe was going to try and repeat what it had done to Warsaw and Rotterdam but this time against Britain's metropolis. So it can be said that it was Bomber Command that caused this fatal switch in the Luftwaffe's attack on Britain. The Command had, by bombing Berlin, initiated the move which virtually saved Fighter Command. By provoking this fatal change, Bomber Command had gone a long way to helping Britain to win the Battle of Britain.

Day 112 – 29 October

Weather: overcast.

Fighter Command Serviceable Aircraft as at 09:00 hours:

- Blenheim – 40
- Spitfire – 211
- Hurricane – 403
- Defiant – 13
- Gladiator – 8
- **Total – 675**

This day represented the last major daylight assault by the Luftwaffe in the Battle but the honours went to the RAF. Notably 602 City of Glasgow Squadron managed to shoot down eight Me109s in almost as many minutes. Unsurprisingly the enemy aircraft turned around and flew for home, but this only further exposed them to another attack in which they lost four aircraft.

Meanwhile, enemy aircraft attacked Portsmouth and Southampton. However, the Italians put in a further appearance by attacking Ramsgate. The final tally that day was nineteen enemy aircraft destroyed for a loss of seven RAF aircraft.

Coventry, Portsmouth, Dover and London were the main targets for this night's raids.

Cyril Shoesmith, 14 years old, Bexhill on Sea – Diary - Tuesday 29 October

At 4:05pm another raid began. Many planes were heard and about 5 o'clock we saw a plane dive and drop two bombs. Not long after this we saw about thirty planes at a great height. And then three low two engine planes flying singly. They were fired at by the Lewis guns and were believed to be Dornier bombers or Messerschmitt two engine fighters. Fighters were seen in pursuit. The raid ended at 5:30, but the night raid came some time later.

(Reproduced by kind permission of the Imperial War Museum and Copyright holder)

Reported Casualties (RAF Campaign Diary):

* Enemy: 27 confirmed, 8 probable, 10 damaged
* Own: 7 aircraft with two pilots killed. Of these, 2 aircraft were destroyed and one pilot killed by bombs when taking off from North Weald aerodrome.

Comments:

Malcolm Smith: I feel I must thank you for the daily reminder of the Battle of Britain.

I was a schoolboy at that time and time spent sleeping in air raid shelters and viewing bomb damage the following morning accompanied by my father a veteran of World War One is still clearly remembered.

The aircraft that are recorded were very familiar to my generation and their pilots our heroes, does this qualify me to ask 'are we worthy of their sacrifice'.

Statistical summary, Week 16:

* *Total Fighter Command Establishment: 1727 planes*
* *Strength: 1735 planes*
* *Balance: over strength 8 planes*
* *Weekly Aircraft Production: 9 Beaufighters, 16 Defiants, 69*
* *Hurricanes, 42 Spitfires*

Weekly Comment: The Significance of the Battle

The fact that the RAF had emerged apparently intact from nearly four months of day to day battle against a concerted attack by three Luftflotten of the Luftwaffe was of enormous significance. Against every expectation, to have won this victory meant that the rest of the world saw that Britain was a serious contender in the war against Hitler. The country was, after all, the only one in Europe still at war with Hitler. It meant that the many governments who had already sought refuge in London knew now that they were safe here. They wouldn't have to move again in a hurry. From Churchill's point of view it meant above all that he could show America that Britain was worth supporting.

For Britain itself, the victory meant that the Germans would not, after all, be marching down Whitehall in a repetition of their victory parade down the Champs Elysees. It meant also, that Britain would not have to experience the nightmare of invasion with the Gestapo making lists of thousands of English people whom they wanted to eliminate. We were to face some appalling dangers in the rest of the war and it would be over two years before we would be able to celebrate a victory on land against German forces. Indeed, we would be in for five years of strife. But we had won our spurs and had not been defeated right at the start, as we might well have been. Our deliverance was, in fact, due to two circumstances. First, the preparation which we had put in before the war so that we were in a position to defend ourselves. Secondly, the small band of young fighter pilots who threw themselves into the fight with such determination. As might have been remarked at the time, it had been a 'good show'.

Day 113 – 30 October

Weather: drizzle.

Fighter Command Serviceable Aircraft as at 09:00 hours:

- Blenheim – 39
- Spitfire – 213
- Hurricane – 391
- Defiant – 11
- Gladiator – 8
- **Total – 662**

Luftflotte 3 joined the action sending a force of over 100 aircraft consisting of fighters and fighter bombers which reached London and bombed a number of targets. However, Kent and Sussex were the main targets that day. The Armstrong Siddeley factory was also hit. North Weald was attacked in the early evening.

The tally that day was eight German aircraft lost against five RAF fighters destroyed.

There were few attacks that night due to the bad weather.

85 Squadron Operational Record Book - 30 October

Night flying training. Sqdn Ldr Townsend and Flt Lt Marshall carried out night patrols.

1 Squadron Operational Record Book -30 October

Blue Section (B Flight) took part in an Army co-operation movement. This section was ordered to scramble base. Personnel: POs G.E. Goodman, R.G. Lewis and Sgt V. Jicha. E/a sighted. Goodman mistook it for a Blenheim. Lewis and Jicha recognised it as a Junkers 88 and shot it down. Sgt J. Dygryn crashed when landing, plane written off.

Reported Casualties (RAF Campaign Diary):

* Enemy: 9 confirmed, 8 probable, 7 damaged
* Own: 5 aircraft with 4 pilots killed or missing.

Top Gun Gallery
Hugh 'Cocky' Dundas

Hugh 'Cocky' Dundas began his career in the RAF when he left Stowe in 1938 and joined the Auxiliary Air Force. He had always been fascinated by the idea of flying. When the war began he was called up to full time service and was posted to 616 Squadron which was flying Spitfires. He was shot down on 22 of August and sustained wounds. However he recovered and rejoined the Squadron in September.

Dundas was one of those fighter pilots who was not only a skilled and successful pilot, but also had great leadership qualities. He was also extremely popular.

He subsequently went on to have an extremely varied and successful flying career. He was awarded the DFC in 1941. This was when he was at Tangmere flying on Bader's wing formation during their sweeps across Northern France.

In September 1941 he was posted to an OTU, but apparently his scruffy appearance did not impress the CO and he was posted as a Flight Commander on 610 Squadron. Then in December 1941, he was posted as CO to 56 Squadron. Evidently his leadership qualities had overcome any problem with his scruffiness. He then went to the Mediterranean and took over of a Spitfire Wing in Malta and remained with them as they moved up into Italy until the end of the war. By this time he had risen in rank to Wing Commander and had won a DSO. A Bar to his DSO was to follow in 1945.

After the war Dundas pursued a very successful professional career ending up as Chairman of Thames Television complete with knighthood. He died in 1995.

The final word on the pilots

In terms of numbers, three quarters of Fighter Command was made up of British pilots. However, the other quarter was made up of pilots from the Commonwealth and from European countries which had been overrun by Hitler's legions.

The Commonwealth contingent was very important and very distinctive. It was made up of young men, either recruited by the RAF before the war, or who had been attracted to the RAF by the excitement of being trained to fly and fight. Either way, their presence in the Battle did much for the relationship in 1940 between the youth of those in the Commonwealth and the youth of Britain. These young men from the Dominions were the natural soul mates of their British counterparts. It wasn't so much that they were part of the Empire and that they were, therefore, responding loyally to the needs of the mother country. The fact was they naturally felt they were part of the British legacy. It was this that made them stand shoulder to shoulder with the youth of this country.

But then there were the many volunteers who came from the countries of Europe which had been overrun by Hitler and who felt that they personally were at war with the Nazi war machine. They joined in the fight for a very different reason from the young men who had come from the Commonwealth. What they had in common with the RAF in 1940 was the opportunity which the service provided to carry on the fight against Hitler. They weren't British at all. They were Poles, Czechs, Belgians and French men. Some, quite a few, in fact, had a problem understanding the English language which they needed to do to operate successfully in Fighter Command. But practically all had one very valuable characteristic in common. They were already experienced fighter pilots. After only a week or two's familiarisation they were capable of being slotted into this or that fighter squadron. Some of them joined one of the specific squadrons formed entirely out of their fellow nationals, for instance, 303 Polish squadron which ended the Battle with the highest score for any squadron in the Command.

These European fighter pilots were an enormous plus for Fighter Command. They were already trained. Many of them had already been in action in the air against the Luftwaffe. They had experience. They proved an invaluable addition to Fighter Command's strength in the summer of 1940.

The fact that the RAF was able to take advantage of this important contribution from overseas and that it was able to provide a place of honour in what might be called the right of the line, was an extremely significant factor in the way the Battle should be seen. It may have been a battle for Britain, but it was also part of what was to become the war for freedom against those who would extinguish it.

Day 114 – 31 October

Weather: cloud and widespread drizzle.

Fighter Command Serviceable Aircraft as at 09:00 hours:

- Blenheim – 40
- Spitfire – 227
- Hurricane – 399
- Defiant – 10
- Gladiator – 8
- **Total – 684**

It seemed that the weather was putting an end to the battle by day. This was in fact officially the last day of the Battle of Britain. The effort put in by the enemy that day seemed half-hearted. However, October as a whole was far from representing a gradual decline in enemy activity. On the contrary, it had put RAF fighters to perhaps the sternest test of the whole encounter. The switch by the Luftwaffe to attacks by fighters and fighter bombers and its abandonment of the twin-engined bomber as its main weapon increased the odds against the RAF. Furthermore, the tactic of sending many of the attacks at what was in those days extreme altitude put a serious extra strain on RAF pilots. All this had resulted in many more fighter-to-fighter combats. The physical strain on pilots of this new form of combat was beginning to tell on RAF capacity to hold their own. The Battle had also taken its toll on the civilian population with the total casualties from the bombing in October being 6,334 civilians killed and 8,695 seriously injured.

However, the RAF kept up its ability to absorb the lessons of every new tactic employed by the Luftwaffe. Whatever the Luftwaffe threw at them, RAF pilots always rose to the challenge. They were doing so on the last day of the Battle as they had done on the first day on July 10.

73 Squadron Operational Record Book - 31 October

Weather terrible – impossible to do any flying, everyone getting 'brassed off' with the mud and general bad conditions.

Reported Casualties (RAF Campaign Diary):

* Enemy: 0 confirmed, 0 probable, 0 damaged
* Own: Nil.

Comments:

Lord Ramsbotham: Thank you for an enthralling series, which I know that you and your colleague spent so much time researching so meticulously. You have reminded your readers not just of an extraordinary episode in our history, but of the fact that, ultimately, it came down to people and how fortunate we were in those whom we had in particular places at that time. Thoughts are provoked thinking about those who received less than their due recognition, but you have done much to redress that balance. I hope that what you have done reaches the widest possible audience, because it is also such a tribute to those who lost their lives on our behalf.

The Final Story: Thank you, but no thank you

The sad thing about the Battle of Britain was that for many of those who had been involved in senior command positions or who had worked behind the scenes to prepare Fighter Command for battle would meet a bitter sweet finale when the fight was over. The pilots who had won the Battle were, Thank Heavens, when the end came, the heroes of the day and still remain so. Churchill saw to that with his famous speeches, particularly the one about 'The Few'. But the other categories of people who made a contribution which was truly vital, were less lucky and just faded from view.

The first category consisted of Dowding, Keith Park and then Brand and Saul. These were the commanders who actually fought the Battle. They had all gone within a few months of the end of the Battle. The ostensible reason was the apparent disagreement over the 'Big Wing' theory led by Squadron Leader Bader of 12 Group with the support of the AOC of that group, Leigh Mallory. But there was more to it than that.

Dowding had run Fighter Command, of which he had been AOC in C, since its formation in 1936, almost as if it had been an air force within an air force He wasn't a man of charm and moreover he wasn't a collegiate colleague. He was just dedicated to a single minded determination to ensure that his command went into the inevitable combat as well prepared as he could possibly make it. He was not a popular figure in the upper echelons of the Service. He had been passed over for the job of Chief of the Air Staff, that is, head of the air force. He was a loner. The top brass were longing to see his back.

Inevitably this meant that his appointees of the group commanders were, of course, totally loyal to him. With just one exception, Leigh Mallory of 12 Group, who had been jealous throughout the Battle of Keith Park, head of 11 Group covering the south of England. They were all destined to be sidelined and fairly soon to be retired. The one exception was Keith Park who had his day, once again in Malta, when he became AOC of the group operating from Luqa.

Could Churchill have saved Dowding or at least ensured that he was made a Marshal of the Royal Air Force as the King had suggested, when he retired? He would have had to run against the collective prejudice of the top brass of the RAF but yes, of course, he could and should have.

To come to the next top individuals who were also overlooked, they were those who were responsible for the five years of preparatory work before the Battle began, ensuring that Fighter Command was furnished with a modern defence system. This included, most importantly, the invention of radar. Henry Tizard was the scientist responsible for this great innovation and Watson Watt was the expert who actually invented radar. Unfortunately, there had been a huge row between Lindeman a fellow scientist and Tizard when the work on radar was just starting. Lindeman had been Churchill's adviser. The two scientists, Tizard and Lindeman, had known each other well but the relationship had broken down between the two men. This meant that when Churchill came to power, he naturally brought Lindeman with him. That spelled the end for Tizard. He moved off to become Master of Magdalene College at Oxford. The new men under Lindeman took over. The old group who had worked on the modernisation of Fighter Command were dispersed.

The third casualty was Chamberlain. He was the politician who ensured that the policy of modernising Fighter Command was adhered to by the pre-war Government. Although he got no thanks for his part in the preparation for war, he nonetheless played an important role in the first few months of Churchill's administration. It was he, Chamberlain, who prevented Lord Halifax from getting his way and allowing talks with Hitler to take place following the fall of France. He vetoed them. He knew how unreliable any agreement with Hitler was bound to be. At least he played this important part, but certainly, like the others in this unfortunate tale, he got no thanks.

In war the honours often fall unevenly. It was certainly the case following the Battle of Britain. At least Keith Park has been honoured by a new statue in London which has been erected in his memory.

Comments:

Philip Cowley: This whole series has been interesting day by day. I have known the details of The Battle for many years but to have it tied to contemporaneous dates was novel and more immediate. Many thanks for all your work

Richard: Thank you for this blog… I have been following this since week one, and it has been an almost surreal experience to witness this battle as it took place, 70 years removed.

I would have loved to see this get better exposure- this blog is a gem that needs to be reissued every year, that we may never forget.

David LaJuett: May I say, first, thank you for the fine action commentary, reading which, day after day, has given us a strong sense of the actual length of time that the Battle lasted, and the stress of the continual German attacks. And you are right to point out the terrible unfairness of the post Battle treatment of Dowding and Park. (the Air Ministry's official booklet 'The Battle of Britain' put out a few months later, did not even mention Dowding or Park!! Even Churchill was shocked by this.)

It should be noted, however, that Dowding himself was too removed from the Park-Leigh Mallory dispute, and allowed it to fester too long, when stronger action might have supported Park, and forced Leigh Mallory into supporting Park more. Dowding's inaction in this dispute is surprising, since throughout the Battle of Britain Leigh Mallory's obvious lack of support for Park's 11 Group contributed materially to the damage that the Luftwaffe was able to inflict on 11 Group's airfields. Why didn't Dowding see this and act more firmly?

It must be accepted, too, that Churchill not only acquiesced in the forcing out of Dowding and Park, but may have encouraged it. Dowding might have incurred Churchill's animosity back in May/June 1940, when Dowding warned about sending too many fighters to France, while Churchill wanted to send many more. Indeed, Churchill's unreliable memoir Their Finest Hour, does not mention Dowding's famous 10-Point letter of warning.

And ironically, among the losers, Kesselring, Sperrle and Milch all continued on. And Goering was never really called to account, and remained with the Luftwaffe until war's end.

History has had the last word, at least.

Appendices

'Dearest Mother' – Published in The Times, 18 June 1940

My Fight With Evil

'My Earthly Mission is Fulfilled'

Among the personal belongings of a young RAF pilot in a Bomber Squadron who was recently reported 'missing, believed killed,' was a letter to his mother – to be sent to her if he were killed.

' "This letter was perhaps the most amazing one I have ever read; simple and direct in its wording but splendid and uplifting in its outlook," says the young officer's station commander. It was inevitable that I should read it – in fact he must have intended this, for it was left open in order that I might be certain that no prohibited information was disclosed. I sent the letter to the bereaved mother, and asked her whether I might publish it anonymously, as I feel its contents may bring comfort to other mothers, and that every one in our country may feel proud to read of the sentiments which support 'an average airman' in the execution of his present arduous duties. I have received the mother's permission, and I hope this letter may be read by the greatest possible number of our countrymen at home and abroad.'

Dearest Mother,

Though I feel no premonition at all, events are moving rapidly, and I have instructed that this letter be forwarded to you should I fail to return from one of the raids which we shall shortly be called upon to undertake. You must hope on for a month, but at the end of that time you must accept the fact that I have handed my task over to the extremely capable hands of my comrades of the Royal Air Force, as so many splendid fellows have already done.

First, it will comfort you to know that my role in this war has been of the greatest importance. Our patrols far out over the North Sea have helped to keep the trade routes clear for our convoys and supply ships, and on one occasion our information was instrumental in saving the lives of the men in a crippled lighthouse relief ship. Though it will be difficult for you, you will disappoint me if you do not at least try to accept the facts dispassionately, for I shall have done my duty to the utmost of my ability. No man can do more, and no one calling himself a man could do less.

I have always admired your amazing courage in the face of continual setbacks; in the way you have given me as good an education and background as anyone in the country; and always kept up appearances without ever losing faith in the future. My death would not mean that your struggle has been in vain. Far from it. It means that your sacrifice is as great as mine. Those who serve England must expect nothing from her; we debase ourselves if we regard our country as merely a place in which to eat and sleep.

History resounds with illustrious names who have given all, yet their sacrifice has resulted in the British Empire, where there is a measure of peace, justice, and freedom for all, and where a higher standard of civilization has evolved, and is still evolving, than anywhere else. But this is not only concerning our own land. Today we are faced with the greatest organized challenge to Christianity and civilization that the world has ever seen, and I count myself lucky and honoured to be the right age and fully trained to throw my full weight into the scale. For this I have to thank you. Yet there is more work for you to do. The home front will still have to stand united for years after the war is won.

For all that can be said against it, I still maintain that this war is a very good thing; every individual is having the chance to give and dare all for his principle like the martyrs of old. However long the time may be, one thing can never be altered – I shall have lived and died an Englishman. Nothing else matters one jot nor can anything ever change it.

You must not grieve for me, for if you really believe in religion and all that it entails that would be hypocrisy. I have no fear of death; only a queer elation...I would have it no other way. The universe is so vast and so ageless that the life of one man can only be justified by the measure of his sacrifice. We are sent to this world to acquire a personality and a character to take with us that can never be taken from us. Those who just eat and sleep, prosper and procreate, are no better than animals if all their lives they are at peace.

I firmly and absolutely believe that evil things are sent into the world to try us; they are sent deliberately by our Creator to test our metal because He knows what is good for us. The Bible is full of cases where the easy way out has been discarded for moral principles. I count myself fortunate in that I have seen the whole country and known men of every calling. But with the final test of war I consider my character fully developed. Thus at my early age my earthly mission is already fulfilled and I am prepared to die with just one regret, and one only – that I could not devote myself to making your declining years more happy by being with you; but you will live in peace and freedom and I shall have directly contributed to that, so here again my life will not have been in vain.

Your loving Son

Comments:

B Vernasco: I am a mother of five boys and this young man's letter is taken into my heart as a message from one of my sons. This was a beautiful tribute to mothers around the world.

Malan's 10 Rules for Air Fighting

The Battle of Britain fighter ace 'Sailor' Malan developed a set of simple rules for fighter pilots, honed during the Battle, which he then had distributed throughout RAF Fighter Command.

TEN OF MY RULES FOR AIR FIGHTING

1. Wait until you see the whites of his eyes. Fire short bursts of one to two seconds only when your sights are definitely 'ON'.

2. Whilst shooting think of nothing else, brace the whole of your body: have both hands on the stick: concentrate on your ring sight.

3. Always keep a sharp lookout. 'Keep your finger out'.

4. Height gives you the initiative.

5. Always turn and face the attack.

6. Make your decisions promptly. It is better to act quickly even though your tactics are not the best.

7. Never fly straight and level for more than 30 seconds in the combat area.

8. When diving to attack always leave a proportion of your formation above to act as a top guard.

9. INITIATIVE, AGGRESSION, AIR DISCIPLINE, and TEAMWORK are words that MEAN something in Air Fighting.

10. Go in quickly – Punch hard – Get out!

Sir Hugh Dowding's 10 Point Memorandum

16 May 1940

Sir,

1. I have the honour to refer to the very serious calls which have recently been made upon the Home Defence Fighter Units in an attempt to stem the German invasion on the Continent.

2. I hope and believe that our Armies may yet be victorious in France and Belgium, but we have to face the possibility that they may be defeated.

3. In this case I presume that there is no-one who will deny that England should fight on, even though the remainder of the Continent of Europe is dominated by the Germans.

4. For this purpose it is necessary to retain some minimum fighter strength in this country and I must request that the Air Council will inform me what they consider this minimum strength to be, in order that I may make my dispositions accordingly.

5. I would remind the Air Council that the last estimate which they made as to the force necessary to defend this country was 52 Squadrons, and my strength has now been reduced to the equivalent of 36 Squadrons.

6. Once a decision has been reached as to the limit on which the Air Council and the Cabinet are prepared to stake the existence of the country, it should be made clear to the Allied Commanders on the Continent that not a single aeroplane from Fighter Command beyond the limit will be sent across the Channel, no matter how desperate the situation may become.

7. It will, of course, be remembered that the estimate of 52 Squadrons was based on the assumption that the attack would come from the eastwards except in so far as the defences might be outflanked in flight. We have now to face the possibility that attacks may come from Spain or even from the North coast of France. The result is that our line is very much extended at the same time as our resources are reduced.

8. I must point out that within the last few days the equivalent of 10 Squadrons have been sent to France, that the Hurricane Squadrons remaining in this country are seriously depleted, and that the more Squadrons which are sent to France the higher will be the wastage and the more insistent the demands for reinforcements.

9. I must therefore request that as a matter of paramount urgency the Air Ministry will consider and decide what level of strength is to be left to the Fighter Command for the defences of this country, and will assure me that when this level has been reached, not one fighter will be sent across the Channel however urgent and insistent the appeals for help may be.

10. I believe that, if an adequate fighter force is kept in this country, if the fleet remains in being, and if Home Forces are suitably organised to resist invasion, we should be able to carry on the war single handed for some time, if not indefinitely. But, if the Home Defence Force is drained away in desperate attempts to remedy the situation in France, defeat in France will involve the final, complete and irremediable defeat of this country.

I have the honour to be, Sir, Your obedient Servant,

H. C. T. Dowding

Air Chief Marshal,
Air Officer Commanding-in-Chief,
Fighter Command, Royal Air Force.

Tatler Magazine, Summer 1940

Overheard in a Village Pub
July 10 1940

Returning from a certain aerodrome a short time ago, I stopped on the way to call at a village inn. There I listened to a conversation which had an almost uncanny bearing on the conversation I had just been taking part in at the aerodrome. Bombs had fallen near the inn two nights before, and two of the more eminent drinkers were voicing the opinion that what we had had up to then in this country was 'just nothing' to what would be coming in the future. They seemed to enjoy the thought of the aerial fury which they expected to descend upon them, and each supported the other in emphasising its probable violence. It seemed that the rain of bombs would be such that not a blade of grass for miles around would survive.

Then up spoke a small pinch faced man who had until then been sipping his beer and listening to the others. 'You say they'll send over hundreds to attack one point' he remarked. 'Thousands' corrected the other two. 'Very well; thousands. But I want to ask you something. D'you think our lads will let them?' The other two looked at one another and said almost simultaneously 'of course not'.

…No one in that inn had the smallest doubt that 'our lads' would let them have it. No one had the slightest fear about the result when 'our lads' got in touch with the enemy. The two solemn drinkers smiled faintly as they solemnly nodded, and gravely asserted that 'our lads' would just 'massacre them'.

Air Defences doing 'marvellously well'….
July 24 1940

Our air defences have been doing marvellously well. This week in which I am writing has been a series of triumphs for the Royal Air Force, and a series of losses for the enemy. And, incidentally, I must mention the finest broadcast I have ever listened too. It was that one by Charles Gardner from a recording van which happened to be at a point where it was possible to actually witness and record a big air-fight in progress. This was a really brilliant piece of broadcasting, and I heartily congratulate Charles upon it. It put into the shade every 'immediate' sports and other 'thrill' type of broadcast that has ever come over the air. It took you right up to watch the battle and share the anxieties and excitements of the participants. And that climax, when the section of 'spitfires' finally hounded after the Messerschmitts, closing up on them as they tore out over the sea, was truly magnificent.

How to prepare for visits to the Air Raid Shelter
July 31 1940

It is quite simple to prepare for visits to the air raid shelter, but it must be done before and not after the warning is given. A bag must be kept packed and should contain among other things a first-aid outfit, rubber gloves (from 1s 6d a pair), air or other cushion, torch, candles or night-light, rubber shock absorbers for the mouth and wax ones for the ears. A packet of food, not overlooking barley sugar. At Marshall and Snellgrove's there is an infinite variety of siren suits from 42s. Some are cut on lines suitable for the older woman who is not as slender as she would like to be, while others are destined for the youthful figure. By the way, the anti-concussion bandeau is also of paramount importance.

(Reproduced with kind permission of The Tatler)

Praise for Blog

Andrew D. Bird: Enjoying reading the diaries – makes it very real.

Joe in Pittsburgh: This is such an interesting site! Keep up the great work.

Hywel Thomas: Your daily diary is a perfect way to appreciate what went on 70 years ago. Thank you.

Adrian F: Just to say that I am enjoying reading this and also re-reading your excellent book, *One Boy's War*, which I would recommend to one and all.

Ken Lodge: Very many thanks for this and all the earlier postings. My eyes still fill with tears as I remember watching the dog fights and hearing Churchill's words although I was too young to fully appreciate, at that time, just what 'The Few' did and at what cost.

Becky Burdick: Thanks to you, Tony, and to those who have been sending such thoughtful comments.

Mike: A GREAT series – thanks!

Lynnerosie: This blog is fascinating – so much hard work has gone into producing it. The lives and experiences of pilots and crews in our wonderful RAF during World War II will never be forgotten.

Michael Deverill: Well done. Should be required reading for the National Curriculum.

Ian Bennett: That was a great piece of work, thank you.

Peter: Thank you. I have enjoyed this tremendously. Great job!

Nick Lawson: This blog has been fascinating to follow. Many congratulations for capturing and delivering the spirit of the Battle of Britain, and presenting the messages it imparts to future generations so clearly. This must now be one of the first points of reference when researching the individual days of the Battle of Britain. Your Blog is a tremendous tribute to The Few.

I have been sharing stories throughout the 70th anniversary about my Great Uncle's personal experiences during the Battle (72 616 and 41 Squadron). Although John died in his Spitfire shortly after the Battle of Britain, John's story continues today.

Thank you for sharing. Never in the field of human conflict was so much owed by so many to so few.

Mark Nevitt: Thanks for doing this it has been first class.

Debra Gendel: Thanks for a wonderful series that we've looked forward to reading each day with great anticipation. Hard work and love of subject is obvious. Congratulations!

Phyllis Earl: And many thanks to you, for a fascinating series and a reminder of those to whom we must all be thankful.

John Kirkham: I really enjoyed reading the series of emails. Many thanks.

Adrian Morrish: What an excellent and informative series which brought to life so many of the participants, some already very well known and many who are not, but to all of whom we owe such an incalculable debt. Many many thanks

Chris: Really enjoyed your efforts, started to look forward to your daily emails and will really miss them now! Thanks, Chris.

Jim Grimm: Thank you very much – the daily posts have become part of my morning read and really brought a sense of the depth and pacing of the Battle – I shall really miss them and look forward to the book, as well as a repeat next year.

Dr Michael J. Butler: What a great series and one that as an ex RAF man, I was pleased to see. The image of the Battle of Britain is all too often one of 'Jolly days", "Yoiks" and "Tally Ho!", and a great deal of fun. Well, nothing could be further from the truth as indeed, my father served in the RAF, during the whole of the war so I know a little about it. As a country, we owe so much to those flying soldiers and indeed, the magnificent Churchill summed it up so well, in his speech, 'Never in the field of human conflict have so many owed so much to so few'.